a CLOSER LOOK at PROPHECY

Richard & Tina Kleiss

T0206690

evelation of Jesus Christ,
God gave him to show his
hat must soon take place; he
nown by sending his angel
John, 2 who testified to the
God and the testimony of
ist, even all that he saw.
ed is the one who reads loud
of the prophecy, and blessed
hear and who keep what
3 hear

A Closer Look at Prophecy

Copyright February 2019
Richard and Christina (Tina) Kleiss
Cover design: M.L. Eckley
Interior Design: Jamie Walton
Editor: Bruce Malone

ISBN : 978-1-939456-35-9
Printed in USA

First Printing - April 2019
Second Revised Printing - September 2020

Unless otherwise indicated, all Scripture quotations
are taken from the King James Bible.

Low-cost multiple copies are available using the order form at the back of the book.

May God bless you as you share the truth with others.

E-mail - truth@searchforthetruth.net
Web - www.searchforthetruth.net
Mail - 3275 Monroe Rd., Midland, MI 48642

DEDICATION:

This book is dedicated to our LORD God and Savior, Jesus Christ, who gave us His Word! He totally supplied every prayer warrior and willing worker from start to finish. May His evidences in prophecy strengthen your faith, provide you with verifiable proof, and feed your passion, as it has ours, to live for, serve, and share the incredible hope, peace, and joy of knowing Jesus and spending eternity with Him.

ACKNOWLEDGMENTS:

This book is the result of the LORD's answers to the hundreds of prayers from many dear and faithful prayer warrior friends. They are not only from our childhood church in Parma Hts., Ohio, Cornerstone church in Gladwin, Michigan, and CRBC in Ocala, Florida, but also from our lifelong friendships and own Kleiss and Pfister families. We love you and could never thank you enough for your faithful and consistent prayers and encouragement.

Without our typist, who wanted to remain anonymous, initial and final proofreaders: Alice Pfister (Tina's mom), Shirley McCoy, Linda Whalen, Robin Malone, Pam Koehlinger, Bryce Gaudian, and Steve Schwarz there would be no written text, and mistakes would not have been found. Without our research and computer assistant, Jonathan Mack, and help from Liz Stobaugh, this book would still be on our computer and not in print. Without the help from M.L. Eckley, the cover would not tell the reader in a visual way that the LORD God of all creation has a fixed, soon approaching time for all things to reach their fulfillment, and He recorded His plan for us to search out. Without Artene Kortright, there would not be an easier way for us to sing God's Word and relinquish our fears about the future. Without our layout coordinator, Jamie Walton, and editor, Bruce Malone, this book would still be on paper stored in a box under the bed. We are also deeply grateful to Dr. Reagan and the contributing authors (listed in the back of the book), on whose shoulders we stand because they dedicated their lives to the God-inspired truth of the Bible. We thank the LORD for all of you from the bottom of our hearts. May God bless you, and may He be honored on every page of this book.

Rich and Tina Kleiss

INTRODUCTION:

Most people are curious about prophecy to one degree or another. It is a topic, however, that many find frightening, confusing, mythical, or they think it deals with too many uncertain interpretations. In other words, why study something no one can understand or agree on? This is precisely why we decided to tackle this subject.

The primary purpose of this book is to show what an incredible Creator Lord and Savior we have and how absolutely **perfect, trustworthy and unchangeable** He is. God said He makes Himself known to mankind through His Creation (Romans 1:19-20), through the Christ-like lives and testimony of those who know Him (John 13:35), and through His Word with its fulfilled prophecies (Psalm 18:30). This book was written to take a "closer look" at the **prophetic biblical evidence** in an easy-to-understand way. It is designed to help **dispel our fears** of the future, **encourage** us in our individual faith, and **inspire** us to share credible reasons for our belief with others.

As part of our study for our previous book on evidences for the existence of God (*A Closer Look at the Evidence* found at www.searchforthetruth.net) and love for biblical research, the authors found that **prophecy** is in a category all its own. The study of biblical prophecy gives us overwhelming evidence that there *is* an all-knowing God. His Word is accurate and verifiable – **something no other book on Earth can verifiably claim.**

Included within this book is the research of many serious, dedicated, and trustworthy Bible scholars. Without them, this book would not have been possible to write. The authors' desire was to avoid all speculation and lay out God's prophecies in a simple format. Our intent is not to interpret the Bible or to force our opinion on the reader. Our prayer is that taking a "closer look" at biblical prophecy will bring a renewed excitement about the certainty of Scripture and an increased sense of urgency to share the blessed hope and **absolute assurance of eternal life with Christ** with as many as possible!

Our hope is that *A Closer Look at Prophecy* will be a useful resource. It includes fulfilled prophecies of the past, those that are being fulfilled in our lifetime, and those still awaiting fulfillment. To help us be better prepared to meet our Creator, the prophecies include both God's warnings and promises. This book cannot possibly include all of the almost two thousand prophecies the Bible records. Hopefully, however, it will whet the readers' appetites to read and examine the Bible for themselves. Excellent resources for further study are listed in the reference section in the back of the book.

A **Topical Index** has been added at the back of this book to make finding specific articles easier to locate. For those who want to study prophecy in a more systematic way, we have also added a closing section containing things that have been a help to us in organizing, remembering, and sharing biblical prophecy with others. We hope these resources (added to the second revised edition) will be a benefit to you.

Fallible people make errors, which is terrifying when dealing with God's Word. It is not the intent of the authors or publisher to distort or mislead in any way; therefore, referring back to the Bible is always best. All confirmed errors will be corrected in future printings.

You may reach us at www.*searchforthetruth.net.*

JANUARY

The Angel Of The Lord

Psalm 34:7

Arlene Faith Kortright

LORD, thank You for assuring us that You literally dwell with those who love and obey You and for Your promise to equip, strengthen and prepare us for all that is ahead. **Amen**

Blessings of Studying Revelation

God gives us a special blessing in Revelation 1:3 for studying prophecy. The following is a list meant to **spur us on** as we edge closer to God's full and final fulfillment of His Word.

Studying Prophecy:

- <u>Keeps us from being deceived</u> by wrong information.
- <u>Moves us to memorize</u> God's promises of guidance, comfort, assurance, and peace in order to prepare for possible persecution.
- <u>Intensifies our desire to share the Gospel</u> with those who don't know Christ.
- <u>Motivates us to get ready</u> for Christ's return by practicing self-control and living pure, God-honoring lives.
- <u>Encourages us to focus</u> on what is most important and avoid wasting time.
- <u>Reminds us</u> that there are consequences to sin.
- <u>Makes us want to know the LORD better</u> and think more of Him and less of ourselves.
- <u>Gives us the assurance</u> that God is in total control, will never leave or forsake us, and wins in the end!
- <u>Removes the fear and confusion</u> of the future.
- <u>Allows us to be more prayerful, thankful, joyful, and hopeful</u> in all circumstances, knowing the best is yet to come.

Blessed is he that reads and those who hear the words of this prophecy, and keep those things which are written in it; for the time is near.
- Revelation 1:3 (NKJV)

The Literal Interpretation of Prophecy

One of the greatest abuses of Bible Prophecy is "spiritualizing." This occurs when a person decides that a passage cannot mean what it says, and so it is interpreted symbolically to mean something else. By spiritualizing, one can make the Scriptures say whatever one pleases. The rule for interpreting all of the Scriptures, including prophecy, is what might be called "The Golden Rule of Interpretation" – **if the plain sense makes sense, don't look for any other sense, or you will end up with nonsense.**

A good example can be found in Revelation 7:1-8. This passage says God is going to seal 144,000 Jews that will serve Him in the Tribulation. Many commentaries spiritualize this passage by saying the 144,000 Jews are a symbol for the Church. They do this because the authors of the commentaries are caught up in Replacement Theology and therefore believe God has replaced Israel with the Church and has no further purpose for the Jews. But the passage says the 144,000 are Jews. It even numbers them by their tribal names. What else would God have to do to convince us that He is talking about the Jewish people?

Although Revelation can be confusing, it is really not difficult to understand. It is difficult to believe. If you are willing to believe it, you will want to study it. If you prayerfully study it, God will help you understand it.

**You shall not add to the word which
I command you, nor take from it....
- Deuteronomy 4:2 (NKJV)**

Scientific Foreknowledge Validates the Bible

In 2 Timothy 3:16, it clearly states that the Bible was given by inspiration of God. One of the many ways God validates this truth is by including scientific facts. The Bible is the only religious book that gives us truths about science that can be tested and proven to be one hundred percent accurate. Even more remarkable is the fact that the **scientific technology to test the accuracy** of biblical statements was only available thousands of years **after** they were recorded.

Below is a **partial** list of scientific foresight and the **approximate** dates of their discovery.

Sci. Foreknowledge	Scripture	Date Discovered
Water cycle	Ecclesiastes 1:7	B. Palissy, 1580
Life is in the blood	Genesis 9:4; Leviticus 17:11	W. Harvey, early1600s
Ocean currents	Psalm 8:8	M. Maury, 1850
Mountains in the sea	Jonah 2:5-6	HMS Challenger, 1872
Springs in the sea	Job 38:16	Submarines, 1930-1945
Subatomic particles	Hebrews 11:3	J.J. Thompson, 1897- today
Uncountable number of stars	Jeremiah 33:22	Hubble telescope, 1990
Circuit of the sun	Psalm 19:4-6	M. Brown, C. Trujillo, D. Rabinowitz, 2005
Stretched out Heaven	Isaiah 42:5, 45:12, Jeremiah 10:12	1960s to the present

All Scripture is given by inspiration of God....
- 2 Timothy 3:16

God's Promise of Peace

Scripture gives us the tremendous promise that if we **keep** our mind on the LORD and **trust in** (*fully lean on*) Him, we **will have** perfect **peace** (*safety, rest, oneness in Him*).

An excellent example of this <u>promise</u> in Scripture is when Peter wanted to come to Christ by walking on the water – as he saw Christ doing. Reading this account in *Matthew 14:28-31* shows us that while Peter trusted Christ and kept his eyes on Him, he could safely walk toward the LORD. As soon as he changed his focus to the winds, his uncertainty and terror returned. **Our full trust and our eyes must remain on the LORD**, Who alone can give us peace in tumultuous times.

Thou wilt keep him in perfect peace, whose mind is stayed on thee: because he trusteth in thee.
- Isaiah 26:3

Amount of Prophecy in Each Book

The *Tim LaHaye Prophecy Study Bible* includes an interesting detail about each book of the Bible. It counts *the number of distinct prophecies each book contains.* Dr. Tim LaHaye included the conditional prophecies, prophetic types, and specific predictions and counted the number of verses involved. With this information, he calculated the percentage of prophecy within each book.

More than one out of four Bible verses are prophetic! Sixteen Old Testament and five New Testament books have over forty percent prophecy in them. The books of the Bible with the highest percentages are as follows:

Revelation 95%	Zechariah 69%
Zephaniah 89%	Joel 68%
Obadiah 81%	Ezekiel 65%
Nahum 74%	Jeremiah 60%
Micah 70%	Leviticus, Isaiah 59%

This research demonstrates that the Bible is **unique** among all others. It includes hundreds of prophecies throughout its sixty-six books, each one both verifiable and one hundred percent accurate. **No other book**, religious or otherwise, can make this claim. This proves that the Bible is worthy of consideration for any person searching for truth.

How God Spoke Through Prophecy

A survey of Old Testament prophecy reveals several methods of prophetic expression:

- **The Writing Prophets** – These are prophets who **wrote books**. These books are referred to as minor and major prophetic books in the Old Testament (depending on their length) and 1 Thessalonians, 2 Thessalonians, and Revelation in the New Testament. The prophets who wrote these books ranged from highly educated men like Isaiah to men with no formal education like Amos.
- **The Oral Prophets** – These are the prophets who **spoke prophetic messages that were written down by other people.** Elijah and Elisha would be examples in the Old Testament. Oral prophets in the New Testament would include Agabus, the daughters of Philip, and Jesus Himself.
- **The Acting Prophets** – Sometimes the Lord would tell His prophets to stop writing or speaking and to start **acting out their prophecies.** This was intended to get people's attention. For example, Isaiah was told to go barefoot and naked for three years (Isaiah 20:3). The immediate message was that if the people of Judah did not repent, God would punish them by bringing an army that would strip them barefoot and naked.
- **Symbolic Prophecy** – A prophecy expressed in an **event**, an **object** or the **life of a person.** Concerning *events*, an example would be the feasts of Israel, all of which pointed to some aspect of the life of the Messiah. An example of an *object* prophetic in nature would be the Ark of the Covenant. Again, every aspect of it pointed to the Messiah. The same is true of the *lives* of key persons in the Old Testament, such as Joseph.

When you begin to look for Jesus in the Old Testament, you will find Him prophesied repeatedly, and the Old Testament comes alive.

God, who at various times and in various ways spoke in times past to the fathers by the prophets... - Hebrews 1:1 (NKJV)

Back to the Future

God is not trapped "in time" (as we are) and is thus able to see the past, present and future. When He speaks of a future event to a prophet, **He often speaks of it in the past tense, as if it has already happened.** This strange phenomenon occurs so frequently in the Bible that theologians have created a special grammatical tense for it that is called the "proleptic tense." Since God is all-knowing and all-powerful, when He wills something, it is done, whether or not it has yet happened in history, and thus He will speak of it in the past tense.

An example can be found in Psalm 2, written by David a thousand years before the birth of Jesus. This is a reference to the Millennial Reign of Jesus that will take place when He returns to Earth at His Second Coming. God speaks of it in the past tense as if it had already happened, yet it is, in fact, a prophecy that is yet to be fulfilled. In the same manner, the Bible speaks of Jesus having been *"slain from the foundation of the world" - Rev. 13:8 (NKJV)* because that is when God willed it.

God has a plan for this universe and for mankind. It will be completed in every detail. No one can derail it. As far as God is concerned, it is already completed because He has foreseen it.

Yet I have set My King on My holy hill of Zion.
- Psalm 2:6 (NKJV)

Israel's Military Victories

The prophet Zechariah tells us that in the last days the armies of the world will come against Israel (Zech. 12:2-3). We know from reading Zechariah 12 that God will intervene on Israel's behalf, and against incredible odds, Israel will be victorious. A study of Israel's recent military victories show how God has already started this process.

- **1948** – A five Arab nation army (Egypt, Syria, Jordon, Lebanon, Iran) attacked Israel within hours of Israel's declaration of independence! Against all odds, Israel defeated them.
- **1956** – An Egyptian-Syrian alliance attacked Israel over the Sinai. Israel won and expanded her territory.
- **1967** – The Six-Day War with Egypt and Jordan attacking – Israel won in an unbelievably short period, leaving Israel in control of a territory four times its previous size!
- **1973** – The Yom Kippur War (Egypt, Iraq and Syria) – Israel forced back the attack, but at great cost of life. Interestingly, the Watergate scandal forced Richard Nixon to shamefully resign his presidency within a year of pressuring Israel to give back some of its previously won land from the Six-Day War. A coincidence?
- **1976** – Operation Thunderbolt – Israel executed a successful counter-terrorism hostage rescue mission in Uganda.
- **1981** – Operation Opera – Israel destroyed a nuclear weapons reactor facility in Baghdad, Iraq.

The entire chapter of Zechariah 12 indicates that Israel will have a strong military force in place in the end times. It states that Israel's strength will be compared to the strength of King David's army – among the most powerful military forces on Earth at that time. Israel is currently one of only few nations upon the earth with a nuclear arsenal. A final prophesied victory for Israel in the end times has come true – she will again call Jerusalem her capital. **Israel took control of Jerusalem in June of 1967,** and the United States officially recognized Jerusalem as the capital of Israel on December 6, 2017.

In that day I will make the governors of Judah like a firepan in the woodpile, and like a fiery torch in the sheaves; they shall devour all the surrounding peoples on the right hand and on the left, but Jerusalem shall be inhabited again in her own place - Jerusalem. – Zechariah 12:6 (NKJV)

Irrevocable Land Promise to Abraham

In Genesis 15:18, God promised Abraham, who was to be the father of the Jewish nation of Israel, a very special section of land. God clearly specified that the land would go from the Mediterranean on the west to the Euphrates River on the east. Ezekiel 48:1-28 tells us the northern border was to be Hamath (about 100 miles north of Damascus), and the southern boundary was to be Kadesh (about 100 miles south of Jerusalem). From the promise of this land to Abraham over 4,000 years ago until today, Israel has never fully occupied this land. This means the promise has yet to be fulfilled. Historical evidence tells us God's track record in fulfilling His promise is one hundred percent, **so we know Israel will receive the land God promised to Abraham.**

We are seeing God moving toward fulfilling this promise. After existing as a nation for over a thousand years, followed by almost 2,000 years of being scattered across the world without a country of their own, Israel miraculously re-emerged as a nation on May 14, 1948. What an encouragement to know that our God kept His promise to Israel regardless of time. He will also keep His promises to all who trust and obey Him.

In the same day the LORD made a covenant with Abram, saying, "Unto thy seed have I given this land, from the river of Egypt unto the great river, the river Euphrates.
- Genesis 15:18 (See also Ezekiel 48.)

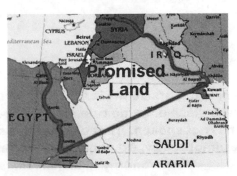

Past Prophecies Fulfilled Deserve Our Attention

The Old Testament records over one hundred different and very specific prophecies about Christ's first coming. These predictions were written down hundreds, and even thousands of years before they happened. There are over thirty prophecies about Jesus' death alone, most of which happened within a twenty-four hour period.

For instance, specific details include how the Messiah's face and body would be marred more than any human (Isaiah 52:14) and how Christ would be spit on, scourged, and have His beard pulled out (Isaiah 50:6). His hands, feet, and body would be pierced, and His bones would be pulled out of joint (Psalm 22:14,16); yet not a bone of Christ's body would be broken (Christ would be the passover Lamb - Numbers 9:12; Psalm 34:20). All of these things happened exactly as foreseen.

Prophecy lets us **test** and **prove** the truth of the Bible, something no other religious book in the world can claim. Since fulfilled biblical prophecies are one hundred percent accurate, wouldn't the Bible be worth investigating and paying close attention to?

If what a prophet proclaims in the name of the LORD does not take place or come true, that is a message the LORD has not spoken. That prophet has spoken presumptuously. Do not be afraid of him.
- Deuteronomy 18:22 (NIV)

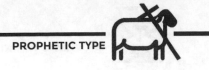
Christ Reveals Himself Through Prophetic Types

The entire Bible points to Christ. Through prophetic types, *Christ* revealed Himself hundreds and even thousands of years ahead of time. Here are a few examples:

<u>Abraham</u> offered his son Isaac to God, giving us a picture of our loving heavenly **Father, who sacrificed His innocent Son** for our salvation. This happened on Mt. Moriah, the same place where Jesus would later be crucified.

<u>Boaz</u> was an example of a **Kinsman-Redeemer** who took the Gentile bride, Ruth, just as Jesus invites believers to be His Gentile bride.

<u>Hosea</u> had a troublesome marriage with his unfaithful wife who rejected his love and sought out others. **This is a picture of God's relationship with unfaithful Israel.** Hosea acted as a prophetic representation of God. He willingly and lovingly paid the price of redemption to make it possible for his wife to be reconciled to him, just as Israel will be redeemed by Christ and will return to God in the future.

<u>Jonah</u> pointed to **Christ's death and resurrection** with his three days in the belly of a great fish.

"These are the words which I spoke to you while I was still with you, that all things must be fulfilled which were written in the Law of Moses and the Prophets and the Psalms concerning Me."
- Luke 24:44 (NKJV)

Prophecy in Ephesians 6:10-12

Ephesians 6:10-12 is an interesting passage in light of the future. Paul warns us to prepare ourselves for the evil day. He said we are not fighting a battle with humans, but the battle is with Satan and the demonic.

Although most people believe in God, many underestimate, ignore, and/or deny the existence of Satan and demons. From these verses we can see the Bible addresses the fact that Satan and his evil forces are real and extremely dangerous. They are dedicated to destroying us. Throughout Scripture we are commanded to stay away from anything contrary to God's Word. We need to understand what the Bible has to say about the Satanic forces. Paul warns us in Ephesians 6:10-18 to put on the whole armor of God, which is **truth**, **righteousness**, the **gospel of peace**, **faith**, **salvation**, the **Word of God** and **prayer**. The Bible says without these we will not be able to stand against Satan. With these, we do not need to live in fear because God will be our protector and shield.

Finally, my brethren, be strong in the Lord and in the power of His might. Put on the whole armor of God, that you may be able to stand against the wiles of the devil. For we do not wrestle against flesh and blood, but against principalities, against powers, against the rulers of the darkness of this age, against spiritual hosts of wickedness in the heavenly places.
- Ephesians 6:10-12 (NKJV)

Israel: A Channel of God's Blessing

When asked if there is one word proving the Bible to be true, that word would be **"Israel."** A look at both the biblical and secular history verifies this.

God chose Abraham to father a nation of people who would be called Israel. The Israelites, or Jews, were to be His *"Chosen People"* for two main purposes:

1. To serve as a **channel of God's blessings.** (Genesis 22:15-18)
2. To serve as a **witness of God.** (Isaiah 43:10)

The following are ways in which the Jews have been a channel of God's blessings:

1. God **revealed Himself** through them. (Matthew 1:17)
2. God gave us the **Bible** through them. (Historical evidence)
3. God provided the **Messiah** through them. (Matthew 1:17)
4. God has enriched the world through their contributions to **education, science, medicine, agriculture, etc.** (Gen.22:18)
5. God will continue to make the Jewish people a channel of His spiritual blessings to the whole world **in the future.** (Isaiah 2:2,3; Isaiah 60-63)

And in thy (Abraham's) seed shall all the nations of the earth be blessed; because thou hast obeyed my voice.
- Genesis 22:18

Israel: God's Miraculous Witness to the World

The Jews are witnesses of God in the following ways:

- They are witnesses of the **existence of God**. The current existence of their nation is a miracle.
- They are witnesses of the **truth of the Bible**. The majority of the Bible was written by Jews, and every historical event of the Old and New Testament has proven to be true.
- They are witnesses of what it means to have a **relationship with God**. From the beginning they have been known as "God's chosen people."
- They are witnesses of **God's unfathomable grace**. Countless times over thousands of years they have turned their backs on God in rebellion. God has allowed punishment in order to draw them back but never rejected them.
- They are witnesses to the **imminent return of Jesus**. Ultimate revival throughout the nation will testify to the reality that Jesus is the Messiah they seek.

God clearly tells us throughout His Word that *both* the Jew and the non-Jew *will know that He is God* by how He worked in the past, works in the present, and will work in the future of the Jewish people.

"You are My witnesses," says the LORD, "and My servant whom I have chosen, that you may know and believe Me, and understand that I am He. Before Me there was no God formed, nor shall there be after Me."
- Isaiah 43:10 (NKJV)

Digging Deeper into Scripture

Understanding the original meaning of words in the language in which they were written helps us to understand God's Word better. The Old Testament was first written in Hebrew and the New Testament in Greek. There are also a few passages in Aramaic.

A **Bible Concordance** is an alphabetical index of the words in the Bible. It gives word *definitions* in the original language and the *verses* where each word is located. It enables one to dig deeper into the meaning of God's Word, allowing us to find treasures of wisdom by opening new understandings of the text.

For example, in Genesis 1:1 it says, "In the beginning God created the heaven and the earth."

A closer look at the Hebrew word for God, *"Elohim"*, means excessively great and mighty. It stresses God's majesty and total power. The *"im"* ending is the Hebrew *plural* ending. **Elohim is a plural name with a singular meaning**, declaring that God is one, yet more than one. This points to the *Trinity* in the very first verse of the Bible!

The Significance of the Number Seven

The number seven is a most sacred number in Scripture. It appears well over 700 times – more than any other number except the number one. Seven signifies completeness. **It represents the completeness of God in spiritual perfection.** For example, the creation week ends with the seventh day, the completion of a perfect creation. God commanded the Israelites to set aside the seventh year for the land to rest and to ensure optimum productivity. God also gave Israel seven specific feast days with prophetic significance that would keep the nation united over thousands of years.

The words "finished" and "it is done" are also connected with the number seven. We can see this in Christ's seven utterances from the final hours on the cross. In the book of Revelation, we find seven final prophetic letters of warnings were sent to seven churches. We see the connection in the completion of history when the seventh angel will sound (Revelation 10:7), leading up to the time when the seventh angel will pour out his vial before God's great voice announces, "It is done" (Revelation 16:17).

In the books of Genesis, Leviticus, Numbers and Revelation, the number seven shows up more than fifty times. A thorough study reveals why. God's completeness and perfection can be seen in Genesis's creation account, His atonement in Leviticus, His character in Numbers, and His completion of history in Revelation. The repeated use of the number seven is evidence of God's fingerprint on His Word, confirming its accuracy.

And the seventh angel poured out his vial into the air; and there came a great voice out of the temple of heaven, from the throne, saying, It is done. – Revelation 16:17

God's Prophetic Plan of Rescue

Sin is "missing the mark" of God's perfection. Our sinful actions are part of our fallen nature and require a payment to a just and holy God. **Salvation means we are delivered from that payment** (*or debt*) and rescued from an eternity in hell – where God's goodness, holiness and love have been totally rejected.

By grace, God came to Earth in the form of a man, Jesus Christ. His desire for us to have a loving relationship moved Him to live as a human and experience what we humans experience. Yet He lived a sinless life. This qualified Christ alone to pay our sin debt.

We can't be perfect. There is *nothing* we can do to qualify ourselves for heaven. This is what makes salvation such an extraordinary gift. It is *free* to all, but it requires humility, confession of our ungodly ways, and acceptance of Christ's amazing sacrificial gift. He promised that when we accept His payment on the cross for our sins and put our trust in Him, we *will* enter His holy presence in heaven. When we truly understand Christ's sacrifice of love for us, how could we help but *desire* to pour our lives out in delighting our Lord and Savior?

For God sent not his Son into the world to condemn the world; but that the world through him might be saved.
- John 3:17

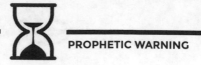

The Wheat and the Tares

In Matthew 13:24-30, Jesus told the parable of the wheat and the tares. He then gave His disciples a clear explanation of the parable in Matthew 13:36-43. Wheat is a useful grain, while *tares* is a word for "darnel" or a type of weed. Tares look like *wheat* but do not produce a useful crop. Christ explained that the wheat represents His followers; they love Him and lead others to know and obey Him. The tares, however, represent those whom Satan plants to hinder the productivity of Christ's true followers. The parable goes on to tell us the two crops grow up side-by-side. The workers were instructed not to pull out the tares because it would damage the roots of the wheat. The landowner would separate them and burn the tares at harvest time.

Peter, Paul, Jude, John and Jesus all warned about apostates (or false believers). They would grow alongside of us (even in the church). We are told to leave the judgment of these apostates to **the Lord, who will separate them out at the end of time**. Our job is not to concentrate on destroying or eliminating them, but rather to *contend earnestly* or "struggle intensely" for the *truth of God's Word*. We are commissioned to study the Bible so well that we will recognize error and won't be led astray or hindered from accurately sharing Christ with others.

...I found it necessary to write to you exhorting you to contend earnestly for the faith which was once for all delivered to the saints.
- Jude 1:3 (NKJV)

The Bible is "PERFECT"

Psalm 18:30 tells us God's way is perfect. The Hebrew word for *"perfect"* means totally true, complete, and without error.

Since God set this standard for His Word, one would expect Him to provide a way to test it, and He does this first and foremost through prophecy. More than twenty-five percent of the Bible, which was written over 2,000 to 3,500 years ago, is prophetic. Hundreds of detailed prophecies have come true with one hundred percent accuracy and are continuing to be fulfilled in our lifetime.

Either the serious student of the Lord's Word or the Bible skeptic can determine that the Bible substantiates its claim to be absolutely *"perfect"* by researching any of the following:

- Its geographic locations confirmed by archaeology
- Its order
- Its scientific statements
- Its historical records
- Its prophetic statements
- Its health information (physical and mental)
- Its design

Throughout this book you will find numerous examples from each of these catagories.

As for God, His way is perfect; the word of the LORD is proven; He is a shield to all who trust in Him.
- Psalm 18:30 (NKJV)

A Prophetic Warning from Isaiah 3

Isaiah 3 foreshadows what is happening in our society today. This prophecy was written to show the decay of ancient Israel, which happened as the people of Jerusalem and Judah *turned away from God*.
Its lessons are applicable to us today:

1-3	*Wise* leaders, counselors, judges, craftsmen, and teachers were removed.
4	Young, inexperienced, and incompetent tyrants ruled over the people.
5	People oppressed each other, and arrogant children ignored and disrespected older and wiser people.
6-7	No one stepped in and corrected the problems.
8-9	People spoke against God, turned from Him, and sinned openly.
12	Children were oppressors, unfit women ruled, and leaders made decisions leading to destruction.
13-15	God pleaded, warned and judged people who wouldn't listen. They wasted food, oppressed the godly, and afflicted the poor.
16-24	Entire towns wallowed in luxury, became haughty, selfish, vain, seductive, and materialistic. God judged them severely because they knew the truth but chose to ignore it.
25-26	War and death destroyed the nation, and cities became desolate.

Too many in America are so proud that they assume such a fate could never happen here. Yet God knows the evil and pain that will ultimately result when human sin is left unchecked. He loves us too much to allow it to continue indefinitely in any nation.

**The LORD standeth up to plead, and standeth
to judge the people. - Isaiah 3:13**

Key Verses to Know About Prophecy

Since **prophecy** is one of the **strongest evidences** for the truth of the Bible, it is important to know these key verses:

- **When a prophet speaks in the name of the LORD, if the thing does not happen or come to pass, that is the thing which the LORD has not spoken; the prophet has spoken it presumptuously; you shall not be afraid of him.**
  - Deuteronomy 18:22 (NKJV)

- **Remember the former things of old, for I am God, and there is no other; I am God, and there is none like Me. Declaring the end from the beginning, and from the ancient times things that are not yet done, saying, "My counsel shall stand, and I will do all my pleasure."**
  - Isaiah 46:9-10a (NKJV)

- **Surely the LORD God does nothing, unless He reveals His secret to His servants the prophets.** *- Amos 3:7 (NKJV)*

- **And we have something more sure, the prophetic word, to which you will do well to pay attention as to a lamp shining in a dark place, until the day dawns and the morning star rises in your hearts, knowing this first of all, that no prophecy of Scripture comes from someone's own interpretations. For no prophecy was ever produced by the will of man, but men spoke from God as they were carried along by the Holy Spirit.** *- 2 Peter 1:19-21 (ESV)*

- **Blessed is he who reads and those who hear the words of this prophecy, and keep those things which are written in it; for the time is near.** *- Revelation 1:3 (NKJV)*

- **For the testimony of Jesus is the spirit of prophecy.**
  - Revelation 19:10b (NKJV)

The Last Trumpet

Trumpets were significant throughout the Old Testament and used for specific purposes. They were blown to **signal the end of something** (like the end of the harvest). They were sounded to **warn of danger, gather the troops for battle, and call God's people together to worship**. Trumpets also have an important place in the prophetic future.

In Paul's discussion about the coming Rapture, he mentions the trumpet twice, making sure we do not miss his point.

- **Behold, I tell you a mystery; we shall not all sleep, but we shall all be changed—in a moment, in the twinkling of an eye, at the last trumpet. For the trumpet will sound, and the dead will be raised incorruptible, and we shall be changed.** *- 1 Corinthians 15:51-52 (NKJV)*

- **For the Lord Himself will descend from heaven with a shout, with the voice of an archangel, and with the trumpet of God. And the dead in Christ will rise first. Then we who are alive and remain shall be caught up together with them in the clouds to meet the Lord in the air. And thus we shall always be with the Lord.** *- 1 Thessalonians 4:16-17 (NKJV)*

Both of these references refer to the same event, the Rapture. The trumpet is used in an exciting anticipatory way, a call signaling the end of the Church age. We are told it will be a call for all believing Christians (the Church) to go meet Christ in the air to be with Him forever. It will be the last trumpet the Church will hear on Earth – we do not want to miss this one. There are more prophetic trumpets for those still on Earth. These trumpets, however, are frightening and will announce judgment on those left behind.

The Revelation Trumpet Prophecies

There are seven trumpet calls that will take place during the Tribulation. According to Christ's own words, this will be the most horrific time on Earth (Matthew 24:21-22). **The seven-trumpet prophecy is the second series in the twenty-one judgments that will be unleashed on the earth for man's rebellion and sin.**

The **seven seal judgments** will be unleashed by Christ himself, and these apparently happen in the first three and a half years of the Tribulation. The **trumpet judgments** come next, followed by the final **seven bowl judgments**. These are so terrible, God said He would have to intervene or else mankind would be destroyed.

The purpose of all these judgments is to show the world that God exists and that He is holy and perfectly just. Because He is a just God, sin must be judged. It would violate God's very nature to allow sin to go unpunished. The penalty of any sin, no matter how great or how small, is the same – death. This coming period of Earth history will be God's final call for those willing to acknowledge Him as Creator, Lord and personal Savior. In His mercy, God had the apostle John describe these coming twenty-one judgments, which include the seven trumpets in the book of Revelation.

The seven trumpets are prophesied to bring the following judgments (Revelation 8-11).

1. *Hail, fire* – 1/3 earth and trees and all grass burn up
2. *Burning mountain* – 1/3 sea is like blood, 1/3 sea creatures die, 1/3 ships are destroyed
3. *Wormwood falls* – waters become polluted
4. *Sun, moon, stars* – lights in the heavens darken
5. *Demonic locusts* – the torment of people across the earth
6. *200 million horsemen* – 1/3 of remaining population dies.
7. *Seven bowl judgments* – the worst warnings are the bowls of judgment which are poured out last.

Surely the LORD God does nothing, unless He reveals His secret to His servants the prophets.   - Amos 3:7 (NKJV)

Prophecy, Praise, History and Science in the Psalms

Language allows us to praise God to the highest degree. It is no accident that the book of Psalms, located in the heart of the Bible, is God's gift to mankind to show us just how to worship and praise Him. Psalms is God's ancient Hebrew songbook which covers praises of the past, present, and future. It addresses our lowest moments as well as gives us ways and words to praise Him beyond explanation.

A sampling of the unique treasures found within the book of Psalms:
- Records over twenty Messianic prophecies
- Uses acrostic arrangement and parallelism – making it easier to memorize
- Is the most frequently quoted book in the New Testament
- Paints a picture of our God and Savior
- Describes the acts of God in both creation and history
- Encompasses over nine hundred years of Jewish history (1410 B.C. to 500 B.C.)
- Includes scientific insights
- Demonstrates the inspiration of the Holy Spirit
- Gives us the means and model for true worship
- Speaks to our hearts in every situation from praise, singing, and comfort to anger, loneliness, joy in the midst of sorrow, and hope in the midst of despair

**Let every thing that hath breath
praise the LORD. Praise ye the LORD.
- Psalm 150:6**

The Promised Blessing of Revelation 1:3

Revelation 1:3 is a unique prophecy about Scripture. It is the only verse in the Bible where a blessing is promised for reading (studying) a book of the Bible.

Revelation or "apokalypsis" in Greek means **disclosure** or **revealing**. In this case, it reveals what is coming in the future. Delving into the original Greek meanings of the words in this verse adds to its understanding.

- *Blessed* – Well-off, happy, fortunate, supremely blessed
- *Reads* – Knows accurately
- *Hear* – Give audience to; come to understand, learn
- *Prophecy* – Prediction
- *Keep* – Watch, guard from loss or injury by keeping an eye upon
- *Near* – At hand, ready

Since the whole book of Revelation is dedicated to revealing the future, and we are promised to be well-off for knowing, understanding, and keeping our eye on its predictions, why wouldn't we want to study it?

Blessed is he who reads and those who hear the words of this prophecy, and keep those things which are written in it; for the time is near.
- Revelation 1:3 (NKJV)

Prophecy in Romans 1:16-32

Romans 1:16-32 is an extraordinary passage of the Bible that outlines crucial information including the exact causes of the past and future demise of cultures.

* *Romans 1:16-17* promises us that everyone can have eternal life through belief and trust in Jesus Christ.
* *Romans 1:18* tells us what brings on God's wrath: mankind's unrighteousness, ungodliness, and the suppression of truth.
* *Romans 1:19-20* informs us that God makes Himself known to everyone. We see evidence in creation, so no one will have an excuse for not knowing Him.
* *Romans 1:21* clearly warns us of the two causes which make God turn from us: 1. lack of glorifying (honoring, magnifying, valuing) God 2. thanklessness.
* *Romans 1:22-32* prophesies the specific progression of man's demise resulting from rejecting God. This process starts with leaving God and His Word out of our thinking. *"Seeking to become wise, they became fools."* (Romans 1:22)

The rejection of God as our Creator can be seen on a global scale for the first time in history since the Flood. Our hope rests in glorifying our Lord Jesus Christ with a heart of thankfulness as we entrust our lives and care to Him.

For whatsoever things were written aforetime were written for our learning, that we through patience and comfort of the Scriptures might have hope.   - Romans 15:4

God's Pattern for Our Witness

Looking at how God dealt with the Israelites when He brought them out of Egypt and called them to be His witnesses to the surrounding nations gives us a prophetic pattern of how Christians are to be God's witness to the world. God went to great lengths to prove Himself to the Israelites.

The series of ten plagues that inflicted Egypt were very specific (Exodus 7-12). Each one tested the authenticity of what the Egyptians worshipped and rendered them totally useless.

- The Egyptians worshipped the Nile, thinking it brought life, so it was turned to blood, bringing death.
- They worshipped frogs and locusts, so they were given in plague proportions.
- They worshipped the sun, so they were plunged into darkness.
- They worshipped eternal life and were struck with misery (boils) in this life.
- They were secure in their future until even the firstborn of every family (their future) was removed.

Their gods could not speak, hear, or act on behalf of the people. **God, on the other hand, visually demonstrated His power over all of creation** – nature, health, life, and death. God spoke, He wrote, and He acted for the good of people. Throughout the Exodus, God demonstrated His faithfulness, patience, and wisdom – as He provided for every need the Israelites had.

Once God revealed Himself, He gave the Israelites the Ten Commandments. They were written to help the people develop a relationship with Him and each other. They would enable the Israelites to live the orderly, peaceful, prosperous, contented, and blessed life which God always intended for His children.

What a perfect example of how we are to witness to the world. May we *reveal God* first by reflecting who He is in our lives through our character and then *demonstrate how His words are written for our good* by obeying them and making a difference in our society.

Battling Our Fears About the Future (Part 1)

In the Ephesians 6:10-18 passage on wearing the "armor of God," we are given the way to combat Satan's attempts to make us sin. **Satan is not all-knowing, but he does realize that fear, including fear of the future, is one of his most effective weapons.**

Ephesians 6:14-17 lists the pieces of armor that help us defend ourselves. Verse 17, however, also gives us an offensive weapon against Satan. God tells us to take up the *sword of the Spirit*, which He defines as the "Word of God." Christ Himself used God's Word three times in Matthew 4 to resist Satan's temptations.

If we learn and obey God's Word, *we will be able to resist* the devil as Christ did, and *Satan will run from us.* In the book of James, God promises us that **we can** resist the temptations of the devil and tells us how to do so. We must both come under the authority of God (submit our lives to His leadership) and purposefully choose to not yield to temptations which come from the devil. If we choose to do these two things, Satan is powerless over us.

Therefore submit to God.
Resist the devil and he will flee from you.
- James 4:7 (NKJV)

Battling Our Fears About the Future (Part 2)

The following are excellent verses to memorize and use against Satan when he attacks us with fears about the future:

- **"Never will I leave you; never will I forsake you."** So we say with confidence, **"The LORD is my helper; I will not be afraid. What can man do to me?"** *- Hebrews 13:5b-6 (NIV)*

- **Fear not, for I am with you; be not dismayed, for I am your God. I will strengthen you, yes, I will help you, I will uphold you with My righteous right hand.** *- Isaiah 41:10 (NKJV)*

- **For God has not given us a spirit of fear, but of power and of love and of a sound mind.** *- 2 Timothy 1:7 (NKJV)*

- **Be anxious for nothing, but in everything by prayer and supplication, with thanksgiving, let your requests be made known to God; and the peace of God, which surpasses all understanding, will guard your hearts and minds through Christ Jesus.** *- Philippians 4:6-7 (NKJV)*

- **When I am afraid, I will trust in you. In God, whose word I praise, in God I trust; I will not be afraid. What can mortal man do to me?** *- Psalm 56:3-4 (NIV)*

- **He shall not be afraid of evil tidings: his heart is fixed, trusting in the LORD.** *- Psalm 112:7 (KJV)*

- **You will keep him in perfect peace, whose mind is stayed on You, because he trusts in You.** *- Isaiah 26:3 (NKJV)*

The Necessity of the Old Testament to Understanding the New Testament

Did you know that the book of Revelation contains over three hundred references to Old Testament prophecies, and not a single one is specifically cited? As an example, consider Revelation 1:7, which presents the theme of the whole book.

This verse is a composite of Old Testament prophecies taken from Daniel 7 and Zechariah 12, but no references are cited. They are just quoted. And so it goes throughout the book of Revelation. Is it any wonder why many Christians who spend little time studying the Old Testament are unable to understand the book of Revelation? In a similar way, Christians often have difficulty understanding what is said in the book of Hebrews about Jesus' death being a fulfillment of the Old Testament sacrificial system.

And what about the seven feasts of Israel (Leviticus 23), every one of which has profound prophetic significance? Many Christians do not even know what the feasts are, much less how four of the seven have been fulfilled in the life of Jesus and the fulfillment of the other three are yet to come.

An understanding of the Hebrew Scriptures is absolutely essential to the full understanding of the New Testament.

BEHOLD, HE IS COMING WITH THE CLOUDS, and every eye will see Him, even those who pierced Him; and all the tribes of the earth will mourn over Him. So it is to be.
- Revelation 1:7 (NASV)

The Practicality of Prophecy

Even though well over one-fourth of the Bible is prophetic, prophecy is one of the most ignored parts of God's Word. Many pastors spend little time preaching on it. There are many reasons for this, but one of the most frequently cited reasons is that "there is no down-to-earth practical value in the study of prophecy." In other word, prophecy is just too vague, futuristic, and irrelevant for today.

Nothing could be further from the truth! For one thing, the strength of one's hope is directly related to the knowledge of God's promises. Bible prophecy gives hope – which is a desperately needed commodity in today's darkening world. **Equally important is the fact that prophecy totally transforms a congregation if they understand the truth of two prophetic promises: 1) Jesus is returning, and 2) His return could occur at any moment.**

Most Christians believe in the return of Jesus intellectually, but not in a heartfelt, imminent way. Thus, the belief has no impact on the way they live, and most have put His return off to the far distant future. Christians who are truly convinced of the return of Jesus at any moment will commit themselves to holiness and evangelism. What could be more down-to-earth and practical?

...But we know that when He is revealed, we shall be like Him...and everyone who has this hope in Him purifies himself, just as He is pure.
- 1 John 3:2-3 (NKJV)

FEBRUARY

Perfect Peace

Isaiah 26:3

Arlene Faith Kortright

Thou dost keep him in per - fect peace, whose mind is stayed on Thee, be - cause he trusts in Thee I - sai - ah twenty - six three

LORD, teach me to trust and obey You. Keep my eyes focused on You so I can have Your peace and be at one with You. My mind wants to wander and when it does, fear and negative thoughts enter. Please remove my wrong thoughts and replace them with Your Word. I love Your Word, help me to memorize it. **Amen**

Preparing for the End Times

God loves us and wants us to know and prepare for the *End Times*. He also tells us *how* to prepare ourselves for His soon return. The Bible seems to address this in the parable of the talents – where the servant who hoards his talents (gifts, possessions, and/or abilities) without putting them to use – is punished (Matthew 25:14-30). The following advice, however, is included to help us:

- Do not be afraid. - *Psalm 46:1-3*

- Remember what Christ did for you. - *1 Corinthians 11:26*

- "Set your mind on things above," not the things on earth. - *Colossians 3:1-4*

- Increase in love toward one another so God can keep you holy until Christ appears. - *1 Thessalonians 3:12-13*

- Teach God's Word and be ready to share it. - *2 Timothy 4:1-2*

- Encourage other believers and meet together. - *Hebrews 10:24-25*

- Be patient and steadfast, and strengthen your heart. - *James 5:8*

- Purify yourself, and follow Christ's example. - *1 John 3:2-3*

- Look for the blessed hope. - *Titus 2:12-13*

- Comfort each other with God's promises. - *1 Thessalonians 4:13-18*

- Build your faith, love God, pray and have compassion for lost and weaker believers. - *Jude 20-23*

I will instruct you and teach you in the way you should go; I will guide you with My eye.
- Psalm 32:8 (NKJV)

Prophetic Picture in an Olive Tree (Part 1)

David makes an interesting and prophetic statement in Psalm 52:8, "I am like an **olive tree** in the house of God." The olive tree is very unique and plays an important symbolic role in Scripture. Particularly fascinating is how it pictures the **nature** of a **mature Christian** as we become passionate followers of Christ.

Olive Tree	Christians
The fruit fresh off the tree is **bitter** and must be treated with lye to neutralize its acid, making it edible.	Our lives are **sinful** until we obey Christ – who removes our sin and makes us a blessing to others.
Better olives develop from **grafted seedlings.**	Only when we are **grafted into Christ** can we grow and become truly productive.
The trees can handle very **tough** weather conditions but need good soil.	We can handle the **toughest of times**, but only with Christ's help and a good foundation in His Word.
The **best oil** comes from the olives after they've been shaken, bruised, crushed, squeezed, ground and the impurities removed.	Christ uses life's troubles, disappointments, failures, humiliation, and sorrow **for our good** (*Romans 8:28*). He removes our impurities to make us the *best* we can be.
Only about 1 in 100 flowers will produce a fruit.	Many claim to be Christians, but **few** produce fruit. (*Matthew 7:12-23*)

Prophetic Picture in an Olive Tree (Part 2)

Olive Tree	Christians
It takes four to eight years to **mature** and produce fruit. Full production takes 15-20 years.	We, too, need to spend **time** praying and studying God's Word in order to produce the best fruit!
It can produce fruit even when it is many hundreds of years **old.**	God tells us in Psalm 92:14-15 that we "Shall still bring forth fruit in **old age.**"
The tree can be chopped down, but many **new shoots** grow in its place to become trees.	We can physically die, but Jesus will use our lives to bring forth **new believers** to continue God's work if our example was rooted in Christ.
The **wood** is twisted and gnarled; yet beautiful ornaments can be made from it.	Our **lives** are a gnarled mess, yet God creates something beautiful out of us when we submit to Him and allow Him to work in us.
The tree trunk grows **hollow** inside, but the **outside layers** grow harder, thicker, and more beautifully grained.	We, too, should grow hollow **(empty of ourselves)** as we age, and stronger in Christ as our **spiritual skin** thickens, making us become beautiful reflections of Christ.
The oil was used in **offerings, food, lamps, and anointing.**	We, too, are **sacrifices and offerings** to God, **feed** the lost with His Word, **light** the darkness, and **honor/live for** Him as His anointed children.

Israel's Trees are Back

At the time of the Jewish exodus from Egypt in 1400 B.C., there were forests in Israel. *Isaiah, Jeremiah,* and *Ezekiel* all mentioned the forests and groves of Israel. During the reign of King Solomon, Israel had many tree planting projects (Eccl. 2:4-6). As Israel declined morally, however, so did its trees (Jeremiah 8:12-13). Destruction of her forests began in 70 A.D. under Titus of Rome. History records trees were used in the following ways:

- *Romans* – Crosses and war machines
- *Muslims* – Mosques
- *Crusaders* – Firewood and building castles
- *Turks* – Railroad ties and stoking engines

In the early 1900s, there were no trees on the mountains of Israel and only a few in cities like Jericho. Isaiah predicted that *Israel would be reforested in the End Times* so people would know that the LORD had His hand in this. **Over 240 million trees were planted in Israel during the twentieth century**. Israel was the *only nation in the world* to enter the twenty-first century with a net *gain* of trees.

I will plant in the wilderness the cedar and the acacia tree, the myrtle and the oil tree; I will set in the desert the cypress tree and the pine and the box tree together, that they may see and know and consider and understand together, that the hand of the LORD has done this, and the Holy One of Israel has created it.
- Isaiah 41:19-20 (NKJV)

Understanding Prophecy (2 Peter 1:19-21)

There are key facts we must understand about prophecy.

1. God **knows** the future. - *Isaiah 46:9-10*

2. God **reveals** the future ahead of time. - *Amos 3:7; Isaiah 46:9-10*

3. **Over one-fourth** of the Bible is prophecy.

4. The Bible is **reliable**. - *Isaiah 14:24; 40:8; 46:10; Matthew 5:18*

5. We have **proof** that Biblical prophecy happened. - *Historical records.*

6. We must **understand** what God says about prophecy. - *2 Peter 1:19-21*
   a. Prophecy is *sure* and *accurate*.
   b. We would be wise to *pay attention* to it.
   c. Prophecy, like a light, *opens up* other parts of Scripture.
   d. Prophecy is *from God*, not man.

And so we have the prophetic word confirmed, which you do well to heed as a light that shines in a dark place, until the day dawns and the morning star rises in your hearts; knowing this first, that no prophecy of Scripture is of any private interpretation, for prophecy never came by the will of man, but holy men of God spoke as they were moved by the Holy Spirit.
- 2 Peter 1:19-21 (NKJV)

Paying Attention to Prophecy Makes Us Wise

God tells us in 2 Peter 1:19 that since prophecy is confirmed or made sure, we would be wise to pay attention to it. Heeding prophecy *increases our wisdom* in the following ways:

1. We will **live knowing we are accountable** to our Creator.
   - *Romans 14:11-18*
2. We are given a chance to **give up our sins** in order to be more like Jesus. - *1 John 3:2-3*
3. We have a chance to **earn the reward** promised for those who love Jesus and look forward to His coming.
   - *2 Timothy 4:8*
4. We learn about heaven, which gives us **reasons to hope** and **share this hope** with others.
   - *Revelation 21*
5. We learn about hell, which offers us (and the people we tell) the **chance to avoid** it. - *Matthew 13:24-50*
6. We are **motivated to obey** Christ and be **patient**.
   - *Hebrews 6:10-12*
7. We **live in the awareness** that the end will come because Jesus said it would. - *Matthew 24*
8. We can **teach others more effectively** because Christ is with us and we want to obey God's command to teach all nations.
   - *Matthew 28:19-20*
9. We will know that we are **pleasing the Lord.**
   - *Revelation 1:3*
10. We will know what warning signs **to look for and how to prepare.** We will learn that God has a plan, is in control, and can be trusted. - *Matthew 24, 25*

**And so we have the prophetic word confirmed,
which you do well to heed....
- 2 Peter 1:19 (NKJV)**

You Can Know for Sure if You Will
Have Everlasting Life with God

Biblical Christianity is the **only religion** in the world in which you **can know for sure** that you will have everlasting life with God. **It is the only belief system that is based on testable ways to support its truth source, the Bible.**

If the Bible's accuracy rate is one hundred percent in its *historical, scientific, geographical, and prophetical* evidence, *then* it can be trusted in its prophecy on how we can know for sure we will have everlasting life with God. John addresses this prophecy most clearly. Below are a few key verses.

- **Jesus said to him, "I am the way, the truth, and the life. No one comes to the Father except through Me."** *- John 14:6 (NKJV)*

- **He who believes in the Son has everlasting life; and he who does not believe the Son shall not see life, but the wrath of God abides on him.** *- John 3:36 (NKJV)*

- **And this is the testimony: that God has given us eternal life, and this life is in His Son. He who has the Son has life; he who does not have the Son of God does not have life. These things I have written to you who believe in the name of the Son of God, that YOU MAY KNOW that you have eternal life, and that you may continue to believe in the name of the Son of God.** *- 1 John 5:11-13 (NKJV)*

- **See also:** *John 3:16; John 6:47; John 12:26; John 14:1-3, 6; John 17:3*

Prophecy of the Marriage Supper

Revelation 19 announces the *marriage of the Lamb.* We are told there will be gladness and rejoicing. Rejoicing means we will literally "jump for joy" as we give honor to the Lamb. Throughout Scripture, the Lamb is the biblical symbol for Jesus Christ. In this passage, the Lamb (the bridegroom) is clearly Jesus *(John 3:28-30).* His bride is the group of saints or godly believers who "made herself ready" for Christ *(Revelation 19:7).*

We discover in Revelation 19:8 that *Christ's wife* is clothed in fine linen, *clean* meaning "pure" and *white* which means "radiant and magnificent in appearance." The *fine linen* is defined as the "righteousness" of saints. Romans 5 instructs us that this *righteousness* can only come through *our faith in Christ*, which is available to all, but rejected by many.

In Revelation 19:9, those who are called to this supper are the *blessed ones.* **This is a feast we will not want to miss.** Those who miss it will be part of the second supper described at the end of the chapter (Revelation 19:21). This is a supper you DO NOT want to attend!

Let us be glad and rejoice, and give honour to him: for the marriage of the Lamb is come, and his wife hath made herself ready. And to her was granted that she should be arrayed in fine linen, clean and white: for the fine linen is the righteousness of saints. And he saith unto me, "Write, Blessed are they which are called unto the marriage supper of the Lamb." And he said unto me, These are the true sayings of God. - Revelation 19:7-9

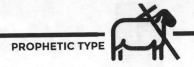

Adam Points Us to Christ

Adam serves as a negative type or symbol of *Christ*. Adam **chose to disobey** God and brought sin into the world. In His mercy, God came to Earth in the person of Christ, God's Son. Christ **chose to obey** God the Father perfectly, even to the point of sacrificing His life on the cross. This qualified Him to make the needed payment for our sins so we could have everlasting life. If we confess our sins, turn from them, and accept Christ's gift of payment for our sins, we are under the "new Adam," Jesus Christ.

Adam	Jesus
A *living soul* - 1 Corinthians 15:45	A *life-giving spirit* - 1 Corinthians 15:45
Of the *earth* - 1 Corinthians 15:47	From *Heaven* - 1 Corinthians 15:47
Rebelled against God - Genesis 3:1-7	*Obeyed* God perfectly - Hebrews 5:8-9; Phil. 2:8
Through him, all were made *sinners* - Romans 5:19	Through Him, all can be made *righteous* - Romans 5:19
Brought *death* - Romans 5:14-19, - 1 Corinthians 15:22	Brought *life* - Hebrews 2:14-15 - 1 Corinthians 15:22
Had but lost dominion - Genesis 1:26-27; 3:17-24	*Won* dominion Hebrews 2:5-9

And so it is written, "The first man Adam became a living being." The last Adam became a life-giving spirit. And as we have borne the image of the man of dust, we shall also bear the image of the heavenly Man.
- I Corinthians 15:45, 49 (NKJV)

Prophecy as an Evangelistic Tool

One of the greatest values of Bible prophecy is its effectiveness as a tool of evangelism. The classic example of this truth can be found in the very first Gospel sermon that was preached by Peter on the Day of Pentecost, as recorded in Acts 2:14-36. This powerful sermon, which produced a response of three thousand salvations, consisted entirely of Bible prophecy from start to finish. Peter quoted one Messianic prophecy after another and then declared that each one was fulfilled in the life of Jesus.

The effectiveness of prophecy as a means of evangelism is also demonstrated in the story of Philip and the Ethiopian eunuch (Acts 8:26-40). Philip, who was one of the Church's first evangelists, encountered an Ethiopian Jew on his way home from having gone to Jerusalem to worship. The Ethiopian was reading a scroll containing the book of Isaiah as he traveled along in his chariot. When Philip flagged him down and asked if he understood what he was reading, the Ethiopian said he did not. The passage in question was Isaiah 53, one of the greatest prophecies in the Bible about the Messiah and His sacrifice for the sins of mankind.

Philip explained that the passage was a prophecy about the Messiah and that Jesus had fulfilled it. The Ethiopian responded by accepting Jesus as his Lord and Savior, and by being baptized in a pond along the side of the road. He then went on his way rejoicing.

**...For the testimony of Jesus is the spirit of prophecy.
- Revelation 19:10**

Messianic Prophecy in Genesis 3:14-15

The very first promise of a coming Savior is given to us after the fall of man in Genesis chapter 3. Genesis 3:14-15 informs us of a conversation between the LORD God and the serpent (Satan). God said there would be **enmity (hatred) between Satan and the woman** ("woman" being a biblical symbol for the Jewish nation). There would likewise be enmity between **Satan's seed and the woman's Seed (Christ).** Satan's hatred for Israel can be traced back in both biblical and secular history. It continues today and is predicted to come to a global climax in the End Times.

Genesis 3:15 is so important that it has been given a special name by theologians. It is known as the Protoevangelium (the *"first gospel"*). It promised the coming and victory of Christ our Savior. He would be the unique Seed of the woman, and not of man's seed. He would be miraculously conceived and virgin-born.

A time of conflict was also predicted where Satan would succeed in grievously injuring Christ and being able to bruise his heel. This happened around four thousand years later at the Crucifixion. The prophecy, however, clearly looked forward to the End Times when Satan's head would be completely crushed by the woman's triumphant Seed, Jesus Christ.

And I will put enmity between you and the woman, and between your seed and her Seed; He shall bruise your head and you shall bruise His heel. - Genesis 3:15 (NKJV)

No Need for Christ's Followers to Fear Death

The fear of death is real, and our Creator Lord and Savior understands this. He clearly addresses this fear in His Word and gives His followers **reasons why we do not need to fear death.**

- Psalm 116:15 – Our entrance to heaven is **precious** to God.
- Hebrews 13:5 – God promises **never to leave us,** which includes before and after death.
- Luke 23:43 – We will **immediately go** to be with Christ at death, like Christ promised the thief on the cross.
- Philippians 1:21-23 – Paul told us our presence with Christ is **far better than life on Earth.**
- 1 John – God tells us we can **know for certain where we will go** when we die.
- Revelation 21 – God gives us a description of heaven so **we can look forward to it** with hope and joy.
- 2 Peter 3:9 – **God wants us** to come to Him.

Precious in the sight of the LORD is the death of his saints.
- Psalm 116:15

Seven Blessings of Revelation

Revelation, the final book of the Bible, has the following **seven blessings.** What wonderful verses to memorize, especially as we look to the time of Christ's return!

1. Blessed is He who <u>reads</u> and those who <u>hear</u> the words of this prophecy, and <u>keep those things which are written in it;</u> for the time is near. - *Revelation 1:3 (NKJV)*

2. ...Blessed are the dead who <u>die in the Lord</u> from now on. "Yes," says the Spirit, "that they may rest from their labors, and their works follow them." - *Revelation 14:13 (NKJV)*

3. ...Blessed is he who <u>watches,</u> and <u>keeps his garments,</u> lest he walk naked and they see his shame. - *Revelation 16:15 (NKJV)*

4. ...Blessed are those who are <u>called to the marriage supper</u> of the Lamb! - *Revelation 19:9 (NKJV)*

5. Blessed and holy is he who <u>has part in the first resurrection.</u> Over such the second death has no power, but they shall be priests of God and of Christ, and shall reign with Him a thousand years. - *Revelation 20:6 (NKJV)*

6. ...Blessed is he who <u>keeps the words of the prophecy</u> of this book. *-Revelation 22:7 (NKJV)*

7. Blessed are those who <u>do His commandments,</u> that they may have the right to the tree of life, and may enter through the gates into the city. - *Revelation 22:14 (NKJV)*

Israel's Flower Prophecy

Israel was desolate at the beginning of the 1900s and regarded as wasteland. As of 2006, this tiny country produces five percent of the world's flowers, only surpassed by the Netherlands and Kenya. **As a major player in the world's flower industry**, Israel has the greatest variety of species year-round. Israel's flower-related industries bring over two hundred million dollars into its economy each year.

Israel's process for picking, packing, and distributing flowers is so efficient that flowers can arrive in Europe on temperature-controlled jets within two days of harvest. Israel is also **a world leader in agro-technology**, especially in growing plants and flowers in hot dry climates. The expertise that Israel has developed is sought after by the European Union, which imports her agricultural technology, such as genetically cloned, climate-adjusted seeds; fruit-picking robots; and drip irrigation systems. One of Israel's most popular horticultural exports to the European Union is a green filler, used for making bouquets of African roses.

Israel is blooming abundantly - just as Isaiah predicted.

**Israel shall blossom and bud,
and fill the face of the world with fruit.
- Isaiah 27:6b**

Truths that Unlock Revelation

There are many false beliefs about the book of Revelation. In order to understand it correctly, we must know the truth.

LIE: No one can really understand Revelation.

TRUTH: God wrote Revelation for the purpose of revealing the future. He meant for us to understand it and even promised a special blessing for doing so. - *Revelation 1:3*

LIE: Revelation is a book of doom and gloom. It is unrelated to the rest of Scripture.

TRUTH: Revelation takes Old Testament prophecies and arranges them so we can better understand the sequence of future events. In fact, of the 404 verses in this book, 278 verses refer back to the Old Testament. Most of Revelation is not new information. Only the last two chapters deal with something totally new, the eternal state of life *after* Christ's 1,000-year rule in the Millennial Kingdom.

LIE: Revelation is a book of "symbols" which can be interpreted in a variety of ways. It is up to the reader as to how they wish to understand it.

TRUTH: The symbols of the Bible, including Revelation, can be interpreted correctly. If the people, places, events, or things can't be taken literally or aren't explained in the passage, their meanings are found elsewhere in the Bible.

**The secret things belong to the LORD our God: but those things which are revealed belong unto us and to our children forever, that we may do all the words of this law.
- Deuteronomy 29:29 (NKJV)**

The Heavens Have a Voice

David wrote Psalm 19 centuries before Christ was born. In the first three verses, he included some scientific foreknowledge. Only God could have known and inspired David to record that the heavens have a "voice." The first three verses of Psalm 19 contain Hebrew words which were translated as: "firmament, speech, voice, and heard."

> *Firmament* – Expanse of the sky
> *Speech* – Utterance, word
> *Voice* – Sound
> *Heard* – Hear intelligently

Before the early 1900s, those who read the Bible could only understand these verses as poetic. Since **radio frequencies** were discovered, however, these verses can now be taken literally. **Objects in space do make sounds!** They give off electromagnetic waves, which can be changed into sound waves. The waves can not only be **measured and recorded**, but also have order and beauty!

The heavens declare the glory of God; and the firmament shows His handwork. Day unto day utters speech, and night unto night reveals knowledge. There is no speech nor language where their voice is not heard.
- Psalm 19:1-3 (NKJV)

Six Main Types of Prophecy (Part 1)

In his book, *Ancient Prophecies Revealed*, author and lecturer
Dr. Ken Johnson lists a number of different types of prophecy.
Explanations and examples are given for the abbreviated list below:

1. **Literal Prophecy** – is the most common form. It needs no
   explanation and occurs exactly as predicted.
   - *Isaiah 7:14* tells us, **"Behold the virgin shall conceive,
     and bear a son and shall call his name Immanuel."**
   - *Matthew 1:23* tells us that this prophecy was fulfilled
     exactly as it was stated.

2. **Timeline Prophecy** – occurs when so many days, months
   or years are given from one event until another specific event
   occurs.
   - *Daniel 9:24-26* records in a riddle the number of days
     from the command to rebuild Jerusalem until the Ruler
     comes. This prophecy was fulfilled to the exact day!

3. **Inscription Prophecy** – is when a word (or group of words)
   in Hebrew or Greek is used prophetically because of its
   specific meaning.
   - *Genesis 5:21-27* describes Methuselah as the son of
     the godly man Enoch and the grandfather of Noah. His
     name is made from two Hebrew words, "meth" meaning
     death and "salah" meaning **sent.** If put in a sentence,
     his name would mean **"when he is dead, it shall be
     sent."** Methuselah died one week before Noah's Flood.
     His name was a prophetic warning to the people. It is
     interesting to note how God, in His mercy, allowed
     him to live 969 years. He lived longer than any man on
     Earth. God is longsuffering and withholds the judgment
     we deserve as long as possible to give us every possible
     opportunity to repent.

Six Main Types of Prophecy (Part 2)

4. <u>**Symbolic Prophecy**</u> – uses symbols to represent things, events, places, or people. The meanings of the symbols are given within the chapter, book, or elsewhere in the Bible.
   - *Revelation 1* – John had a vision and saw seven lampstands and seven stars. Within the chapter we are told that the lampstands are seven churches. The stars are the seven angels, or messengers, of the seven churches.

5. <u>**Double Fulfillment Prophecy**</u> – is fulfilled at one time in history and is fulfilled again in the *same* way at a later date. This can be hundreds or thousands of years later.
   - *Daniel 11* – An antichrist type would place an abomination in the Temple. ***Antiochus Epiphanes*** fulfilled this in 167 B.C.
   - *Matthew 24:14-15* – Jesus warned that Daniel's prophecy would be fulfilled again by the ***Antichrist*** in the End Times.

6. <u>**Dual Purpose Prophecy**</u> – is given and fulfilled at one time in history and also serves as a type of prophecy for the future, yet is a totally different prophecy.
   - *Genesis 6:3-7* – God warned the world of a Worldwide Flood to judge sin. He also used this prophecy as a warning that He will judge sin again. This time, however, will be the **final** judgment and will happen with **fire** - 2 Peter 3:3-7.

Psalm 46 Complements Jesus' End Times Prophecy

In Matthew 24:3 the disciples asked Jesus what "signs" would signal the end of the world. His answer to them is fully recorded in Matthew 24 and 25.

Jesus first addressed the things that would be the *beginning* of "the sorrows to come." He said there would be deception, wars, and rumors of wars. Nations and kingdoms would rise up against each other, and famines, plagues, and earthquakes would occur in various places. **Psalm 46 tells us not to fear such things.**

Hundreds of years earlier, God gave words of assurance through the writer of Psalm 46. We are reminded that God is an all-powerful God who is our *refuge* (shelter) and *strength* (security) in all circumstances. We do not need to fear.

As we draw closer to the end of time, Jesus predicted more disasters would come. The Hebrew psalmist reminds us that no *trouble* (adversity, affliction, anguish) or *natural disaster* (volcano, flood, earthquake) keeps us outside of God's refuge and strength. We can trust Him completely.

God is our refuge and strength, a very present help in trouble. Therefore we will not fear, even though the earth be removed, and though the mountains be carried into the midst of the sea; though its waters roar and be troubled, though the mountains shake with its swelling.
- Psalm 46:1-3 (NKJV)

Heaven's 18 "No More" Promises

Revelation 21 gives us more specific details about heaven than any other chapter in the Bible. Reading about its "heavenly" prophecies gives us much to look forward to. May it motivate us to keep *our focus on Jesus* and live our remaining days on Earth for our Lord and Savior. **One of the interesting aspects about Revelation 21 is what it says will NOT be part of our heavenly home:**

Revelation 21:1	No more old heaven, no more old earth, no more sea
Revelation 21:3	No more having to dwell without God
Revelation 21:4	No tears, no death, no sorrow, no pain, no crying, no former things, no lacking of anything
Revelation 21:22	No temple in the holy city of New Jerusalem
Revelation 21:23	No need of the sun and moon to shine in it
Revelation 21:25	No closed gates, no night in the city
Revelation 21:27	No things that are unholy, detestable, or a lie

But as it is written, "Eye hath not seen, nor ear heard, neither have entered into the heart of man," the things which God hath prepared for them that love Him.
- 1 Corinthians 2:9

Prophecy More Certain than Science

Science is based on repeatable experimentation and observation. Yet events of the past cannot be directly observed or repeated. Much that masquerades as science is really just storytelling and guesswork. No one has ever seen: chemicals come alive; one body structure transform into another; any new organ arise within a creature; matter or energy appear from nothing; any new star form; or coded information (such as the DNA code) write itself. Every experiment and observation of science tells us things do not happen by themselves.

2 Peter 1:19 tells us that prophecy is actually a surer way of knowing the truth than observation. The context of this passage is Peter's account of seeing Jesus transformed into the glorious light of God and hearing a voice from heaven proclaiming, "This is my beloved Son, in whom I am well pleased." Peter saw and heard these things, yet he tells us that prophecy is an even "more sure" way of knowing that Jesus is God than his eyewitness observations.

Prophecy shows that Scripture is inspired by God Himself because it predicts the future with unerring accuracy. before it happens. Over three hundred Old Testament passages pertain to the first coming of the Messiah. They cover His lineage, birth, life, death, and resurrection. The statistical odds (i.e. scientifically observable and testable probability) of these events happening by chance are a scientific impossibility. Thus, prophecy makes it "more sure" than direct observation that Jesus was who He claims to be – God, in human flesh, who came to take away our sins.

> **We have also a more sure word of prophecy;**
> **whereunto ye do well that ye take heed,**
> **as unto a light that shineth in a dark place...."**
> **– 2 Peter 1:19**

Israel's Land Rejuvenation Prophecy (Part 1)

Ezekiel 36:33-36 tells us that God will clean Israel of all her sins on a specific day in the future. He says God will also enable Israel to **dwell in her cities, rebuild her ruins, and till her land so it will not lay desolate** in the sight of anyone who passed by. The passage goes on to tell us that Israel will **become like the garden of Eden** and **the land inhabited.** Verse 36 of this passage tells us God will do this because, *"I the LORD, have spoken it, and I will do it."* - *Ezekiel 36:36* The nations all around will <u>know</u> the LORD did it.

Although this prophecy will be completely fulfilled when Christ returns to Earth to reign, we saw its beginning coming to pass in the 1900s, and most rapidly after 1948, when Israel became a nation.

Consider the following signs of fulfillment:
- In the early 1900s, land was purchased, small collective farms were started, and swamps were drained via canals dug to the sea.
- More than 240 million trees were planted in the twentieth century.
- The Nation Water Carrier was inaugurated in 1964. Eighty percent of its water was allotted to agriculture.
- Drip irrigation was developed to distribute water more effectively.

The desolate land shall be tilled instead of lying desolate in the sight of all who pass by.
- Ezekiel 36:34 (NKJV)

Israel's Land Rejuvenation Prophecy (Part 2)

In just the last sixty years, many innovations have made Israel a unique "garden country":

- Water treatment systems were developed in Israel that recapture eighty-six percent of used water for irrigation. (Spain comes in second at nineteen percent.)
- Desalination plants were designed to convert sea water into fresh water. In 2013, the world's largest desalination plant, the Sorek Plant, opened ten miles south of Tel Aviv. It can produce seven million gallons of drinkable water every hour. Altogether, Israel's desalination plants provide fifty-five percent of the water used in the country.
- Israel's dairies produce the highest amounts of milk per animal in the world.
- Israel is one of the world's leading fresh citrus producers and exporters. It is considered the breadbasket of the Middle East.
- The world's first long shelf life tomato varieties were developed in Israel.
- Overall, Israel is the world's leader in agricultural research and development.
- Israel has devised water conservation techniques to save the one inch of rain per year in the Negev Desert (this single desert covers fifty-five percent of Israel's land).
- Israel has genetically engineered plants to grow on brackish water reservoirs that lie below the desert's surface.
- The United Nations declared Israel "the most agriculturally efficient land on Earth."

And they shall say, This land that was desolate is become like the garden of Eden....
- Ezekiel 36:35a

An Unbiblical Prophecy

There is no prophecy in the entire Bible stating that God is finished with Israel. Scripture clearly tells us in Jeremiah 30:11 that He will justly chasten Israel and punish her, but He *will not* completely destroy her. God also makes it clear that He will allow Israel and His beloved Jerusalem to be destroyed for a time but *will also* bring her back as a nation. This took place on May 14, 1948.

In order to claim that God is finished with Israel, one has to deny the truth of many verses in the Bible including the following:

- God will raise an ensign (flag, banner) for Israel.
  - Isaiah 11:12a
- The time will come when Israel will take root again.
  - Isaiah 27:6
- God will gather His people back to Israel.
  - Isaiah 11:12b; 43:5-7
  - Jeremiah 16:14-15; 23:3; 29:14; 30:3; 32:37
  - Ezekiel 11:16-17; 28:25-26; 34:12; 37:21
  - Amos 9:11-15
- Israel will live in the land God gave them.
  - Jeremiah 23:8; 30:3
  - Ezekiel 34:13-15; 37:21-22

God is not finished with Israel!

**I say then, has God cast away His people? Certainly not!...
God has not cast away His people whom He foreknew...
- Romans 11:1-2 (NKJV)**

Prophecy: Suffering Will Bring Joy

God's prophetic promise through Peter gives us hope during suffering. We are told in 1 Peter 1:3-5 that our living hope is in Jesus. He died for our sins so we would be able, by His power through our faith in Him, to have eternal life. 1 Peter 1:6-7 goes on to encourage us to stay focused on this and the fact that though we face trials, **our suffering on Earth has purpose**. The Lord reminds us that suffering (whether physical, emotional, or spiritual), compared to an unending eternity with Him, is really only a little while, and **God teaches us much through it.**

This suffering weans us away from dependence upon the world, points us to heaven, and helps us value His blessings more than ever. Suffering enables us to help others, keeps us from sin, and strengthens our spiritual character. Through suffering, we are refined for greater usefulness. It proves God's grace is sufficient and at the same time is proof of our faith in Him. God tells us our faith through suffering is far more precious than gold. It will **result in praise, glory, and honor** not only *to* but also *from* our Lord God and Savior!

In this you greatly rejoice, though now for a little while, if need be, you have been grieved by various trials, that the genuineness of your faith, being much more precious than gold that perishes, though it is tested by fire, may be found to praise, honor, and glory at the revelation of Jesus Christ.
- 1 Peter 1:6-7 (NKJV)

The Sufficiency of Old Testament Prophecy

Old Testament prophecy alone is sufficient to bring a person to acceptance of Jesus as the promised Messiah of God. A good example can be found in a very familiar verse that the Apostle Paul wrote to a young disciple named Timothy. Paul declared: *"...from childhood you have known the sacred writings which are able to give you the wisdom that leads to salvation through faith which is in Christ Jesus"* (2 Timothy 3:15).

Christians reading this verse today tend to visualize Timothy's parents sharing with him New Testament Bible verses. **But the New Testament didn't even exist when Paul wrote these words in the First Century.** The "sacred writings" Paul refers to are the Hebrew Scriptures which we refer to today as the Old Testament. And since those Scriptures do not specifically mention Jesus, Paul must be referring to the Messianic prophecies that Jesus fulfilled.

Those prophecies are vitally important today if you want to try to lead a Jew to Jesus as his Messiah. Jews don't read the New Testament because they consider it to be an apostate, Gentile book. Witnessing to a Jew must be out of his own 'sacred writings' – what we call the Old Testament.

But sanctify the Lord God in your hearts: and be ready always to give an answer to every man that asketh you a reason of the hope that is in you with meekness and fear.
- 1 Peter 3:15

Understanding Conditional and Unconditional Prophecies

God demonstrated His control and planning at the beginning of creation. He spoke all things into being out of nothing. He laid the foundation for predictive prophecy. God's pattern of prophecy and fulfillment began in Genesis. He spoke, which is <u>predictive prophecy</u>, and then it happened, which is <u>prophetic fulfillment</u>. An example of this is first found in Genesis 1:3: *"Then God said, Let there be light; and there was light."* God followed this pattern throughout the first chapter of Genesis (Genesis 1:3,6,9,14,24,26).

It is important to know that all the prophecies of the Bible are either conditional or unconditional. The fulfillment of **conditional prophecies depends on human responses.** For example, God told Adam if he ate from the tree of knowledge of good and evil he would surely die. This prophetic fulfillment depended on the actions of Adam (Genesis 2:16-17).

<u>Unconditional prophecies</u>, on the other hand, **do not depend on man's response.** Genesis contains three of the most important unconditional prophecies in the Bible:
1. The triumph of the "Seed of the woman" over the serpent (Genesis 3:14-15). This was fulfilled by Jesus Christ at the cross. We do nothing to earn or deserve our salvation.
2. God's prophetic covenant with Abraham promised him three major provisions: land, descendants (including Christ), and worldwide blessings (Genesis 12:1-3; 15;1-21; 17:1-21).
3. God's prophetic blessing through Jacob on the twelve tribes of Israel (Genesis 49).

The last two prophecies have yet to reach complete fulfillment and *will* be filfilled since they depend on God alone.

Prophecy in a Land Covenant

The conditions for the Jews' current possession and enjoyment of Israel are set forth in the Jewish Land Covenant of Deuteronomy 28, 29, and 30. Only God could have inspired the **biblical writers to describe the historical events regarding the Jews and the Land promised to them thousands of years in advance.**

1. **Dispersion** among the nations as punishment for idolatry. - *Deuteronomy 28:64-65*
2. **Persecution** by the nations where the Jews are dispersed. - *Deuteronomy 28:65-67*
3. **Affliction** of the land of Israel until it becomes a "wasteland." - *Deuteronomy 29:22-28*
4. **Regathering of the Remnant** to the land of promise. (This began in 1948 and will be completed at the Second Coming.) - *Deuteronomy 30:3-4*
5. **Repentance** of the Jewish people. - *Deuteronomy 30:1-2*
6. **Spiritual regeneration** of the repenting remnant. (God will change the hearts of the people.) - *Deuteronomy 30: 6,8*
7. **Repossession of the Promised Land** by the Jews. (This happened on May 14, 1948, and will be completely fulfilled at the Second Coming.) - *Deuteronomy 30:5*
8. **Punishment of the enemies** of Israel. (Christ Himself will complete this at the Second Coming.) - *Deuteronomy 30:7*
9. **Blessing of the re-established nation** of Israel with more material prosperity than ever before. (Christ grants this after His Second Coming.) - *Deuteronomy 30:5,9*

Prophecy in the Zodiac

In Genesis 1:14, God was in the midst of creating the heavens when He said He made the lights in the heavens for the purpose of "*Signs and for seasons, and for days and years…*" The Hebrew word for "*signs*" in this verse means a signal as a beacon, monument, or distinguishing mark.

Through a careful study of ancient writings concerning the constellations, we can see a prophecy. Virtually all the ancient civilized nations – Babylonia, Assyria, Persia, Egypt, Greece, and Italy – have descriptions of the twelve major star systems, the "Constellations of the Zodiac." What is interesting is the fact that nearly all had the *same* twelve signs, in the *same* order, with the *same* representations for the signs. This points to a common original source.

An in-depth study of the constellations reveals God's prophetic "gospel" in the stars. For instance, the constellation Virgo is commonly acknowledged to represent a virgin, and constellation Leo represents a Lion (one of the names for Christ). Other constellations have similar biblical meanings and implications. Most have already occurred, but the complete fulfillment of this Gospel in the sky (the final defeat of Satan) has yet to occur. It will be fulfilled by Jesus Christ at the end of time.

He telleth the number of the stars;
he called them all by their names.
- Psalm 147:4

MARCH

God Did Not Give Us ... Fear

2 Timothy 1:7

Arlene Faith Kortright

For God did not give us a
spir - it of fear, but of po - wer and of
love and of a sound mind, for
God did not give us a spir - it of
fear, but of po - wer and of love and of a
sound mind mind
Two Tim - o - thy one sev - en

LORD, I thank You for reminding me that none of my fears, especially those of the future, come from You. Instead You give me strength, love and a disciplined mind. **Amen**

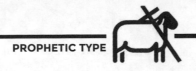
The Tabernacle: Prophetic Type of Christ

The Tabernacle of Moses was built as a prophetic type of Christ. Every aspect turns our eyes toward Jesus Christ and who He is.

The Tabernacle of Moses as a Prophetic Type

1.	The Gate	Jesus as the **Door**	*John 10:9*
2.	The Altar	Jesus as the **Sacrificial Lamb**	*John 1:29*
3.	The Laver	Jesus as the **Spirit Baptizer**	*John 1:33*
4.	The Shewbread	Jesus as the **Bread of Life**	*John 6:35*
5.	The Candlestick	Jesus as the **Light of the World**	*John 8:12*
6.	The Incense	Jesus as the **Intercessor** offering prayers of the Saints to God	*Romans 8:26-27*
7.	The Veil	Jesus as the **One who would rend the veil**, enabling the Saints to have direct access to God through Him	*Matthew 27:51*
8.	The High Priest	Jesus as our High Priest who enters the Holy of Holies in heaven as our **Mediator** before God	*Hebrews 8:1-2, 9:24*

Then have them make a sanctuary for me, and I will dwell among them. Make this tabernacle and all its furnishings exactly like the pattern I will show you.
- Exodus 25:8-9 (NIV)

The "Worldwide Blessing" Through the Jews

God promised Abraham in Genesis 12:1-3 that He would make Abraham the "father of a great nation." God also said that *"all of the families of the earth"* would be blessed through him. **Christ, the direct descendant of Abraham, truly is the *"greatest blessing"* the world has ever known.**

The prophecy, however, does not end here. If one takes a look at the Nobel Prize winners from 1901 to 2015, we get another glimpse of the truth of this remarkable prophecy.

Jewish people currently make up *two-tenths* of one percent of the *world* population, yet of all the people who were awarded the Nobel Prize, *22 percent* were either Jews or people of ½ to ¾ Jewish ancestry. In the fields of scientific research, we find that *26 percent* of the awards went to Jewish recipients. Even when we look at the organizations that were awarded the Nobel Peace Prize, we find that *22 percent* were founded by Jews or people of half-Jewish descent.

**And I will bless them that bless thee, and curse
him that curseth thee: and in thee shall
all families of the earth be blessed.
- Genesis 12:3**

Hope from Habakkuk

As we see the moral decline and hatred of Christians increase worldwide, we can get very discouraged and wonder why God hasn't judged the depravity, cruelty, violence, injustice, and persecution of the righteous.

The book of Habakkuk addresses this question. The same moral climate existed in Judah many hundreds of years before Christ was born. The prophet Habakkuk was deeply troubled and confused. In his book, he shares certain truths about God that were applicable in his day and continue to be so today:

1. God often judges nations who know better by using nations who are even more evil, violent, and cruel. (Hab. 1:6-11)
2. Bloodshed and violence cry out for the judgment of the Holy God. (This is mentioned three times in Hab. 2:8b, 12, 17b.)
3. God is consistent in His prophetic promise that the ungodly "*will* be held guilty" and the "just *will* live by his faith" in God. (Hab. 2:4)
4. We need to take our fears and cries for justice to God in our prayers. **When we recount all the things God has done in the past (Hab. 3:3), we get the confidence that He will be our strength in the future. (Hab. 3:17-19)**

Yet I will exult in the LORD, I will rejoice in the God of my salvation. The Lord GOD is my strength...
- Habakkuk 3:18-19a (NASV)

Jesus is Clearly Identified as the "Messiah" In the Old Testament

The *name of God*, **YHWH**, is made up of four letters of the Hebrew alphabet: **Yud, Hey, Vav,** and **Hey.** It is the most important of all the names of God and is used almost seven thousand times in the Old Testment, which was written in the Hebrew language. The English spelling and pronounciation of this word is "Yahweh" or "Jehovah." Ancient Hebrew has a *pictogram* (picture) for each letter as well as a specific *meaning*. The combined letter meanings of YHWH in the most ancient pictograms are remarkable and clearly reveal the Messiah.

The first letter of the Hebrew word for God is **Yud**. It has a pictogram of a *hand*, which means "mighty work." The second letter, **Hey**, has a pictogram of a *stick figure man with his arms raised up in amazement*, which means "to behold or look upon." The third letter, **Vav** - represented by the pictogram of a *nail or spike*, means - "to secure or save." The final letter repeats the letter Hey - (to behold or look upon). Taken together, YHWH declares the name of God: **"Behold the hand, behold the nail."** The *idea* reveals: **"Behold! The mighty hand that saves and secures."**

The *original Hebrew alphabet* made it possible for all Jewish readers to recognize *Jesus* as Messiah. He would be the *mighty* one (as shown by his power over all, including nature, animals, disease, the demonic, etc.). He would be nailed to the cross, bear the nail marks on His hands, and save mankind from hell. The Messiah, in fact, is God and is revealed from the very beginning of Genesis to the end of Revelation.

**In the beginning was the Word, and the Word was with God, and the Word was God.
- John 1:1**

Reasons for Looking Forward to
the Rapture and Second Coming

Revelation describes the seven-year Tribulation period as the worst time in history, yet some will come to accept Jesus as their Lord and Savior. In spite of the horrific natural disasters, violence, starvation, mass epidemics, evil, persecution and martyrdom, some believers will survive and go into the Millennial Kingdom. They will have these among many other wonderful promises to look forward to:

- Satan will be bound and *Jesus will reign* and be worshipped by all.
- The Jews will recognize their Messiah.
- Multitudes of people will be saved.
- Creation will be *completely* restored once again.
- There will finally be *perfect* peace, justice, and righteousness on Earth.

The raptured believers (those who had accepted Christ and were removed prior to the Tribulation) will also be blessed by these promises. They, however, also have the following additional incredible blessings among many others to look forward to, and be both comforted and blessed by:

- They will not go through the Tribulation. They will meet their bridegroom, Christ, in the air in their newly glorified bodies, never to leave His presence again.
- Many will receive rewards.
- They will rule with Christ in the Millennial Kingdom.
- They can live without fear *right now* in the present.

**Looking for that blessed hope, and the glorious appearing of the great God and our Saviour Jesus Christ.
- Titus 2:13**

The Jewish Population Prophecy

Almost 3,400 years ago, over a thousand years before the Jewish people were scattered throughout the world, Moses predicted this dispersion would happen. According to Roman records, in the first century there were about eight to ten million Jews. Their final dispersion came in 135 A.D. by the Romans. Since then, the Jews have been scattered worldwide just as Moses predicted. They have also been persecuted wherever they went, exactly as Moses also prophesied in Deuteronomy 28:65-67.

Between 1840 and 1939, the Jewish population increased from 4.5 million to 16.7 million. The Nazi Holocaust, however, killed six million Jews. This reduced the worldwide Jewish population to about ten million. Now their numbers have grown to 14 million, with about 6.5 million Jews living in Israel. Had no persecution ever occurred, demographers estimate there *should be* 400 to 500 million Jews alive. **Instead, there are only about four million more than two thousand years ago.** This lower population is a direct fulfillment of the Deuteronomy 4:27 prophecy.

And the LORD will scatter you among the peoples, and you will be left few in number among the nations where the LORD will drive you. - Deuteronomy 4:27 (NKJV)

A Prophecy *Not* in Scripture

Jesus described what the world will be like in the global, spiritual, moral, religious, political, economic, and heavenly spheres at the end of time. If one reads Matthew 24, Mark 13, Luke 17 and 21, as well as the many verses from *almost every book* in the Bible concerning this future coming time, they will not be caught unaware as to what to expect. It is estimated that as much as ten percent of the Bible deals with End Times, yet *most people know little* about this extremely important topic.

The one prophetic piece of information that people do want to know, however, is the *exact date* the world will end. **This date is not given anywhere in the Bible.** Christ simply tells us the way the world will be when He returns; and in Revelation 16:15, He gives a special blessing to those who watch for Him.

If we are serious Christ followers, then we are serious readers of His Word, which in turn enables us to be serious watchers. May we *focus* on the prophecies that are in the Scriptures, *avoid* those that are not, and *keep from becoming* part of the 2 Peter 3:3-4 crowd.

Knowing this first, that there shall come in the last days, scoffers, walking after their own lusts, and saying, Where is the promise of his coming?...
- 2 Peter 3:3-4

The Revival of Ancient Hebrew Language

During the Diaspora that began in 70 A.D., the majority of Jews were scattered over all nations of the world. They had to learn the language of the country into which they relocated. Many continued to speak Hebrew, but over the centuries, the language became corrupted. As more and more Jewish people began to migrate to Israel in the early 1900s, communication was a real problem. Not only did they speak different languages, but the distorted Hebrew dialects were not understood.

Through the tremendous efforts of Eliezer Ben Yehuda and others, the Hebrew language was revived, and **in 1928 it was recognized as the official language of the returning Jewish people.**

Throughout the Old Testament, God gave many specific prophecies concerning Israel that would serve as a sign of the End Times. The revival of the pure Hebrew language after almost two thousand years is one of those remarkable signs.

**"Therefore wait ye upon me, saith the LORD, until the day that I rise up to the prey: for my determination is to gather the nations, that I may assemble the kingdoms, to pour upon them mine indignation, even all my fierce anger: for all the earth shall be devoured with the fire of my jealousy. For then I will return to the people a pure language, that they may call upon the name of the LORD, to serve him with one consent."
- Zephaniah 3:8-9**

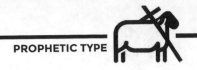

Boaz Points to Christ

According to the Jewish law of kinship, the next of kin was expected to marry and redeem (to free or rescue by paying a price) the widow that the kinsman or relative left behind. In the book of Ruth, Boaz became Ruth's kinsman – redeemer. He voluntarily married Ruth, purchased her deceased husband's family property, and dedicated their first child in Ruth's former husband's name.

The Old Testament points to Jesus Christ. **Boaz portrayed a striking type or picture of Jesus Christ in the following ways:**

Boaz offered Ruth protection and safety from evil under his care.	Jesus offers protection and safety from Satan under His care.
Boaz offered to redeem the Gentile bride, Ruth, who came to him for help and redemption.	Jesus offers to redeem all, Jews and Gentiles alike, who come to Him for redemption from sin.
Boaz paid the full price required by law to have Ruth come into his family as his wife.	Jesus paid the full price for our sins with His death on the cross to bring us into His family.
Boaz took Ruth because she left her old life and turned from her false gods to the one true God.	Jesus takes all who forsake their old life of sin and ask Him to be their Savior.

For whatsoever things were written aforetime were written for our learning, that we through patience and comfort of the scriptures might have hope.
- Romans 15:4

Look for the Blessed Hope

How wonderful to know that Christ tells us to look for His return *not with fear* but *with excitement.* This can motivate us to turn from our sins, spur us on to be more like Christ, and become passionate about doing good works. We desire this because we recognize that:

- Hope is the *confident expectation* of good things to come.
- Our awesome God and Savior Jesus Christ *died to pay the ransom to set us free from the penalty we owe God* for breaking His laws.
- Jesus did this to cleanse us for Himself and to call us His *special people* who eagerly desire to do good deeds.

No wonder Paul, as he wrote to Titus, described this as a "blessed hope." It is because those who have accepted Christ as their Savior and the Lord of their lives have been blessed not only as they follow Him here on Earth, but also for *eternity.*

Looking for the blessed hope and glorious appearing of our great God and Savior Jesus Christ, who gave Himself for us that He might redeem us from every lawless deed and purify for Himself His own special people, zealous for good works.
- Titus 2:13-14 (NKJV)

Psalm 8:8 - Inspiration for Oceanography

Scripture is unique when compared to every other religious book. It is full of remarkable insights and foreknowledge leading mankind to many useful discoveries when diligently studied. Psalm 8:8 is one such example which led to the discovery of the field of oceanography.

During a long illness, Matthew Fontaine Maury (1806-1873) had his son read to him from the Bible. Matthew Maury was drawn to the book of Psalms during his suffering. **After recovering, Maury dedicated his life to finding out about the "paths of the sea" mentioned in Psalm 8:8.** As a result, he was the first to recognize that the seas contained circulating systems which interact between wind and water. Maury's book on physical oceanography is still considered the foundational textbook on this subject. In 1927, the United States Naval Institute issued a book by C.L. Lewis titled *Matthew Fontaine Maury: Pathfinder of the Seas*, which describes Maury's work and inspiration.

The birds of the air, and the fish of the sea that pass through the paths of the sea.
- Psalm 8:8 (NKJV)

Ten Prophetic Events Revelation Reveals

One thing that makes Revelation so valuable is its insight into the future. The following is a partial list of places in Revelation (and other books of the Bible) which mention specific events of the future. Knowing what lies ahead keeps us focused on and motivated for holy living and warning others.

- The rise of a final world ruler (Rev. 13; Dan. 7:8; Thess. 2:3-4)
- The seven-year Tribulation (Dan. 9:27 [1 week = 7 years]; Rev. 13:5 – the last 3½ years)
- A global government/economy (Rev. 13:16-17; 17:13)
- A global religion (Rev. 13:5)
- The Second Coming of Christ (Acts 1:9-11; Heb. 9:28; Rev. 19:11-21)
- The great war of Armageddon (Joel 3:12-14; Rev. 1:7; 19:11-21)
- The 1,000-year rule of Christ on Earth (Rev. 20:1-4)
- The final judgment of unrepentant sinners (Rev. 19:20; 20:13-15)
- The final state of the wicked in hell (Rev. 21:8; Matt. 13:42,49,50)
- The New Heaven and New Earth (Rev. 21)

As we watch the news, we can see how some of these prophecies are already beginning to unfold. God tells us, however, not to be afraid. He is with those who put their trust in Him.

**Fear not, for I am with you; be not dismayed, for
I am your God. I will strengthen you, yes, I will help you,
I will uphold you with My righteous right hand.
- Isaiah 41:10 (NKJV)**

"Running To and Fro" and "Increased Knowledge"

A closer look at Daniel 12:4 reveals something beyond a prophecy pointing to increased travel (many shall "run to and fro") and a tremendous "increase in knowledge." During the last 150 years, we have seen travel go from horses to rockets, and the doubling of knowledge taking centuries is now happening on the average of every thirteen months. Digging into the text, however, reveals even more insights:

1. *"Sealing"* a book (Daniel 12:4) was a process of **making sure a document could not be changed** in any way and preserving it so it would be available when it was needed in the future,
2. In this context, the *"time of the end"* refers to the Tribulation period.
3. The Hebrew verb form *"run to and fro"* used always refers to the **movement of a person searching for something.**

In other words, many people will **search for the answers** to the devastation of the Tribulation and will discover **increased knowledge** as they search the Bible.

But thou, O Daniel, shut up the words, and seal the book, even to the time of the end: many shall run to and fro, and knowledge shall be increased.
- Daniel 12:4

Antichrist Defined, Deception Avoided

All references using the word *"antichrist"* are found in the writing of John the apostle. 1 John 2:22-23 calls these individuals "liars" and defines the word "antichrist" as those who "deny the Father and the Son". 2 John 1:7-8 adds that they "deny Jesus Christ as coming in the flesh". In other words, all those who attack the work and person of Christ are a type of antichrist.

Scripture is clear that there will be a final tyrannical Antichrist who will be the ultimate master of deception. It also states that there have been and will continue to be many antichrist types and that we should not be deceived.

In order to keep from being deceived by an antichrist, we have to know the work and person of Jesus Christ ourselves. When we ask Christ to be the Lord of our lives and seriously want to know Him, Christ will guide us to the truth about Himself. Reading, studying, testing, and accepting God's Word as truth will keep us from being deceived when we are confronted with things that are in any way false or altered. With God's guidance and a prayerful desire to be watchful and obedient, we have God's promise that we can know the truth.

If ye continue in my word, then are ye my disciples indeed; and ye shall know the truth, and the truth shall make you free.
- John 8:31-32

Advice from Peter

Since the Bible can be trusted in its history, geography, science, physical and mental health advice, and past prophecies, **then** it can be trusted in its promises concerning our future. 1 Peter 1:13 is such a promise. Notice the meaning of the language in this passage:

- *Gird up* - Gather up, prepare, discipline
- *Loins of your mind* - Procreative power of your deep thoughts
- *Be sober* - Think clearly, keep control of
- *Rest your hope fully* - Keep your expectations and full trust
- *Grace* - Benefit, favor
- *That is to be brought* - That will come, be carried to you
- *At the revelation* - At the coming, appearing, revealing

We can rest on the foundational truth that God reveals Himself to everyone (Romans 1:19-20). If we search out and clearly think through the truths of God's Word and put our complete trust in it, God *promises* He will give us His undeserved favor at the final and full revelation of Himself.

**Therefore gird up the loins of your mind, be sober, and rest your hope fully upon the grace that is to be brought to you at the revelation of Jesus Christ.
- 1 Peter 1:13 (NKJV)**

The Exodus – Prophecy Fulfilled to the Day

Galatians 3:16-17 records two interesting fulfilled prophecies that were given to Abraham, the father of the Jewish people, 430 years before they happened. They not only predicted that Christ would come through Abraham's lineage, but also **the exact day** of the "Exodus from Egypt."

...He does not say, "And to seeds" as referring to many, but rather to one, "And to your seed," that is Christ. What I am saying is this: the Law, which came four hundred and thirty years later, does not invalidate a covenant previously ratified by God, so as to nullify the promise. - Galatians 3: 16-17 NASV

Exodus 12:41 tells us that this prophecy was fulfilled on the very day God told Abraham that it would take place.

And it came about at the end of four hundred and thirty years, to the very day, that all the hosts of the LORD went out from the land of Egypt. - Exodus 12:41 NASV

The Lord told Moses on the evening of the Exodus that this night was to be remembered and honored by the Jewish nation throughout their generations. How remarkable it is to find that over three thousand years later, the Jewish people worldwide still observe this feast day which God instituted and called "Passover." (Exodus 12)

Remember the former things of old: for I am God, and there is none else; I am God, and there is none like me, declaring the end from the beginning, and from ancient times the things that are not yet done, saying, "My counsel shall stand, and I will do all my pleasure." - Isaiah 46:9-10

A Personal Prophecy

For God so loved the world that He gave His only begotten Son, that whoever believes in Him should not perish but have everlasting life. For God did not send His Son into the world to condemn <u>the world</u>, but that <u>the world</u> through Him might be saved. - John 3 :16,17 (NKJV)

For since the creation of the world, His invisible attributes are clearly seen, being understood by the things that are made, even His eternal power and Godhead, so that <u>they</u> are without excuse. - Romans 1:20 (NKJV)

**The Lord is not slack concerning His promise,
as some count slackness,
but is longsuffering toward us,
not willing that <u>any</u> should perish
but that <u>all</u> should come to repentance.
- 2 Peter 3:9 (NKJV)**

These prophetic promises are personal. The underlined words are intentional. *Every* person on Earth can insert his or her name in each place on the underlined words and apply God's promises. God gave us enough evidence and more than ample opportunity to accept or reject Him as Lord of our lives. If our choice is to *reject* Him, it will be the final and most terrifying choice we will ever make. If we *accept* Him, it will be more wonderful than anything we can imagine.

**"...Eye has not seen, nor ear heard, nor have entered into the heart of man the things which God has prepared for those who love Him."
- Isaiah 64:6 & 1 Corinthians 2:9 (NKJV)**

The "Strong Force"

Colossians 1:16-17 is an interesting passage that tells us that Christ *created all* things in heaven and on Earth, the visible and the invisible. It also reveals that Christ *sustains all* things in creation. Only God could have inspired the writer in such a way that reflects the principles of physics, which have only recently come to be fully understood.

All matter consists of atoms. Atoms contain a nucleus, or center, with neutral particles called neutrons and positively charged particles called protons. Atoms also contain negatively charged particles called electrons that move around and outside the nucleus at the speed of light. As with magnets, positive and negative particles attract, while like charges repel. **The positively charged protons, however, exist next to each other in the atom's nucleus with a tremendous force that holds them together.** Scientists call this unknown force the "strong nuclear force". We really cannot explain exactly what this "force" is that holds atoms together. We simply give it a name and acknowledge that it must exist.

The word "consist" translates into the Greek word *sunistano* from which we get the word "sustain." The Bible says that Christ sustains all things. If it were not for Him, all matter would come apart.

And He is before all things, and in Him all things consist.
- Colossians 1:17 (NKJV)

The First Law of Thermodynamics

The most basic of all scientific principles is implied in Colossians 1:16-17. The First Law of Thermodynamics states that **the total quantity of mass and energy cannot be created or destroyed; it can only be changed from one form into another.** This is the best-proven law of science, but science cannot tell us *why* it is true. The Bible, on the other hand, can. **Nothing is now being created** because Christ created all things in the past. Creation was complete by the seventh day.

Thus the heavens and the earth, and all the host of them, were finished. And on the seventh day God ended His work which He had done.... - Genesis 2:1-2 (NKJV)

**For by Him all things were created that are in heaven and that are on earth, visible and invisible....
- Colossians 1:16 (NKJV)**

All things were made through Him, and without Him nothing was made that was made. - John 1:3 (NKJV)

The reason matter and energy are now *not being destroyed* is that all things "consist," which means they are *sustained* in Christ.

**And He is before all things, and in Him all things consist.
- Colossians 1:17 (NKJV)**

God Authenticates Himself Through Prophecy

God proves Himself to be who He claims to be throughout His Word. The history, geography, science, and prophecy recorded in the Bible, as well as its wisdom concerning our physical, mental, and spiritual well-being, are one hundred percent accurate and can be tested. The strongest of these proofs are the Bible's prophecies. **God Himself tells us fulfilled prophecy proves He is God.**

The following are **key verses worth memorizing** concerning God's proof of Himself through prophecy:

- **Behold, the former things have come to pass, and new things I declare; before they spring forth I tell you of them.** *- Isaiah 42:9 (NKJV)*

- **Remember the former things of old, for I am God, and there is no other; I am God, and there is none like Me, declaring the end from the beginning, and from ancient times things that are not yet done, saying, "My counsel shall stand, and I will do all My pleasure."** *- Isaiah 46:9-10 (NKJV)*

- **"Now I tell you before it comes, that when it does come to pass, you may believe that I am He…."** *- John 13:19 (NKJV)*

- **Worship God! For the testimony of Jesus is the spirit of prophecy.** *- Revelation 19:10b (NKJV)*

Joy Promised for Reaching Others for Christ

In 1 Thessalonians 2:19-20, Paul specifically addressed the Thessalonian believers. He told them that they would be his victor's crown. Notice the meaning of the words used in this passage:

- **Hope** – Expectation, confidence
- **Joy** – Cheerfulness, calm delight, great gladness
- **Crown** – Winner's wreath or prize, symbol of honor
- **Presence** – In front of, in sight of
- **Coming** – Being near, return
- **Glory** – Honor, praise

Paul says that one of our greatest rewards in heaven will be the incredible joy of seeing the people God reached through us. This is a tremendous motivation for us to want to be a reflection of Christ in our words, attitudes, actions, and thinking so that God *can* use us to draw and help others grow closer to Him. When Christ returns, there will be great rejoicing as we all stand together in His presence!

For what is our hope, or joy, or crown of rejoicing? Is it not even you in the presence of our Lord Jesus Christ at His coming? For you are our glory and joy.
- 1 Thessalonians 2:19-20 (NKJV)

The Prophetic Parable of Trees (Part 1)

Trees are often used as symbols or examples of nations in the Bible. In Judges 9:8-15, there is a parable about trees that were determined to anoint a king over them. The trees went to the *olive tree* first and asked it to be their ruler. When it refused to take on the responsibility, the *fig tree* was asked, followed by the *grapevine*, but both refused. Lastly, the trees asked the ***bramble bush*** to be their ruler. The bramble bush agreed to lead them on the condition that the rest of the trees would put their trust in its shadow. If they didn't, the bramble bush said it would cause many trees to burn. (*Read* **Judges 9:8-15.**)

Scripture is the primary guide for interpreting other Scriptures. Using this principle, we discover that the *olive tree* is symbolic of God's **"Spiritual Israel"** (Jeremiah 11:15-16). Under the judges, Israel had the opportunity to lead all nations in righteousness but was unwilling. **"National Israel,"** who was ruled by a series of kings, is symbolized by the *fig tree* (Joel 1:7, Jeremiah 8:13). Israel was also given the opportunity to be a leader in righteousness but refused. The *grapevine*, symbolic of **"Messianic Israel,"** was then given the opportunity to lead the nations in godliness. Christ even offered Himself to Israel as the vine, the king, the very one who could help them usher in the kingdom, but the people rejected Christ's righteousness. They said, *"We will not have this man to reign over us."* (Luke 19:14)

The Prophetic Parable of the Trees (Part 2)

The *bramble bush* represents the "**Antichrist,**" who will set himself up in Israel as God over all.

The **parable of the trees** is a prophetic type of **Israel's opportunities to display righteous rule under God.** In each case, such rule was rejected until the last. By choosing the bramble bush, or false messiah, Israel and the world will have to go through deep sorrow and tribulation. Revelation tells us that in the end, the rebellion of people will bring about the burning of all the grass and one-third of all the trees. A Jewish remnant, however, will have their eyes opened and will finally see the Lord Jesus Christ as their only hope and Savior. At last, God's original plan to use Israel to lead the nations in holiness and worship of God will be fulfilled.

Today as we watch Israel, we can see the final part of this parable unfolding before our eyes. The Jewish nation is looking for a "messiah" who will bring them peace. This is setting them up to allow the bramble bush, or Antichrist, to take control.

As Christians, God calls us to watch, pray, dedicate ourselves to the study of the Bible, and share the gospel. The time is short.

**But the end of all things is at hand; therefore, be serious and watchful in your prayers.
- I Peter 4:7 (NKJV)**

Humanity in the Last Days (Part 1)

Just before Paul died, he wrote 2 Timothy. In this letter, Paul encouraged Timothy, his co-laborer for Christ, to *remember* what Paul taught him and *stand firm* in his faith and in the truth of God's Word. Paul wanted Timothy to be assured of the gifts God gave him to teach and pass on the knowledge of Christ to *faithful* men. He said evil men would come, and he warned Timothy not to follow the world, but to stay pure.

In Chapter 3, Paul included a list of twenty very specific characteristics that would describe humanity and characterize the perilous times of the last days:

¹ **This know also, that in the last** (final) **days perilous** (difficult, dangerous) **times shall come**.

² **For men shall be**

Lovers of their own selves (self-centered),

Covetous (wanting what someone else has),

Boasters (bragging about themselves),

Proud (thinking they are better than others),

Blasphemers (hurtful, vulgar, false and malicious accusers, misrepresenting God),

Disobedient to parents,

Unthankful,

Unholy (wicked, having no respect for God).

These charactoristics of societies worldwide are becoming increasingly apparent.

Humanity in the Last Days (Part 2)

This list of sins which will characterize mankind in the last days continues in 2 Timothy chapter 3:

³ **Without natural affection** (hard-hearted, without family love)

Trucebreakers (unwilling to get along or harmonize),

False accusers,

Incontinent (unwilling to control themselves),

Fierce (brutal, savage),

Despisers of those who are good (hostile, detesting good),

⁴ **Traitors** (betrayer),

Heady (rash, reckless),

High-minded (proud, conceited),

Lovers of pleasure (desires, enjoyment) **more than lovers of God,**

⁵ **Having a form of godliness** (holy and godly),

But denying (rejecting, refusing, contradicting)

The power thereof (force, especially miraculous power)

Although these traits are not new to mankind, they have intensified and accelerated on a global scale. Christ warned His disciples this would happen in Matthew 24:8. He said certain signs would be "the beginning of sorrows," which in Greek refers to "birth pains." Just as a mother's birth pains intensify in strength and frequency, so will these sorrows.

But evil men and seducers shall wax worse and worse, deceiving, and being deceived. But continue thou in the things which thou hast learned and hast been assured of....
- 2 Timothy 3:13-14

Prophetic Promise of an Inheritance

Colossians 3:23-24 clearly tells us *to do everything* with all of our breath and spirit as to the Lord and *not for other people.* It states that we can be absolutely sure God, the very One we do everything for, *will reward* us with an *inheritance.* Notice the meaning of the words:

- **Heartily** – Breath, spirit
- **Knowing** – Be sure, understand
- **Inheritance** – Heirship, possession

In Ephesians 1:18, we discover that God can give us the understanding and knowledge of exactly how valuable and honorable this inheritance will be. 1 Peter 1:4 records **God's promise** that this inheritance is **incorruptible** (not subject to decay) and is **undefiled** (pure). God says it does not **fade away**, is **kept by His power** through faith for salvation, and that it **will be revealed** in the End Times.

There is not another inheritance even close to being as worthy!

And whatever you do, do it heartily, as to the Lord and not to men, knowing that from the Lord you will receive the reward of the inheritance; for you serve the Lord Christ.
- Colossians 3:23-24 (NKJV)

Naaman's Leprosy (Part 1)

In 2 Kings 5:1-19 God included a unique account of a man named Naaman. He was a great and honorable commander of the Syrian army. Naaman contracted the terrible, dreaded disease of leprosy and was miraculously healed by God through the prophet Elisha. Although Naaman was angered at the way he was told he would be healed, he decided to humble himself and follow Elisha's very specific instructions.

This true account gives us a prophetic picture of the ugliness of sin and its amazing cure. The unusual parallels of sin and Naaman's leprosy are listed below.

	2 Kings 5:1-19 Naaman's Leprosy:	Sin of Mankind:
1.	Could attack anyone regardless of race, gender, or status.	All have sinned. (*Romans 5:12, 6:23*)
2.	Brought both physical and emotional harm.	Brings both physical and emotional harm.
3.	Is extremely contagious.	Sinful behavior infects others. (*Romans 5:12*)
4.	Kills the sensitivity of the nerves.	Numbs the sensitivity of the conscience. (*1 Timothy 4:2*)
5.	Leads to death.	Leads to death. (*Romans 6:23*)
6.	Payment for the cure was rejected by Elisha.	Forgiveness can't be earned. (*Ephesians 2:8-9*)

Naaman's Leprosy (Part 2)

The many parallels between Naaman's leprosy
and sin is continued below:

	2 Kings 5:1-19 Naaman's Leprosy:	Sin of Mankind:
7.	Required Naaman's humility to admit his disease and seek help.	Sin requires humble confession. (*Psalm 51:2-3, John 13:8*)
8.	Required washing in the Jordan River to get rid of the disease.	Sin requires Christ's blood to wash it away . (*Isaiah 1:16, Heb.10:12*)
9.	Required Naaman to turn from his anger.	Requires turning from sin. (*1 John 1:6-9*)
10.	Demanded obeying Elisha's instructions.	Demands obeying Christ's words (*John 14:23*)
11.	Naaman only had one way to be cured.	Sinners only have one way to be saved. (*John 14:6*)
12.	Naaman's belief in what Elisha told him to do saved him from leprosy.	Belief in Christ brings salvation. (*John 3:16*)

Poor Excuses for Not Studying Prophecy (Part 1)

Excuse #1 Prophecy is too difficult.
Scripture itself promises the Holy Spirit's help in reading God's Word (John 14:26). God tells us to study the Bible diligently (2 Timothy 2:15).

Excuse #2 Prophecy creates disunity and discord.
Over one-fourth of the Bible is prophecy. God told us to study all of it and clearly wrote how we are to handle His Word as Christians (2 Timothy 2:15). If one creates discord, it is not of God (Titus 2:7-8).

Excuse #3 Prophecy is too scary and full of bad news.
The Bible has a lot of frightening prophecies for the unbeliever. However, God is not a God of fear (2 Timothy 1:7), and He promised all believers perfect peace if we trust and obey Him (Isaiah 26:3, John 14:23,27). By studying God's prophecies, we are better equipped to share the "good news" of safety in Christ while there is still time for unbelievers to come to Him and be spared the terrors of the End Times.

Excuse #4 Prophecy is confusing.
God tells us He is not a God of confusion (1 Corinthians 14:33). Not all prophecies can be understood by all people at all times, but each one can and will be understood in God's specified time (Daniel 12:4).

For whatsoever things were written aforetime were written for our learning, that we through patience and comfort of the scriptures might have hope.
- Romans 15:4

Poor Excuses for Not Studying Prophecy (Part 2)

Excuse #5 Prophecy does not apply to me.
We are told all Scripture, which includes prophecy, was written for our learning and was inspired by God. It is profitable for doctrine (instruction), reproof (to tell a fault), correction, and instruction in righteousness (2 Timothy 3:16). Prophecy offers both warnings (Hebrews 3:12-13) and promises (2 Peter 1:4) for all people in all ages.

Excuse #6 All prophecies have been fulfilled in the past.
A careful study of the Bible will prove it has many hundreds of detailed prophecies. By comparing historical records to these biblical prophecies, one can clearly see many have come to pass since the Bible was written, including some in our own lifetime. Prophecies of a third Temple, peace in Jerusalem, and a one-world religion, economy, and government, the Millennial Kingdom, and many others, however, are yet in the future.

Excuse #7 Prophecy is contradictory.
Prophecy cannot contradict itself because "the testimony of Jesus is the spirit of prophecy" (Revelation 19:10b). Christ also told us He is the truth (John 14:6) and God cannot lie (Titus 1:2). A thorough investigation of ALL the Scripture dealing with the same subjects, which includes prophecy, proves there are no contradictions in Scripture.

**Blessed is he that readeth, and they that hear
the words of this prophecy, and keep those things
which are written therein: for the time is at hand.
- Revelation 1:3**

Complete History of a Nation Prophesied

Biblical prophecy is an evidence God uses to authenticate Himself. **One of the most remarkable prophecies is when God laid out Israel's future.** No other country in the world has ever had their existence outlined from before they existed to thousands of years into the future. This prophecy is certainly a witness to our all-knowing, all-powerful, all-present God. He is like no other.

- Abraham would father a new nation. (Genesis 12:1-3)

- The new nation would be *given a specific piece of land.* (Genesis 15:18)

- Israel's Temple and the city of Jerusalem would be *destroyed.* (Daniel 9:26)

- The Israelites would be *exiled.* (Deuteronomy 4:25-27; 28:36-37)

- The exiles would be *scattered* throughout the world. (Leviticus 26:33; Deuteronomy 28:64)

- The land of Israel would lay *desolate.* (Leviticus 26:27-33)

- The Israelite exiles would be *persecuted.* (Deuteronomy 28:65-67)

- The people of Israel would be *preserved.* (Jeremiah 30:11)

- The people of Israel would be *regathered* to their own land. (Jeremiah 32:37-41; Isaiah 43:5-6)

- Israel would be *restored.* (Deuteronomy 30:3-5; Ezekiel 36:8-12)

- Israel would become the *center of the world.* (Ezekiel 5:5)

APRIL

Fear Not, For I Am With You

Isaiah 41:10

Arlene Faith Kortright

Fear not for I am with you be not dis-mayed for I am your God I will strength-en you, yes, I will help you, yes, I will up-hold you with my right-eous right hand Fear hand I- sa-i-ah for-ty one ten

LORD, help me memorize this verse and sing it out when fear overcomes me. I know You are true. Remind me of those times You have proved it to me. **Amen**

Prophecy in a Worm

In Psalm 22:6, the psalmist used the crimson worm as a *prophetic type* of Christ. This chapter was written about one thousand years before Christ was born, yet clearly describes what He would experience on the cross. The psalmist stated that Jesus saw Himself as a worm that people would shame and despise.

The Hebrew word for worm is *"tolath"*, which is translated a *"scarlet or crimson worm."* In ancient times, this worm was used as a source for making red dyes.

It is interesting that God inspired the psalmist to use this particular worm in light of the following facts:

- The mother worm permanently implants her body in a tree before she gives birth.
- Her body provides protection and sustenance for the young until they can leave and fend for themselves.
- As the mother dies, red fluid comes out of her body and stains her body, her babies, and the wood of the tree.

It is no coincidence that Christ called Himself this worm. He shed His blood on a wooden cross and gave His life to cover the sins of His children if we confess our sins and turn from them. His death gives us life, protects us from hell, and permanently changes our lives.

**But I am a worm, and no man;
a reproach of men, and despised of the people.
- Psalm 22:6**

Restoring the Shekel

As the Jews came back to Israel from different countries, they brought their various currencies – francs, dollars, pounds, rubles, etc. It was difficult to buy or sell in Israel because there was no basic exchange unit. The British pound or U.S. dollar was most commonly used. In 1980, the Knesset, the ruling body in Israel, voted on an official currency. Amazingly, they chose the **shekel,** the same currency used in the time of Moses (Exodus 30:11-16).

Ezekiel 45:12-13, 16 contains a very interesting prophecy concerning the End Times. **Ezekiel predicted that the "shekel" would be the currency used in the offering brought to Christ when He returns and sets up His kingdom.**

Restoring the shekel as the official Israeli currency after thousands of years of not even existing as a nation is another remarkable prophecy that affirms the truth of God's Word.

The shekel shall be twenty gerahs...This is the offering which you shall offer.... All the people of the land shall give this offering for the prince in Israel.
- Ezekiel 45: 12-13, 16 (NKJV)

Understanding Revelation

The word "revelation" (Greek – apokalupis) means *"an uncovering, unveiling, or disclosure."* A closer look at Revelation shows us that it is not a book of secrets and hidden meanings. On the contrary, Jesus's disciple John wrote it to reveal truth. Revelation is the final chapter in God's account of redemption and His last written Word. It was written by the last living disciple who explains the last things that will take place before Christ's return. In all of Scripture, the book of Revelation gives us the most detailed look into the future. The following points are crucial to a better understanding of Revelation:

- The very first verse tells us this book was written to all **Christ's devoted followers.**

- It is the only book that God sent and communicated to mankind **through an angel.**

- God promises to **bless** those who read, hear, and keep His Word.

- It offers **the grace and peace** of the one and only true God of the past, present, and future.

- While the **Gospels** *(Matthew, Mark, Luke, John)* focus primarily on Christ's life, earthly ministry, and crucifixion, the book of **Acts** describes the history of the Church. The **epistles** *(letters in the New Testament)* primarily explain and apply the meaning of the life, death, and resurrection of Christ to the life of the Church in the present. The book of **Revelation** reveals Jesus Christ in His majesty, power, and glory and focuses mainly on the future.

The Revelation of Jesus Christ, which God gave unto him to show unto his servant's things which must shortly come to pass; and he sent and signified it by his angel unto his servant John.
– Revelation 1:1

The Completion of Prophetic Fulfillment

The Law of Moses refers to the first five books of the Hebrew Scriptures. The Jews today call them the Torah. The Pentateuch is a Greek term used for these books. The *Psalms* were used to describe all the poetic wisdom literature, including Job, Psalms, Proverbs, Ecclesiastes, and the Song of Solomon. *The Prophets* included historical books like Joshua, Judges, First and Second Samuel, First and Second Kings, First and Second Chronicles, and the major and minor Prophets.

Some people interpret Luke 24:44 to mean that all Old Testament prophecies about Jesus were fulfilled in the First Coming of Jesus, but that is not what Jesus said. **He said they must be fulfilled.** A careful study of both the Old and New Testaments shows that specific prophecies have not yet been fulfilled. They include hundreds of prophecies about Christ's Second Coming, up until the Millennial Reign has ended and eternity begins.

Then He said to them, "These are the words which I spoke to you while I was still with you, that all things must be fulfilled which were written in the Law of Moses and the Prophets and the Psalms concerning Me."
- Luke 24:44 (NKJV)

We Will Appear with Christ in Glory

If we are *raised* or "spiritually revived" in Christ, we die to our own selfish nature and allow Christ to control our words, thoughts, and actions. Money, power, possessions, and worldly pleasures lose their hold on us. To the extent we allow it, Christ's priorities become ours and we set our mind on the reality of heaven. Our lives become hidden or concealed in Christ because His nature shines through us.

In Colossians 3, we are promised that when we are "in Christ" **we will appear in union together with Him when He appears on Earth at His Second Coming** and makes Himself visible to everyone in His full honor, dignity, and majesty.

If then you were raised with Christ, seek those things which are above, where Christ is, sitting at the right hand of God. Set your mind on things above, not on things on the earth. For you died, and your life is hidden with Christ in God. When Christ who is our life appears, then you also will appear with Him in glory.
- Colossians 3:1-4 (NKJV)

Exhorting One Another

In 2 Timothy 3:1-9, Paul clearly describes what mankind will be like in the Last Days. Selfishness, deceit, lovelessness, and evil will be rampant. Knowing that godly believers will be terribly discouraged as they face increasingly evil times, God inspired the author of Hebrews to both forewarn and encourage them with words of advice.

We are to care about one another's needs and spiritual growth. We should encourage each other in the most God-pleasing and worthy undertakings. **The best way we can do this is by living the example Christ gave us in Philippians 2:3-4, where He put the needs of others before His own.**

It is interesting that the writer of Hebrews specifically addresses how important it is *not to stop* gathering together with fellow believers (like some do). Instead, he encourages believers to meet together to *exhort* one another, a word that entails earnest encouragement which both warns and comforts. True followers of Christ are urged to do this with *increasing fervency* as Christ's return approaches.

And let us consider one another in order to stir up love and good works, not forsaking the assembling of ourselves together, as is the manner of some, but exhorting one another, and so much the more as you see the Day approaching.
- Hebrews 10:24-25 (NKJV)

Hebrews 11:3 and the Atom

Only God, with His foreknowledge of the atom and its subatomic particles, could have known over two thousand years ago that visible matter was made from invisible subatomic particles. When God inspired the author of Hebrews to write this fact in Hebrews 11:3, He already knew that someday we would be able to understand the meaning and profound significance of this verse more fully.

Today we know that all matter in the universe is made up of particles called atoms. We also know that individual atoms can contain as many as eighteen subatomic particles. These particles cannot be seen with our eyes, but we can infer they exist by the effects they produce. Therefore, we can have a well-justified faith in these particles and their properties. Similarly, we cannot see God with our eyes. **We can see His overwhelming power, design, order, complexity, and beauty displayed throughout the universe, however, from the smallest bosons and quarks (subatomic particles) to the largest galaxies.** God has given us abundant evidence to validate faith in Him, mankind will be without excuse. (Romans 1:20)

By faith (defined in Hebrews 11:1 as "evidence of things not seen")
we understand that the universe was created by the word of God, so that what is seen was not made out of things that are visible.
- Hebrews 11:3 (ESV)

God Reveals His Will in His Word

In her book, *Prayer that Works*, Jill Briscoe comments on how God's will is revealed in His Word and confirmed by the Spirit of God. She relays how boldly Elijah, a true prayer warrior, could confidently announce to King Ahab a drought would come due to Israel's spiritual idolatry (1 Kings 17:1).

A closer look at Scripture shows us that many years earlier, Israel's King Solomon had prayed a prayer of dedication for the new Temple in Jerusalem (1 Kings 8:35-36). In that prayer, Solomon predicted the very consequence Elijah told King Ahab was about to happen if Israel sinned against God. In ancient times, God revealed His will with His Word. These predictions always came true.

Today we see ourselves, like ancient Israel, leaving God's path of biblical morality (in parenting, marriage, abortion, administering justice, our work ethic, incurring debt, etc.). We have exchanged God's will for that of idolatry (placing people, things, pleasures before God). **We can also look to the Bible and see our predicted outcome** (Romans 1:18-2:16). God clearly *sets forth* His will in His Word, *warns* of the consequences for disregarding it, and consistently *follows through with every word!*

Thy word is true from the beginning: and every one of thy righteous judgments endureth forever.
- Psalm 119:160

The Fiery Tongue of the Last Days

In the third chapter of James, we find a very interesting and fitting verse for these End Times. James not only tells us the tongue is "set on fire of hell," but that it cannot be tamed, is unruly, and is a deadly poison (v.8). It offers curses and blessings out of the same mouth, which "ought not to be so" (v.10).

In looking at Matthew 24, where Christ gave His disciples the signs of His return, **we can see the tongue is either directly or indirectly involved in most of the End Time signs (outside of the natural disasters).** It truly is a fire, and now in our days of cell phones, tweets, and other electronic messaging, our tongues are spreading their poison at the speed of light.

As we prepare ourselves to be Christ's faithful bride at His coming, shouldn't we work more diligently than ever to bridle our tongues (James 3:2-3). This can only happen with God's help.

**And the tongue is a fire, a world of iniquity:
so is the tongue among our members, that it
defileth the whole body, and setteth on fire
the course of nature; and it is set on fire of hell.
- James 3:6**

The Wife of Jehovah (Part 1)

Israel has been portrayed as the wife of Jehovah throughout the Bible in many ways. In his book, *The Footsteps of the Messiah*, Dr. Arnold G. Fruchtenbaum lays out **six distinct stages** through which this relationship develops. His analysis and biblical support is well worth studying. The various stages of the marriage and some key verses of Scriptures are listed below.

Israel: The Wife of Jehovah

Stage 1: The Marriage Contract
The prophets always saw this covenant relationship as a marriage contract.
>*Deuteronomy 5:1-3* God covenanted with His people at Mt. Sinai.
>*Deuteronomy 6:10-15* God declared His jealousy over His wife, Israel.
>*Deuteronomy 7:6-11* God calls Israel His "chosen one."
>*Ezekiel 16:8* The wedding night is described.

Stage 2: The Great Adultery
>In *Jeremiah 3:1-5,20,* Israel was warned to stay faithful to her Husband but was guilty of great adultery with the many false gods of the Egyptians, Assyrians, and Babylonians that she chose to worship as well.

**"Surely, as a wife treacherously departs from her husband,
so have you dealt treacherously with Me,
O house of Israel," says the LORD.
- Jeremiah 3:20 (NKJV)**

The Wife of Jehovah (Part 2)

In *Ezekiel 16:15-34,* the marriage contract between Jehovah and Israel became null and void – Israel did not want to turn from her harlotry with other gods.

Stage 3: The Separation
Due to Israel's adultery, a separation took place between God and Israel.
> *Deuteronomy 24:1* If a husband divorced his wife, he had to write out a bill of divorcement.
> *Isaiah 50:1* Israel's adultery with foreign gods was great, so God withheld His blessings and separated Himself from her.

Stage 4: The Divorce
After 100 years of separation and withheld blessings, Israel still did not return to God. God was forced to issue the bill of divorcement due to her adultery.
> *Jeremiah 3:6-10* God divorces Israel, again declaring her guilty of adultery.
> *The Book of Hosea* God's bill of divorcement of the Northern Kingdom.
> *The Book of Jeremiah* God's bill of divorcement of the Southern Kingdom.

Stage 5: The Punishment
Deuteronomy was the original marriage contract between Israel and God. It clearly stated that if Israel were faithful, she would be blessed, but if unfaithful, God would punish her severely.
> *Ezekiel 16:35-43* God describes Israel's punishment. She would be destroyed by the very nations with which she committed adultery (worshiped their gods). The punishment was to make Israel stop her sin and come back to God.
> *Hosea 2:6-13* God further describes His program of punishment.

This is what the LORD says: "Where is your mother's certificate of divorce with which I sent her away? Or to which of my creditors did I sell you? Because of your sins you were sold; because of your transgressions your mother was sent away." – Isaiah 50:1 (NIV)

The Wife of Jehovah (Part 3)

In *Jeremiah 3:11-18,* throughout the punishment period there is a continual call for Israel to repent and come back to Jehovah, her Husband. Today, Israel is in this fifth stage of her historical and prophetical relationship with Jehovah, her God.

Stage 6: The Remarriage with Restored Blessings
The Bible does not leave things in a hopeless state. It speaks clearly that there will be a day when Israel will become the restored wife of Jehovah with a brand-new marriage contract found in Jeremiah 31:31-34.

> *Ezekiel 16:60-63* These verses also describe the new, everlasting covenant with Israel in the future.
> *Isaiah 54:1-8* Describes the restoration of Israel as Jehovah's wife.
> *Hosea 2:14-23* Speaks of Israel's reunion with her husband.

A study of the prophets, as well as the history of Israel, reveals the remarkable integrity of Scripture. If Israel's past has been accurately fulfilled to the most minute detail, then its future will be as well. In light of what is happening in Israel today and the Bible's clear prediction of her future, it would be prudent to *read* the Scriptures and *watch* Israel.

**"The time is coming," declares the LORD, "when I will make a new covenant with the house of Israel and with the house of Judah. It will not be like the covenant I made with their forefathers when I took them by the hand to lead them out of Egypt, because they broke my covenant, though I was a husband to them," declares the LORD. "This is the covenant I will make with the house of Israel after that time," declares the LORD. "I will put my law in their minds and write it on their hearts. I will be their God, and they will be my people. No longer will a man teach his neighbor, or a man his brother, saying, 'Know the LORD,' because they will all know me, from the least of them to the greatest," declares the LORD. " For I will forgive their wickedness and I will remember their sins no more."
- Jeremiah 31:31-34 (NIV)**

Has Our Evil Become Good? (Part 1)

Throughout the Bible, God gives us a clear description of what is: *good* and brings peace, and what is *evil* and leads to a person's and a nation's downfall. As we see in both biblical and secular history, God's words prove one hundred percent accurate. It is tragic that we do not heed His wise counsel.

We need to consider what God says in Scripture concerning the current culture. Our obedience to or rebellion against His Word is a good indicator of how far down the road we are in calling evil good and good evil, which invokes God's wrath.

- Abortion – *Psalm 139:13-14; Proverbs 6:16-17*
- Homosexuality *Leviticus 18:22; 1 Corinthians 6:9-10; Romans 1:24-32*
- Healthy marriages and family – *Colossians 3:18-21; Matthew 19:4-6; Ephesians 5:21-31*
- Training, disciplining, and obedience of children – *Proverbs 6:20-23; 22:6,15; 23:13-14,22*
- Passing on the knowledge of God to the next generation – *Deuteronomy 6:5-9*
- Telling of lies (half-truths, fake news) – *Proverbs 6:16-17,19*
- Deciding what is acceptable to see, say, hear, and think – *Ephesians 4:29-32, 5:3-4; Philippians 4:8*
- Addiction to money and pleasures – *1 Timothy 6:10; 1 John 2:15-16*
- Self-control in eating, drinking, buying – *Proverbs 23:20-21; Matthew 6:19-20; 1 Corinthians 10:31; Romans 13:13-14*
- How we treat our bodies – *1 Corinthians 3:16*
- Debt – *Romans 13:7-8*
- Work ethic – *Psalm 90:17; Ecclesiastes 9:10; Colossians 3:17, 23; 1 Thessalonians 4:11-12*
- Laziness – *Proverbs 12:24*
- Harmony in the church – *Proverbs 6:16-19; Philippians 2:1-8*
- Respect for authority and fellowman – *Romans 13:1-10*

Woe unto them that call evil good, and good evil....
- Isaiah 5:20

Has Our Evil Become Good? (Part 2)

How well do our culture, our churches, and our personal behavior and beliefs line up with Scriptural mandates in these and other areas?

- Intercessory prayer for the government and leaders – *1 Timothy 2:1-4*
- Pride – *Proverbs 6:16-17; 8:13; Romans 1:30-32*
- Selfishness – *Philippians 2:3-8*
- Music – *Psalm 33:1-3; Colossians 3:16-17*
- Punishment – *Ezra 7:26; Proverbs 21:7*
- Thankfulness – *1 Thessalonians 5:18; Psalm 100:4-5; Romans 1:21*
- Religious compromise – *Deuteronomy 6:14-15*
- God – *Matthew 22:37-38; 1 Peter 1:15-16*
- Jesus Christ – *John 14:6*
- The Bible – *Psalm 119:160*
- Creation – *Romans 1:20; 2 Peter 3:3-5*
- Sin – *Romans 3:23; 5:12*
- Prayer – *Psalm 66:18*
- Speech – *Ephesians 4:29*

Although we cannot force societal obedience to God's Word, **we can have inner peace and be the light to the world that God calls us to be.** We do this when we demonstrate our own personal obedience to the Bible, especially in these End Times, when too few are doing so.

**The way of the fool is right in his own eyes,
but he who heeds counsel is wise.
- Proverbs 12:15 (NKJV)**

Undeniable Proof of the Crucifixion (Part 1)

The crucifixion of Jesus Christ is an event documented in both biblical and secular history. Some details were given over one thousand years prior to the event. With one hundred percent accuracy of both timing and details, "chance" cannot even be considered. This event was foreseen by the Creator of the universe.

The following partial list of fulfilled prophecies concerning the crucifixion of Christ was compiled by Dr. David Reagan. Each Old Testament passage, the detailed prophecy and the New Testament fulfillment are listed below.

OT Passage	Prophecy	NT Fulfillment
Dan. 9:25-26	Timing of death	483 yrs. after edict to rebuild Jerusalem
Zech. 9:9	Entry into Jerusalem on donkey	John 12:12-15 Matt. 21:1-11 Mark 11:1-10
Is. 53:3-5 Ps. 55:12-14	Experience of profound grief and agony	Matt. 26:37-39 Mark 14:32-36 Luke 22:39-44
Ps. 41:9	Betrayal by friend who ate with Him	Matt. 26:20-25, 47-49
Zech. 11:12-13	Betrayal for 30 pieces of silver	Matt. 26:14-16
Zech. 11:13	Disposition of betrayal money	Matt. 27:3-7
Zech. 13:7	Forsaken by disciples	Matt. 26:55-56
Ps. 35:11 12	Accused by false witnesses	Matt. 26:59-63
Is. 53:7	Silent before His accusers	Matt. 27:14; 1 Pet. 2:23
Is. 50:6	Spat upon	Matt. 26:67
Micah 5:1	Hit on face	Matt. 26:67
Isaiah 50:6	Scourged	Matt. 27:26
Isaiah 52:14	Beaten to extreme	Matt. 27:26,29-30
Ps. 22:6-18 Ps. 69:19-20 Is. 50:6	Humiliated	Matt. 26:67-68 Matt. 27:28-31 Mark 15:17-19

Undeniable Proof of the Crucifixion (Part 2)

This table continues the incredible list of specific and predicted events surrounding the crucifixion of Christ.

OT Passage	Prophecy	NT Fulfillment
Ps. 22:16 Zech. 13:6	Crucified	Luke 23:23
Is. 53:12	Identified with sinners	Mark 15:27
Ps. 22:6-8 Ps. 69:20 Ps. 109:25	Despised and mocked	Luke 23:35-36, 39
Ps. 22:15 Ps. 69:3, 21	Thirsty	John 19:28
Ps. 69:21	Given vinegar to drink	Matt: 27:48
Ps. 38:11	Friends stand far away	Luke 23:49
Ps. 22:17	Stared at	Luke 23:35
Ps. 22:18	Clothing divided among enemies	John 19:23
Ps. 22:18	Lots cast for clothes	John 19:23-24
Amos 8:9	Darkness at noon	Matt. 27:45
Ps. 22:1	Cry due to separation from God	Matt. 27:46
Ps. 109:4 Is. 53:12	Prayer for persecutors	Luke 23:34
Ps. 22:31	Cry of victory	John 19:30
Ps. 31:5	Voluntary release of His life	Luke 23:46
Ps. 34:20	No bones broken	John 19:32-33
Zech. 12:10	Pierced in side	John 19:34
Ps. 22:14	Reference to heart	John 19:34
Is. 53:9	Buried in rich man's grave	Matt. 27:57-60

For prophecy never came by the will of man, but holy men of God spoke as they were moved by the Holy Spirit.
- 2 Peter 1:21 (NKJV)

Why Israel Is Always in the News

In his book, *The Prophecy Answer Book*, Dr. David Jeremiah poses the question why such a small and relatively new country as Israel (born in 1948) – with a population of only around nine million and a total land space only slightly larger than New Jersey – is mentioned so often in the nightly news. In answering that question, he shows why Israel is so important in prophecy by making these following interesting points from Scripture:

1. God reveals His sovereign purpose for Israel from the beginning of the Bible, in Genesis.
2. Most of Genesis (thirty-eight of fifty chapters) deals with the accounts of the lives of Abraham, Isaac, and Jacob – the forefathers of the Jewish people.
3. "Israel is important because the fulfillment of God's covenant with Abraham greatly affects every one of us."
4. By watching Israel and seeing biblical prophecy being fulfilled, we can discern we are close to the End Times and can know God's prophecies about the future will also be fulfilled.
5. Against what seems to be impossible odds, God demonstrates His divine guidance, care, and ability to accomplish His purpose.
6. Biblically, Israel is center stage in both the beginning and end of time.

For the LORD hath chosen Zion…. - Psalm 132:13

The Prophecy of Psalm 22

Psalm 22 is known as the Messianic Psalm. It describes in detail what Christ would experience on the cross one thousand years in advance and long before crucifixion was practiced or *even known*. The following is a partial list of the detailed predictions in Psalm 22 that were fulfilled:

- **v. 1** What Christ would *say* on the cross – **"...My God, my God, why hast thou forsaken me?"**
- **v. 6** Specific *creature* to which Christ would compare Himself – a worm
- **v. 6, 7, 13** How people would *despise*, *mock*, and *laugh* at Him
- **v. 8** The exact *words* with which people would taunt Him
- **v. 14-16, 22** Exactly what would happen to Christ's physical body – all His *bones* would be out of joint; His *hands* and *feet* would be pierced; He would experience extreme *thirst*
- **v. 18** What would happen to His *clothes* – they would be gambled for
- **v. 22-31** That Christ would be *victorious*, *worshipped*, and *praised* forever

Psalm 22 is evidence that points to the truth and perfection of the Bible. The science of probability supports the fact that chance could never have produced this passage or the events of the crucifixion and resurrection.

...My God, my God, why hast thou forsaken me? (v. 1) ...All they that see me laugh me to scorn (v. 7) ...[A]ll my bones are out of joint (v. 14)... [M]y tongue cleaveth to my jaws (v.15)...[T]hey pierced my hands and my feet (v. 16)...and cast lots upon my vesture (v. 18)... [A]ll the kindreds of the nations shall worship before thee (v. 27)   - Psalm 22

Prophetic Warning from the Tower of Babel

The biblical account of the Tower of Babel is recorded in Genesis 11:1-9. Scripture tells us that the people all spoke one language at that time and joined together to defy God. The people were in direct rebellion against God's earlier command *"be fruitful, and multiply upon the earth." - Genesis 8:17*

God responded to the rebellion with this statement:

"...[B]ehold the people is one, and they have all one language; and this they begin to do: and now nothing will be restrained from them, which they have imagined to do." - Genesis 11:6

Today we are at the same point once again. We can communicate in one language through a computer and are in full rebellion against God's commands. We have put ourselves in His place as masters of our own fate, following our hearts in an unrestrained fashion. A look at what we are doing with technology in the areas of artificial intelligence, genetic manipulation, robotics, and nano-technology, as well as biological, chemical, and nuclear weapons, is sobering. We are on the path to self-destruction. Scripture says God will step in to judge mankind. We can choose to ignore God's warning or get serious about what the Bible teaches us about salvation and godly living.

...[L]et us build us a city and a tower, whose top may reach into heaven; and let us make us a name, lest we be scattered abroad upon the face of the whole earth.
- Genesis 11:4

Foundational Verses About God's Word (Part 1)

In order to share our faith with others, it helps to know those foundational verses that validate Scripture:

- **Thy Word is true from the beginning: and every one of thy righteous judgments endureth forever.**
  - *Psalm 119:160*

- **As for God, His way is perfect; the word of the LORD is proven; He is a shield to all who trust in Him.**
  - *Psalm 18:30 (NKJV)*

- **...Indeed I have spoken it; I will also bring it to pass. I have purposed it, I will also do it.**
  - *Isaiah 46:11b (NKJV)*

- **So shall My word be that goes forth from My mouth; it shall not return to Me void, but it shall accomplish what I please, and it shall prosper in the thing for which I sent it.**
  - *Isaiah 55:11 (NKJV)*

- **In the beginning was the Word, and the Word was with God, and the Word was God. He was in the beginning with God. All things were made through Him, and without Him nothing was made that was made.**
  - *John 1:1-3 (NKJV)*

Foundational Verses About God's Word (Part 2)

Here is a sampling of more key verses that point to the authority of God's Word:

- **For assuredly, I say to you, till heaven and earth pass away, one jot or one tittle will by no means pass from the law till all is fulfilled. - Matthew 5:18 (NKJV)**
  - Jot – the smallest Hebrew letter
  - Tittle – The highest point of a Hebrew letter

- **For whatever things were written before were written for our learning, that we through the patience and comfort of the Scriptures might have hope. - Romans 15:4 (NKJV)**

- **All Scripture is given by inspiration of God, and is profitable for doctrine, for reproof, for correction, for instruction in righteousness, that the man of God may be complete, thoroughly equipped for every good work. - 2 Timothy 3:16-17 (NKJV)**
  - Doctrine – Teaching from God
  - Reproof – To tell a fault
  - Correction – To correct or straighten up
  - Instruction – Training

- **For I testify to everyone who hears the words of the prophecy of this book: If anyone adds to these things, God will add to him the plagues that are written in this book; and if anyone takes away from the words of the book of this prophecy, God shall take away his part from the Book of Life, from the holy city, and from the things that are written in this book. - Revelation 22:18-19 (NKJV)**

Prophetic Warning About Satan (Part 1)

Scripture tells us a great deal about Satan. It gives us evidence of his existence and desire to destroy mankind. In Terry James' book, *Deceivers*, Dr. Billy Crone, wrote an excellent chapter on Satan. Dr. Crone states that only thirty-five percent of American Christians say they believe Satan is real. He points out over twenty-five verses in the Bible where Satan is directly referred to and gives dozens of different names Satan is called, each with a specific meaning. **God saw fit to clearly identify and describe Satan in the Bible in order for us to recognize and avoid his schemes.**

We are told Satan is an **angel of light,** one who appears as good when actually evil (2 Cor.11:14). He is a **deceiver** (Rev.12:9), an **enemy** (Matt.13:28), an **evil one** (John17:15). He is a **devil**, one who slanders and falsely accuses (Matt. 4:1), and a **liar** (John 8:44). Satan is a **tempter**, soliciting people to sin (Matt. 4:3), the **wicked one** who turns us away from God's Word (Matt.13:19), a **murderer** who leads people to physical, emotional, spiritual, and eternal death (John 8:44). He is described as a **roaring lion** (1 Pet. 5:8) and the **ruler** or chief leader behind world systems (John 12:31).

Satan desires more than anything to be God and be worshipped as God. He spells out his intentions in Isaiah 14:13-14. God, however, prophesied his doom.

Yet thou shalt be brought down to hell, to the sides of the pit.
- Isaiah 14:15

Prophetic Warning About Satan (Part 2)

God is holy, all-knowing, and all-powerful. He promised that Satan would ultimately be destroyed (Genesis 3:15). Knowing this, Satan attacks mankind, who was created in God's image. **He wants us to reflect *him*, not God** and seeks to destroy any relationship we might have with our Creator, Lord and Savior.

Satan has watched humans and over time has used many methods to accomplish his goal. For the first time in history, he now has access through *"mass media"* to instantly and simultaneously reflect his character worldwide. His first step is to slowly and increasingly numb the world to evil behavior. We see sex, violence, and corruption portrayed in books, music, television, movies and the internet. This evil is accessible not only to adults, but children as well.

Second, Satan uses the media to draw us in and get us to join him by showing us the "how-to" of evil and the occult. Finally, he transforms his evil character into an "angel of light", enticing us not only to watch, think, and act on the evil which reflects him, but ultimately convinces us to call evil "good" and what God calls good, as clearly revealed in His Word, "evil."

God, however, does not leave us defenseless. Although we know evil will continue to increase as we edge towards the End Times (Matthew 24, 2 Timothy 3:1-4), we have the *Bible* to guide, arm, and defend us. *God calls us to be faithful to His truth until He returns.*

I have fought the good fight, I have finished the race, I have kept the faith. Finally, there is laid up for me the crown of righteousness, which the Lord, the righteous Judge, will give to me on that Day, and not to me only but also to all who have loved His appearing.
- 2 Timothy 4:7-8 (NKJV)

God Always Sends a Warning

In Amos 3:7, God tells us that He does nothing without revealing His secret to His servants, the prophets. As we look through biblical history, we see this to be true.

- **Noah** was told to prepare for the coming worldwide Flood. He warned the people. *Genesis 6:17*
- **Joseph** was told the interpretation of the Pharaoh's dreams to warn the people of the seven years of plenty which were to be followed by seven years of severe famine. *Genesis 41*
- **Jonah** was sent by God to warn Nineveh of her coming destruction. *Jonah 1:1-2*
- **Jeremiah** was told to warn the people of the coming seventy year captivity of the Israelites. *Jeremiah 25:11*
- **Jesus** Himself warned the people of the destruction of the Temple, which happened in 70 A.D. *Matthew 24:1-2*

These are just a *few* of the many biblical examples from the past which show Amos 3:7 to be true. The biblical prophets in both the Old and New Testaments, like Isaiah, Jeremiah, Ezekiel, Daniel, Peter, Paul, and Christ Himself, also warn us of the coming worldwide Tribulation and the future return of Christ. If all the words of the prophets came true in the past, their future warnings will also come to pass as well, and they are worthy of our attention.

Surely the Lord GOD will do nothing, but he revealeth his secret unto his servants the prophets.
- Amos 3:7

Where Does the Soul Go at Death?

Many wonder what happens to our souls when we die. Does our soul go to sleep in the grave or does it go directly to heaven? The Bible gives us these clues:

- **Ecclesiastes 12:7** – The body goes to *dust* and "the spirit shall *return unto God* who gave it."
- **Luke 23:43** – Christ told the repentant thief on the cross next to Him, "**Today** thou shalt be with me in paradise."
- **Luke 16:20-31** –
    - *Angels carried* Lazarus' soul *to a place of comfort.*
    - The rich man in Hades could *see, speak, feel unbearable pain, and remember* his five brothers.
    - Abraham, who had died over 1,800 years earlier, was able to *communicate* with the rich man in Hades.
- **1 Thessalonians 4:14-16** – When Paul wrote about the resurrection of believers, he said they *would rise from the grave* and also that *Christ would bring them with Him* when He returns to Earth. Since the believers both rise and are brought from heaven, the body and the soul must be separated at death and later reunited. Sleep is the term applied to the body, not the soul.
- **Revelation 6:9-11** – John tells us he *saw the souls* of the martyrs in heaven. He *heard them ask* the Lord how long it would be before He would judge and avenge their blood on the people that dwell on Earth. The martyrs were *given white robes and told to rest just a little longer.*

We are confident, I say, and willing rather to be absent from the body, and to be present with the Lord.
- 2 Corinthians 5:8

Heaven: Ethereal or Tangible?

Most Christians seem to believe that Heaven, which will serve as their eternal home, is going to be an ethereal spirit world where they will exist as tangible spirits.

The Bible teaches no such thing. We are told in several passages of Scripture that our bodies will be supernaturally resurrected, glorified, and perfected to be like the body that Jesus had after His resurrection (1 Corinthians 15:42-44 and Philippians 3:21). Further, the Bible teaches that the Redeemed are going to live eternally on a New Earth – this earth renovated by fire (2 Peter 3:7-13) and perfected (Revelation 21:1-7). And their home on that New Earth is going to be a New Jerusalem of incredible size and beauty (Revelation 21:9-23).

The eternal destiny of the Redeemed is going to be as tangible as the world in which we currently live in – but it is going to be a perfected world in which there is no sin, no illness, no natural calamities, and no death.

Heaven is coming to Earth. Heaven is where God resides. When the Eternal State begins with life on the New Earth, the Bible says God will live among His people and they will see His face (Revelation 22:4). That means we will have intimate fellowship with our Creator eternally.

And they shall see his face…. - Revelation 22:4

Isaiah's Reminder for Handling Calamity

Isaiah 8:9-22 is an interesting passage which gives us hope, encouragement, and motivation as we go through great trouble. It is as vital today as it was in Isaiah's day.

Isaiah had warned Israel of impending doom. While in the midst of it, he addressed the believing remnant and told them not to get caught up in fear of what was happening. **It was not a time to panic (v. 12). Instead they could be beacons of light in a dark world by demonstrating real trust in God.** Isaiah reminded them that *God* is our holy sanctuary and our security (vs. 13-14).

In verses 16-18, Isaiah wrote practical advice on how to stay calm in the midst of calamity. The original Hebrew words convey the idea of "securing or sealing up" God's Word. Its teaching is accurate, unchangeable, and trustworthy. The people were to look to God and wait with confident expectancy that God would prevail. In verse 18, Isaiah goes on to say that one's trust and calm reliance on God through times of panic, confusion, and upheaval are marvelous examples of faith in God, and by acting in this way we serve as His signs to the world.

Bind up the testimony, seal the law among my disciples. And I will wait upon the LORD...and I will look for him. Behold, I and the children whom the LORD hath given me are for signs and for wonders in Israel from the LORD of hosts, which dwelleth in mount Zion.
- Isaiah 8:16-18

The Bible's Integrity Prophesied and Proven (Part 1)

In Isaiah 46:9-10, God tells us He is unique, He alone is God, there is no other like Him, and He alone can declare the beginning from the end.

In John 1:1, we are told that Jesus is the Word, and the Word was with God from the beginning.

We are told in Revelation 19:10 that the testimony or evidence of Jesus is the spirit of prophecy.

If these statements are all true, then we would expect to find God *is* His Word, and every word of the Bible is true – past, present, and future. We would also find the Bible is a one-of-a-kind book, greater than *any* other. If we take a "closer look" at the evidence, this is exactly what we find.

Consider these facts about the Bible:

- It had over forty authors living on three continents, writing in three different languages over a period of more than sixteen hundred years. The authors covered many different controversial subjects and had **absolute continuity and harmony.**
- The Bible covers history, science, geography, and psychology with **one hundred percent accuracy.**

Remember the former things of old, for I am God, and there is no other; I am God, and there is none like Me, declaring the end from the beginning, and from the ancient times things that are not yet done....
- Isaiah 46:9-10 (NKJV)

The Bible's Integrity Prophesied and Proven (Part 2)

The Bible alone authenticates itself by making and fulfilling many hundreds of detailed, long and short predictions. No other book even comes close.

The Bible is the only book on Earth that can claim the following:

- Accurate in transmission over time (it can be compared to the Dead Sea Scrolls, which were written over two thousand years ago and uncovered in 1948)
- Closest in date to the original documents
- Closest writing in date to the actual events
- Accuracy in information (history, science, geography etc.)
- Perfect harmony from beginning to end with one unfolding account, "God's redemption of man"
- Continuity throughout
- Most influence on surrounding literature
- Most read book on Earth
- Most purchased book every year
- Most translated book on Earth
- Most number of books in circulation
- Most often sought to be destroyed
- Harmonious coverage of controversial subjects among all of its forty plus authors
- Book with most hope – offers assurance of heaven for those who put their trust in Christ
- Most influence on people in history and in all the world
- Verifiable in its claims
- Most life-changing book on Earth

The entirety of Your word is truth, and every one of Your righteous judgments endures forever.
- Psalm 119:160 (NKJV)

The Prophecy of the Three Cursed Cities

There is an interesting prophecy in Matthew given by Jesus where three very specific cities are cursed. Scripture tells us Jesus did most of His miracles in the cities of Chorazin, Bethsaida, and Capernaum. *Capernaum* was Jesus' "own city." He had relatives, called His apostles, and taught in the temple in Capernaum. *Bethsaida* was the home of Andrew and James, and *Chorazin*, located about five miles north of Capernaum, was a fairly large town with many buildings and a well-built synagogue.

The people of all three cities were very familiar with Christ's teaching. They actually *heard* His messages and *saw* firsthand how people were miraculously healed! Their hearts were hard, however, and they would not acknowledge their sins or repent. This brought on Christ's rebuke. **Unlike other Jewish cities and towns that exist in Israel today, those cities were destroyed and never rebuilt, just like Jesus prophesied almost two thousand years ago.** His words are always accurate.

**Then He began to rebuke the cities in which most of His mighty works had been done, because they did not repent: "Woe to you, Chorazin! Woe to you, Bethsaida! For if the mighty works which were done in you had been done in Tyre and Sidon, they would have repented long ago in sackcloth and ashes….And you, Capernaum, who are exalted to heaven, will be brought down to Hades; for if the mighty works which were done in you had been done in Sodom, it would have remained until this day."
- Matthew 11:20-21, 23 (N**

MAY

Finally Brethren, Whatsoever Things Are True

Philippians 4:8

Arlene Faith Kortright

Final - ly Breth - ren, what - so - ev - er things are true, hon - est, just, pure and love - ly, of good re - port, if there be an - y vir - tue, if there be an - y praise think on these things

1. things

2. things Phil - ip - pi - ans four eight

LORD, etch these words on my heart. Help me discern what is true, honest, just, pure, lovely, virtuous and praise-worthy. Please help me think on these things. Drive away anything that is not pleasing to You, and let my life reflect You. **Amen**

A Prophecy from Psalm 2

Although Psalm 2 was penned over three thousand years ago, it is being fulfilled before our eyes. We see the nations in an uproar on a global scale as never before.

A look at the original Hebrew words translated into English (*the underlined words below in bold italics*) gives a vivid picture of what is happening worldwide today:

Rage:
We truly see the nations of the world in *tumultuous commotion.*

"Plot" a vain thing:
They *imagine and study* things that are *empty and worthless.*

Counseling together against:
The leaders *sit down together and settle on* things *contrary* to Christ and His teachings.

Breaking God's bonds:
They *tear themselves away from* all biblical *restraints.* Mankind wants to *draw away from and throw off* everything God has to say.

Just consider how we have torn ourselves away from God's Word on marriage, gender identity, abortion, and raising children. Many in America have turned far away from obeying God's Word on finances, the Ten Commandments, or good work ethic, and putting Christ first in our lives with the needs of others before our own. Psalm 2 goes on to tell us the inevitable result, but not without God's warning to come back to Him, where we can find peace, safety, and blessings. Psalm 2 is a sobering psalm to contemplate.

Why do the nations rage, and the people plot a vain thing? The kings of the earth set themselves, and the rulers take counsel together, against the LORD and against His Anointed, saying, "Let us break Their bonds in pieces and cast away Their cords from us."   - Psalm 2:1-3 (NKJV)

A Warning from Christ's Brother

Jude was certainly qualified to write on what "false Christs" and "false prophets" were like. According to biblical scholars, Jude was Christ's half-brother. Just as we have the *Bible* as our standard for comparison, *Jude* had *Jesus* (John 1:1) with whom to compare to everyone else.

Jude's one-chapter book devotes itself exclusively to warning believers not to be fooled by these false teachers. **Within Jude's verses, we get the following list of specific characteristics to watch for.** They not only help us *identify these imposters*, but also allow us to *evaluate ourselves* to make sure *we* are not one. It is interesting to note that the warning of false Christs and false prophets was not only the very *first* thing Christ mentioned in His list of warning signs leading into the End Times (Matthew 24:4-5), but also the *last* (Matthew 24:23-26).

Jude's Profile of an Apostate

1. Ungodly v. 4
2. Morally perverted v. 4
3. Denying Christ v. 4
4. Defiling the flesh v. 8
5. Rebellious v. 8
6. Reviling holy angels v. 8
7. Dreaming v. 8
8. Ignorant v. 10
9. Self-destructive v. 10
10. Grumbling v. 16
11. Fault-finding v. 16
12. Self-seeking v. 16
13. Arrogant v. 16
14. Flattering v. 16
15. Mocking v. 18
16. Causing division v. 19
17. Worldly minded v. 19
18. Lacking the Spirit v. 19

**...I felt the necessity to write to you appealing
that you contend earnestly for the faith
which was once for all delivered down to the saints.
- Jude 3 (NASB)**

Prophecy from the Fig Tree (Part 1)

In the New Testament, Jesus gave us three major prophetic teachings about the *fig tree*. In each case, **Christ used the fig tree to represent Israel.**

In the first passage of Luke 13:1-9, Jesus used a parable to *warn Israel to repent and bear fruit.* From the Old Testament, we know that God chose Abraham to be the father of the new nation of Israel. He picked the Jewish people to be His witness to show the world who He was. Israel was to be the leader of righteousness and draw others to the one and only true God. This parable points out that Israel, like the fig tree, was not bearing fruit. The Lord had warned Israel early on that His blessings rested on their obedience to Him.

In this parable, the owner planted the fig tree just as God planted Israel in her land. The owner came to seek fruit for three years. The Jewish people had the unique opportunity to see great miracles. They saw how Christ reacted to the most unfair trial on Earth. They also saw Christ crucified, the veil torn in the temple, the sky going pitch black at noon, an earthquake, Christ's empty tomb, dead people resurrected, willing martyrdom for Christ's sake, Pentecost, and the miracles of the disciples. Even with all these evidences, Israel still refused to repent and bear fruit.

He also spoke this parable: "A certain man had a fig tree planted in his vineyard, and he came seeking fruit on it and found none."
- Luke 13:6 (NKJV)

Prophecy from the Fig Tree (Part 2)

The second prophetic teaching about the fig tree is recorded in both Matthew 21:18-22 and Mark 11:12-24. In both accounts, Jesus went to the fig tree which symbolized Israel. Even after the Messiah Himself came to the Jewish nation and demonstrated that *He* was the predicted Messiah through His miracles, the Jews refused to accept and present Jesus to the world as His witnesses. As a result, **Christ predicted Israel, just like the fig tree, would be cut off as a nation.**

Jesus and His disciples passed that same fig tree the following day. Peter was shocked to see how it had withered from the roots. Strangely enough, Christ responded by telling His disciples to have "faith in God."

This prophecy's fulfillment began in 70 A.D. with the total destruction of Jerusalem. It was completed in 135 A.D. when the Jewish people were scattered throughout the world and Israel disappeared as a nation. Just as Christ predicted, they would be cut off, but the prophecy does not end there.

**And seeing from afar a fig tree having leaves, He went to see if perhaps He would find something on it. When He came to it, He found nothing but leaves, for it was not the season for figs. In response, Jesus said to it, "Let no one eat fruit from you ever again." And His disciples heard it.
- Mark 11:13-14 (NKJV)**

Prophecy from the Fig Tree (Part 3)

Christ's final teaching on the Mount of Olives, known as "the Olivet discourse," is the third and final prophecy about the fig tree. It is recorded in Matthew 24, Mark 13, and Luke 21.

In this parable, Christ prophesied about a specific time in history, a time that would point to the nearness of His return. **It was the time when the fig tree (or Israel) would bud (become a nation).** We saw this prophecy fulfilled after almost two thousand years on May 14, 1948, when the nation of Israel was reborn. Luke makes mention in his account that Christ also said we should look at "all the trees". In other words, *many nations* would be born around this same time.

According to records, there were about seventy-five recognized sovereign countries when Israel was born in 1948. In the 50 years that followed from 1950-2000, 109 new countries came into existence. Since 2000, only about five additional nations have formed. Christ's statement, *"When you see these things happening, know that the kingdom of God is near,"* should definitely get our attention.

Then He spoke to them in a parable: "Look at the fig tree, and all the trees. When they are already budding, you see and know for yourselves that summer is now near. So you also, when you see these things happening, know that the kingdom of God is near."
- Luke 21:29-31 (NKJV)

Old Testament Prophecies of the "Second Coming"

Throughout the Old Testament the "First Coming" of the Messiah was prophesied. Christ's purpose was to provide a way for sinful man to come into the presence of a Holy God. Over one hundred prophecies were recorded hundreds and even thousands of years before Christ's birth. Every single prophecy was precisely fulfilled. The Old Testament also records prophecies about His physical "Second Coming." They will happen with absolute certainty in every detail. The following list includes some of these prophecies:

The Lord's second appearance upon the earth will:

- Happen for certain - Habakkuk 2:2-4
- Be when His feet touch the Mount of Olives - *Zechariah 14:3-4*
- Come when Israel is under attack - *Isaiah 29:5-8; Zechariah 14:1-4*
- Be visible - *Isaiah 35:2-4; Zechariah 12:10*
- Bring His Holy Ones (the church) with Him - *Zechariah 14:5*
- Be in glory - *Habakkuk 3:3-4*
- Be in wrath - *1 Samuel 2:10; Isaiah 26:20-21; Zephaniah 1:14-18*
- Be as a defender and deliverer - *Isaiah 31:4-5*
- Be as a judge - *1 Samuel 2:10; 1 Chronicles 16:33*
- Be as a king - *Daniel 7:13-14; Zechariah 14:9*
- Bring upheaval in nature - *Micah 1:3-4; Isaiah 24:17-20*
- Defeat the Antichrist - *Daniel 7:24-28*
- Save a Jewish Remnant - *Isaiah 54; Joel 2:32; Zechariah 13:9*
- Bring in a reign of righteousness, justice, and peace - *Isaiah 11*

**The LORD of hosts hath sworn, saying,
Surely as I have thought, so shall it come to pass;
and as I have purposed,so shall it stand.
- Isaiah 14:24**

Biblical Claims Unmatched

The Bible is unique above all other religious books in the *claims* it makes about itself - and then *fulfills*. The Bible claims and proves to be the following:

1. "Thy word is <u>true</u>, from the beginning."
    - *Psalm 119:160; John 17:17*
2. "Every word of God is <u>pure</u>.... Add thou not to his words lest he reprove thee, and thou be found a liar." - *Proverbs 30:5-6*
3. "The Word of the LORD is <u>right</u>...." - *Psalm 33:4*
4. "Forever O LORD, thy Word is <u>settled</u> in heaven."
    - *Psalm 119:89*
5. "As for God, His way is perfect; the Word of the LORD is <u>proven</u>." - *Psalm 18:30 (NKJV)*
6. "So shall my word be that goeth forth out of my mouth: it shall <u>not return unto me void</u>, but it <u>shall accomplish</u> that which I please, and it <u>shall prosper</u> in the thing whereto I sent it." - *Isaiah 55:11*
7. "Word...was written for our <u>learning, comfort, and hope</u>."
    - *Romans 15:4*
8. "Heaven and earth shall pass away, but my words <u>shall not pass away</u>." - *Matthew 24:35; Isaiah 40:8*
9. Word will <u>all be fulfilled</u>. - *Matthew 5:18*
10. The Scripture <u>cannot be broken</u>. - *John 10:35*
11. "For all the <u>promises of God in him</u> are yea, and in him Amen, unto the glory of God by us." - *2 Corinthians 1:20*
12. The Word of God is <u>quick, powerful, sharp, piercing, and discerns the thoughts and intents</u> of the heart. - *Hebrews 4:12*
13. "<u>In the beginning was the Word</u>, and the <u>Word was with God</u> and the <u>Word was God</u>." - *John 1:1*
14. We have something more <u>sure</u>, the <u>prophetic word</u>...men spoke <u>from God</u>. - *1 Peter 1:19-21*

A Closer Look at Psalm 32:1-4

Thirteen psalms are labeled as being a *maschil* or "instructive" psalm. A closer look at Psalm 32 reveals that it instructed us in the field of psychology (the science of the mind and behavior) over three thousand years before it became a science. The first two verses in the psalm teach **us how to attain true contentment,** something everyone desires.

As Christians, we know that ultimate contentment only comes by accepting Christ as our Lord and Savior. It is *only through Christ's forgiveness* that our rebellion and missing the mark or perverting God's standards will *not be held against us.* What a blessing, indeed!

Blessed is he whose transgression is forgiven, whose sin is covered. Blessed is the man to whom the LORD does not impute iniquity, and in whose spirit there is no deceit.
- Psalm 32:1-2 (NKJV)

Verses 3 and 4 are equally insightful. We are told that "keeping silent" or concealing our wrong-doing affects us physically, mentally, and spiritually. It wears on us and becomes burdensome, even robbing us of sleep and vigor. "Selah," the Hebrew term signifying a pause of silence, concludes this psalm. It allows us a moment to think about this truth.

When I kept silent, my bones grew old through my groaning all the day long. For day and night Your hand was heavy upon me; my vitality was turned into the drought of summer. Selah.
- Psalm 32:3-4 (NKJV)

Rapture Prophecies (Part 1)

The next major prophetic event will be the *rapture*. **It is an event for all who accept Jesus as their personal resurrected LORD and Savior (who died for their sins).** This group of people, whose purpose in life should be to *obey* God, *pattern* themselves after Christ, and *share* Him with others, is called "the Church" (Greek, ekklesia) in the New Testament. *"The Church"* is not a building or a denomination but a specific group of people. At the rapture, this Church will be caught up or "snatched away" to meet Christ in the air and taken to heaven. The rapture is a completely separate event from the Second Coming when Christ returns to the earth at the Mount of Olives. There are several key New Testament passages which describe this event:

Let not your heart be troubled; you believe in God, believe also in Me. In my Father's house are many mansions (dwellings); if it were not so, I would have told you. I go to prepare a place for you. And if I go and prepare a place for you, I will come again and receive you to Myself; that where I am, there you may be also. - John 14:1-3 (NKJV)

Behold, I tell you a mystery: We shall not all sleep, but we shall all be changed-in a moment, in the twinkling of an eye, at the last trumpet. For the trumpet will sound, and the dead will be raised incorruptible, and we shall be changed. - 1 Corinthians 15:51-52 (NKJV)

But I do not want you to be ignorant, brethren, concerning those who have fallen asleep, lest you sorrow as others who have no hope. For if we believe that Jesus died and rose again, even so God will bring with Him those who sleep in Jesus. For this we say to you by the word of the Lord, that we who are alive and remain until the coming of the Lord will by no means precede those who are asleep. For the Lord Himself will descend from heaven with a shout, with the voice of an archangel, and with the trumpet of God. And the dead in Christ will rise first. Then we who are alive and remain shall be caught up together with them in the clouds to meet the Lord in the air. And thus, we shall always be with the Lord. Therefore comfort one another with these words. - 1 Thessalonians. 4:13-18 (NKJV)

Rapture Prophecies (Part 2)

The *rapture* is not mentioned in the Old Testament because the "Church" (Greek ekklesia) did not come into existence until Pentecost, forty days after Christ's resurrection. Paul tells us in 1 Corinthians 15:51-52 that he had a *mystery* to share with New Testament people.

Behold, I tell you a mystery: We shall not all sleep, but we shall all be changed – in a moment, in the twinkling of an eye, at the last trumpet. For the trumpet will sound, and the dead will be raised incorruptible, and we shall be changed. - 1 Corinthians 15:51-52 (NKJV)

The mystery was that Christ would come back and rapture the "Church."

For the Lord Himself will descend from heaven with a shout, with the voice of an archangel, and with the trumpet of God. And the dead in Christ will rise first. Then we who are alive and remain shall be caught up together with them in the clouds to meet the Lord in the air. And thus we shall always be with the Lord. - 1 Thessalonians 4:16-17 (NKJV)

The New Testament was written in Greek. **The Greek word for "caught up" is** *harpazo* **which is defined as "to suddenly remove or snatch away, to seize, to carry off, or take by force."** This word was translated into the Latin word ***raptus*** which became the English word "rapture." Harpazo is used fourteen times in the New Testament (Matthew 11:12; 12:29; 13:19; John 6:15; 10:12, 28-29; Acts 8:39; 23:10; 2 Corinthians 12:2-4; 1 Thessalonians 4:17; Jude 23; Revelation 12:5). Each use is consistent with the original Greek word "harpazo." Christ is coming to "catch away" the Church.

Prophecy from Obadiah (Part 1)

Obadiah is the shortest Old Testament book. Its twenty-one verses were written by the prophet Obadiah to the strong and well-protected nation of Edom. Edom was founded by *Esau*, Isaac's son and Abraham's grandson (Genesis 36:1,8-9). Esau and his descendants proved to be a proud, bitter, and resentful enemy of Jacob (Esau's twin brother) and Jacob's descendants (the nation of Israel).

Unlike Israel, Edom rejected God and refused to live under His authority. Obadiah exposes the ugliness of Edom's pride and shameful treatment of Israel in the following ways:

- Edom *prided* itself in its own strength and invincibility, v. 3-4
- Edom was *violent* against Jacob (Israel), v. 10
- Edom had *no compassion* and did nothing to help Israel when Israel was attacked by an enemy, v. 11
- Edom *took pleasure* in Israel's destruction, v. 12
- Edom *joined Israel's enemies* to *loot and plunder* her when she was taken captive, v. 13
- Edom *refused to give Israel refuge* when she needed it most and *betrayed her* to her enemy, v. 14

History proved that God in His justice did not let Edom go unpunished for her pride, her treatment of Israel, and her total rejection of Him. She ultimately ceased to exist.

"...[S]hame shall cover you, and you shall be cut off forever."
- Obadiah 10 (NKJV)

Prophecy from Obadiah (Part 2)

Just as God had Obadiah record Edom's sins, God also had him predict their judgment. Obadiah made the following prophecies:

- Edom would be **despised** and **made small** among the nations. v. 2
- God said He would **destroy** them. v. 4-5
- Edom would **be betrayed** by its allies and friends. v. 7
- God would **remove** the **wise** men and **understanding**. v. 8
- The mighty men would be **dismayed and slaughtered**. v. 9
- "The house of Esau shall be stubble...**no survivor** shall remain of the house of Esau," for the Lord has spoken. v. 18

Edom's judgment was not immediate, but history shows a series of events that led to her downfall. By the sixth and fifth centuries B.C., foreigners owned the lands of Edom. The Maccabean Jews got control of the land in 2 B.C., and in 70 A.D. the Edomites ceased to exist. This once proud, violent, and uncompassionate nation was destroyed exactly as God had said.

A study of the rise and fall of Edom in her prideful, rebellion against God and cruel treatment of Israel is a warning to all nations and even us as individuals. A lapse in time does not erase judgment. God's holiness and faithfulness to His Word demand His justice. We will reap what we sow.

**For the day of the LORD upon all the nations is near;
as you have done, it shall be done to you;
your reprisal shall return upon your own head.
- Obadiah 15 (NKJV)**

Prophecy from Obadiah (Part 3)

Obadiah does not end his prophecy with the gloom and doom of coming judgment. He concludes it with prophetic promises for Israel that have yet to be fulfilled (verse 15). The fact that the promises were given to Israel well over two thousand years ago does not negate their fulfillment. Obadiah prophesied the following:

- *Israel* will **be delivered**, saved from destruction. v. 17
- *Israel* will **live in holiness**. v. 17
- *Israel* will **own the land** God originally promised her in Genesis 15 through the Abrahamic Covenant. v. 18-20.
- *Esau* will **be judged**. v. 21
- The *Kingdom* will **be the LORD's**. v. 21

From these promises to the nation of Israel, we can find tremendous encouragement. As we see Edom's many prophecies fulfilled hundreds of years after they were given, we can expect these prophecies for Israel to be fulfilled as well. We should also be encouraged, because if God's promises have been fulfilled to nations with one hundred percent accuracy, we can expect that every promise He gives to us will also come to pass. Like Esau and Jacob, we must make the choice to follow or reject God and His Word. In both cases, God's judgment and His promises are certain.

The grass withereth, the flower fadeth:
but the word of our God shall stand forever.
- Isaiah 40:8

Esau and Jacob: A Prophetic Type of Two Natures

Through Esau and Jacob, the writers of the Old Testament give us a type of the **old nature** (the flesh) and **new nature** (the spirit) that the New Testament describes in Galatians 5:17-25. We can compare them in the following ways:

Esau (Old Nature)	**Jacob** (New Nature)
Rejected God's authority	Wrestled with, but finally submitted to, God
No interest in God's blessings	Sought God's blessing
Prideful, rebellious heart	Humble, repentant heart
No compassion for others	Compassion for others
Followed after gods of power, prestige, possessions	Followed after the true and living God of the Bible
Declared ability to live without God	Clung to God
Cruel and Violent	Loving and gentle
Gloried in self and man-made fortresses	Gloried in God

We have these two natures struggling within us, just as the generations of Esau and Jacob struggled even to this day. God gives us a choice as to which nature we allow to become dominant. It is a lifelong battle. The blessing is that God will help us want to do His will and give us the power to do it if we ask Him (Philippians 2:13).

For the flesh lusteth after the Spirit, and the Spirit against the flesh: and these are contrary the one to the other: so that ye cannot do the things that ye would. - Galatians 5:17

For it is God which worketh in you both to will and to do of His good pleasure. - Philippians 2:13

Prophetic Encouragement from Psalm 42

As the Lord Himself predicted in Matthew 24, Paul warned in
2 Timothy 3:1-9, and John revealed in the book of Revelation, times
will get increasingly more difficult as we head toward End Times.
Psalm 42 is one of the thirteen Maschils (instructional psalms) in the
book of Psalms. It addresses the discouragement which followers of
Christ have faced throughout history, and will continue to face, until
Christ's return.

The psalmist lays before us not only his deep discouragement, but
also leaves us with his course of action. It not only helped him but is
still useful today. In Psalm 42, the author:

1. Openly lays out the <u>cause</u> of his discouragement.
   **...Mine enemies reproach me; while they daily say unto
   me, Where is thy God?** *v. 10*

2. Records how deeply he is affected <u>emotionally</u>.
   My tears have been my meat day and night, *v. 3;* **My soul
   is cast down...disquieted in me.** *v. 5,6,11*

3. Describes how his discouragement affected him <u>physically.</u>
   He cannot sleep well, since he cries 'day and night *v. 3*
   The enemies' afflictions are as the crushing of his bones
   v. 9, 10

4. Specifically details what he did and encourages us to do in <u>fighting
   discouragement.</u>

   a. Craves God's presence (and Word), *v. 1,2*
   b. Pours out his soul to God, *v. 4,9*
   c. Recounts how God helped him in the past, *v. 6*
   d. Remembers God's promises, *v. 8*
   e. Talks to God in praise, *v. 5,8,11,* and in prayer, *v. 8*
   f. Disciplines himself to do what he must do – puts his hope in
      God as he praises Him with a thankful heart, *v. 11*

Rapture Prophecies Compared (Part 1)

John in <u>John 14:1-3</u> and *Paul* in <u>1 Thessalonians 4:13-18</u> provide the same information about the "rapture" or time when Jesus will bring believers to live with Him. From these passages, we can see the Bible does not contradict itself. Jesus and Paul are in complete agreement. The actual passages are shown on the next page (May 17).

- **We are to be comforted.**

John 14:1 "Let not your heart be troubled…."
1 Thessalonians 4:18 "Therefore, comfort one another with these words."

- **We must have a personal faith in Jesus.**

John 14:1 "…you believe in God, believe also in Me."
1 Thessalonians 4:14 "For if we believe that Jesus died and rose again, even so God will bring with Him those who sleep in Jesus."

- **We can take God at His Word.**

John 14:2 "…if it were not so, I would have told you."
1 Thessalonians 4:15 "…[T]his we say to you by the word of the Lord…."

- **The Lord promised He would return.**

John 14:3 "…I will come again…."
1 Thessalonians 4:16 "For the Lord Himself will descend from heaven…."

- **We will be removed from Earth.**

John 14:3 "…I will come again and receive you to Myself…"
1 Thessalonians 4:17 "Then we who are alive and remain shall be caught up together with them in the clouds to meet the Lord in the air."

- **We will be where Christ is.**

John 14:3 "…that where I am, there you may be also."
1 Thessalonians 4:17 "And thus we shall always be with the Lord."

Rapture Prophecies Compared (Part 2)

In Scripture we are encouraged to study God's Word (Acts 17:10-11; 2 Timothy 3:16).   As we prayerfully read these two passages, may the Holy Spirit guide us.

[1]Let not your heart be troubled; you believe in God, believe also in Me. [2]In My Father's house are many mansions; if it were not so, I would have told you. I go to prepare a place for you. [3]And if I go and prepare a place for you, I will come again and receive you to Myself; that where I am, there you may be also.   - John 14:1-3 (NKJV)

[13]But I do not want you to be ignorant, brethren, concerning those who have fallen asleep, lest you sorrow as others who have no hope. [14]For if we believe that Jesus died and rose again, even so God will bring with Him those who sleep in Jesus. [15]For this we say to you by the word of the Lord, that we who are alive and remain until the coming of the Lord will by no means precede those who are asleep. [16]For the Lord Himself will descend from heaven with a shout, with the voice of an archangel, and with the trumpet of God. And the dead in Christ will rise first. [17]Then we who are alive and remain shall be caught up together with them in the clouds to meet the Lord in the air. And thus we shall always be with the Lord. [18]Therefore comfort one another with these words.   - 1 Thessalonians 4:13-18 (NKJV)

Joel's Warning About the Tribulation

The book of Joel gives us some wise advice in the light of the End Times. The "Day of the LORD" is mentioned five times (1:15; 2:1, 11,31; 3:14) in his three chapters.

Joel was a prophet called by God (1:1) to use a destructive locust swarm as a picture of the coming devastating, end-time Tribulation. As is often the case in the Bible, prophecy was given that would come to pass in both the *near and distant future*. God wanted people to understand that His judgment on the ungodly is *certain*. **God is holy and just, so He cannot withhold punishment indefinitely.**

The following lessons can be learned from Joel:

1. God warns in advance of His judgment. We are to teach the lessons of God's judgment to the following generations. - *Joel 1:1-3*
2. God's judgment is thorough; no one escapes. - *Chapters 1-2*
3. God hates sin, and His judgment is fierce, grievous, and complete. - *Chapters 1-2*
4. God calls everyone to mourn for their sins and repent. This is the only way to God's forgiveness and salvation. - *Joel 1:5-20, 2:12-17*
5. The coming Tribulation is a fact. There has never been anything like it, nor ever will be again. - *Joel 2:1-2, 10-11*
6. God is merciful and clearly tells us how to avoid His wrath. - *Joel 2:12-17*
7. God promised to and will restore Israel in the End Times. - *Joel 2:18-27; 3:1, 16-20*
8. Nations will be judged for how they treat Israel. - *Joel 3:2-8,19,21*

Joel's End Time Promises for Israel

The focus of Joel's book is End Times. He devotes much of his book to God's specific promises to Israel after He returns to judge the nations (following the Tribulation). Jesus clearly tells us in John 14:6 that He is the *only way* to God. Christ's Words are meant for all. This includes the Jews. Their belief in God the Father only is not enough. **Zechariah 12:10 tells us God will pour His Spirit on the house of David and inhabitants of Jerusalem and they will recognize Jesus Christ as their Messiah.** Through Joel we learn that God guaranteed Israel the following promises at the end of time:

- "...Behold, I will send you grain and new wine and oil." - *Joel 2:19 (NKJV)*
- "...I will no longer make you a reproach among the nations." - *Joel 2:19 (NKJV)*
- "Be glad then, you children of Zion, and rejoice in the LORD your God; for He has given you the former rain faithfully...the threshing floors shall be full of wheat...the vats shall overflow with new wine and oil." - *Joel 2:23-24 (NKJV)*
- "You shall eat in plenty and be satisfied..." - *Joel 2:26 (NKJV)*
- "...My people shall never be put to shame...you shall know that I am in the midst of Israel: I am the LORD your God...." - *Joel 2:26-27 (NKJV)*
- "...But the LORD will be a shelter for His people, and the strength of the children of Israel." - *Joel 3:16b (NKJV)*
- "...Then Jerusalem will be holy, and no aliens shall ever pass through her again." - *Joel 3:17b (NKJV)*
- "...The mountains shall drip with new wine, the hills shall flow with milk, and all the brooks of Judah shall be flooded with water; a fountain shall flow from the house of the LORD...." - *Joel 3:18 (NKJV)*
- "But Judah shall abide forever, and Jerusalem from generation to generation...for the LORD dwells in Zion." - *Joel 3:20-21 (NKJV)*

Recesses of the Deep Foretold

The Bible is full of scientific insights revealed long before man discovered them. One example is a question God asked Job, *"Have you walked in the recesses of the deep?"* In another passage, David referred to the *"channels of the sea"* (2 Samuel 22:16). The Hebrew word for *recesses* refers to that which is *"hidden and known only by investigation."* **What are these recesses of the deep?** The Hebrew word for *"deep"* is the same word used for seas or oceans.

For thousands of years, mankind considered the ocean as nothing more than a relatively shallow, sandy extension from one continent to another. It wasn't until the Glomar Challenger expedition (1973-1976) that the first comprehensive scientific exploration of the ocean floor took place. One of the discoveries was a five-mile-deep canyon under the Pacific Ocean. **Numerous other "recesses" have been found since that time, including one near the Philippines which is almost seven miles deep!** One wonders how the writer of Job knew there were "recesses in the deep." Was it just a lucky guess, or was it revealed to him by our Creator?

Have you journeyed to the springs of the sea or walked in the recesses of the deep?
- Job 38:16 (NIV)

The "Sidon" Prophecy

The prophet Ezekiel prophesied that the city of Sidon, twenty miles north of Tyre, would have a miserable and bloody future due to its horrible sinfulness. A study of history shows that this prophecy came true exactly as predicted.

Throughout the centuries, Sidon has been one of the bloodiest locations in history. Soon after the prophecy was given, the city was captured by the Babylonians. Later, over forty thousand died in a rebellion against the Persians. The Greeks then captured it under Alexander the Great in 330 B.C. It continued to be the scene of many fierce battles during the Crusades and various Turkish wars. Today, this city is part of Lebanon, only twenty miles south of Beirut. This area seems destined to continue its unhappy history (indefinitely), just as the Bible predicted over two thousand years ago.

The Bible is filled with prophetic statements. Every single prediction has come or is in the process of coming true because the Bible is inspired by the Holy Spirit. Only God is outside of time and capable of seeing all of time in advance. This is possible because time is part of the physical universe, and God, who created the entire universe, is outside of time. Only the Bible validates itself by predicting specific future events in advance.

Behold, I am against you, O Sidon....I will send
pestilence upon her, and blood in her streets;
the wounded shall be judged in her midst
by the sword against her on every side....
- Ezekiel 28:22-23 (NKJV)

Avoiding Confusion in the Last Days

Paul's teaching in 1 Corinthians 14:33 was important for the church at Corinth. It also has significant implications into the prophetic future. Reading both the Old and New Testaments will show that **"confusion" was never a part of the will of God in people's lives.** In fact, confusion was often used to defeat Israel's ungodly enemies.

- At the Tower of Babel (Genesis 11:9)
- When God looked down at the Egypian army (Exodus 14:24)
- As the Philitines drew near to atttack while Samuel was offering up the burnt offering (1 Samuel 7:10)

In our day, we see Satan's use of confusion to destroy the Christian faith and families. There is confusion over key doctrinal issues such as the inerrancy of Scripture, the dual nature of Christ's humanity and deity, and how one can get to heaven. There is also much confusion over evolution versus creation, the definition of marriage, abortion, sexuality, the raising of children, and many more issues.

None of this catches God by surprise. Throughout the Old and New Testaments, we are warned to read and diligently study God's Word. We will find God is clear on these issues. The confusion comes when we refuse to accept them as His final Word because we don't like what they say.

**For God is not the author of confusion,
but of peace, as in all churches of the saints.
- 1 Corinthians 14:33**

Is the Exodus a Type of The Tribulation? (Part 1)

The book of Exodus is prophetical in that it gives us insight into the coming Tribulation period. We know God's plan for the future can be understood by looking into the past. Throughout Scripture God calls us to remember His past dealings in history so we can learn about His eternal attributes and the nature of love and grace, as well as see our nature of sin, rebellion, and selfishness. God wants mankind to understand that it is *through Christ alone* that we can become what He created us to be and be saved from hell.

By *comparing* the **Exodus of the Israelites** from the bondage of Egypt with the end time **Tribulation,** we can learn the following:

- God always blesses, protects, and saves those who love and trust Him.
- God always warns people not to turn from Him. Turning from God leads to moral depravity, confusion, and death.
- God's judgments are meant to draw us back to Him, and they come with increasing severity when we do not listen to Him.
- God is Holy and cannot tolerate sin.
- God is not partial to male or female, rich or poor, Jew or Gentile.
- God's judgment is final. There are no second chances.
- God was, is, and always will be victor over Satan. There is no contest!
- All mankind *will* acknowledge God is LORD!

...In this thou shalt know that I am the LORD.... - Exodus 7:17

...Fear God, and give glory to him; for the hour of his judgment is come.... - Revelation 14:7

Is the Exodus a Type of The Tribulation? (Part 2)

Coincidence or God-ordained? Notice the similarities between the plagues of the Exodus and the series of Tribulation judgments:

The Exodus Exodus 7-12	The Tribulation Revelation 6-16
The Nile River became blood. Ex. 7:17-21	One third of the sea will become blood. Rev. 8:8; 16:3-4
The rivers brought up frogs. Ex. 8:3-6	Frogs will come out of the dragon, beast, and false prophet's mouths. Rev. 16:13
The plague of lice couldn't be duplicated by the magicians. Ex. 8:16-18	People will not duplicate or stop God's witnesses. Rev. 11:3-6
Flies bothered only the Egyptians. Ex. 8:21-24	Locusts will only harm the ungodly. Rev. 9:3-6
Animals died. Ex. 9:3-6	Animals will die. Rev. 8:9
Boils came on Egyptians and their beasts. Ex 9:8-9	Sores come on those with the beast's mark. Rev. 16:2
Hail and fire killed people, plants, animals, trees, and crops. Ex. 9:22-25	Hail and fire will come down. Rev. 16:8-9, 21
Locusts covered and destroyed everything. Ex. 10:12-15	Locusts will come up out of the earth. Rev. 9:2-10
Darkness covered Egypt for three days. Ex. 10:21-23	Darkness will come upon the earth. Rev. 8:12; 16:10
Death angel killed all the first-born. Ex. 12:29	Death kills a third of all mankind. Rev. 9:18

The Exodus always has been part of Jewish culture. The Jewish New Year and Passover Feast were instituted by God Himself to remind His people of His provision and protection as well as certain judgment for disobedience and unbelief. **It was a perfect way to illustrate what the future Tribulation will be like.**

Is the Exodus a Type of The Tribulation? (Part 3)

The parallels between the Exodus and the Tribulation do not end with the plagues. The following points show how well God knows man's nature and the measures He takes to reveal Himself and draw us to Him:

- God heard and responded to the Israelites' cry. - Exodus 3:7
  God will hear and respond to the martyred saints. - Rev. 6:10-11

- God called Aaron and Moses to speak and perform signs for Him. - Exodus chapters 3-4
  God will call two witnesses to speak and perform signs for Him. - Revelation 11:3-6

- Magicians performed false signs. Exodus 7:11; 22; 8:7
  The false prophet will perform false signs. - Rev. 13:11-15

- God warned the Israelites through His prophets. - Amos 3:7
  God's prophets in the Bible warn us today. - Amos 3:7

- God promised His children a land of milk and honey.
  - Exodus 3:8
  God promised His children will inherit all things, have life, and enter His city. - Revelation 21:7; 22:14

- Plagues resulted in God bringing His rule through Moses, prophets, judges, and kings. - Various Scriptures
  The overthrow of the Antichrist will bring in the Millennial Kingdom. - Revelation 20

- The godly were mistreated by the Pharaoh. - Exodus 3:7
  The Antichrist will kill the Jews and Christians. - Rev. 13:15-17

- The Egyptians were glad to get rid of the Israelites. - Exodus 10:28; 12:33
  The Antichrist's worshippers will be glad to be rid of the two witnesses. - Revelation 11:9-10

Is the Exodus a Type of The Tribulation? (Part 4)

The following are true about *both* the Exodus and Tribulation accounts:

- Judgments are certain and increase in severity.
  Exodus 7-11, Revelation 5-18

- Successive judgments increase the anger of the ungodly.
  Exodus 7-11, Revelation 9:20-21; 16:9-11

- Judgments are to bring man to acknowledge God.
  Exodus 14:4,17-18, Zechariah 13:9

- Death awaits those who do not heed God's warning.
  Exodus 14:27-28, Zephaniah 1:15-18

- The LORD fights the battle alone/the godly stand by.
  Exodus. 14:24-28, Revelation 19:11-16

- God's victory is celebrated with a "Special Song."
  Exodus 15:1-21, Revelation 5:9-14

- Saints are saved by the blood of the Lamb.
  Exodus 12:21-23, Revelation 12:11

The Day Jesus Declared Himself Messiah

The book of Daniel contains a remarkable prophecy that accurately predicts the exact day on which Jesus declared himself Messiah. **A passage that begins in Daniel 9:24 indicates that 483 years would pass from the day that the order was given to rebuild Jerusalem until the day of the declaration of "Messiah the Prince."** We know from other Old Testament texts that the order to commission the rebuilding of Jerusalem was given on March 14, 445 B.C. If we count forward exactly 483 Jewish years (a Jewish year was 360 days long), this equals 173,880 days; and we come to the date of April 6, 32 A.D. What happened on that day in history? It was the exact day on which Jesus arranged to have Himself declared the Messiah of the Jewish people by riding into Jerusalem on a donkey.

The Messiah's entry into Jerusalem on a donkey was predicted hundreds of years earlier in Zechariah 9:9. Exactly on the day predicted by Daniel, 173,880 days after the proclamation that Jerusalem be rebuilt, Jesus rode into Jerusalem, revealing Himself as the Messiah. As the people sang a Messianic song, the Jewish religious authorities (understanding what was implied) told Jesus to stop the worship. Jesus responded, "I tell you that, if these should hold their peace, the stones would immediately cry out" (Luke 19:40).

> **Know and understand this: from the time the word goes out to restore and rebuild Jeruselum until the Anointed One, the ruler comes, there will be seven 'sevens' and sixty-two 'sevens.'**
> **- Daniel 9:25 (NIV)**

(In Hebrew, the word "week" represents a "seven" of years, months, or days. In this passage it means seven years.)

Isaiah's Dead Sea Scroll Prophecy

There is an unusual passage recorded in Isaiah 29. It says that when Ariel, the symbolic name for Jerusalem, is brought back as a nation, it will be attacked. Isaiah 29:2 tells us Israel will grieve and face much sorrow. The following verse states that enemies would surround her and adversaries will set up a mound (military post) in order to lay siege against her. In Isaiah 29:4, we are told Israel will be brought down and humiliated.

The prophecy does not end here, however. Verse 4 also predicts that **Israel shall speak out of the ground.** Her words would mumble or whisper forth. Isn't it interesting that the *very day* the Israeli War of Independence started, Jordan attacked Jerusalem (as predicted in Zechariah 12), and *that same day* the Dead Sea Scrolls fell into Jewish hands. One of the first scrolls discovered was the very one Isaiah wrote, *which included this prophecy* over 2,500 years earlier.

Woe to Ariel, to Ariel, the city where David dwelt! Add year to year; let feasts come around. Yet I will distress Ariel; there shall be heaviness and sorrow, and it shall be to Me as Ariel. I will encamp against you all around, I will lay siege against you with a mound, and I will raise siegeworks against you. You shall be brought down, you shall speak out of the ground; your speech shall be low, out of the dust; your voice shall be like a medium's, out of the ground; and your speech shall whisper out of the dust.
- Isaiah 29:1-4 (NKJV)

Prophecy from Hosea

The book of Hosea was written well over seven hundred years before Christ to the nation of Israel. In her God-given peace and prosperity, the people turned from God and followed the nations around them into idolatry and deep moral corruption. **God called Hosea, the prophet, to use his own love and marriage to his wayward wife, Gomer, as a real-life example of God's love and marriage to His chosen people, Israel.**

Hosea's life demonstrated how he loved and provided for his wife, but she left him for luxuries and pleasures, just as Israel had done to God. This resulted in destroying both. Gomer's lack of appreciation and desire to be satisfied with other lovers paralleled Israel's craving to indulge herself in paganism and its worldly enticement. As Gomer was warned and refused to repent, so did Israel. Both were determined to leave their husband and forgot all that had been done for them. God separated Himself from Israel as did Hosea from Gomer. They grievously watched their "wives" self-destruct. The amazing thing, however, was that in the end, when Gomer and Israel came to their lowest point, Hosea and God were there. Hosea bought his wife back from slavery. Although God's promise to bring Israel back as His wife is yet in the future, He will ultimately fulfill His promise to her also.

> "And it shall be in that day," says the LORD,
> "that you will call Me 'My Husband'...."
> - Hosea 2:16 (NKJV)

> "I will betroth you to Me forever...in
> faithfulness and you shall know the LORD."
> - Hosea 2:19-20 (NKJV)

Is Hosea Holding Up a Mirror for Us?

Within his book, Hosea detailed the causes of Israel's downfall.
This list is worth reviewing because it mirrors society today.

- "…There is no truth or mercy or knowledge of God in the land. By swearing and lying, killing and stealing and committing adultery, they break all restraint, with bloodshed upon bloodshed."
  - Hosea 4:1b-2 (NKJV)
- "My people are destroyed for lack of knowledge…you have rejected knowledge…you have forgotten the law of your God."
  - Hosea 4:6 (NKJV)
- "The more they increased, the more they sinned against Me…"
  - Hosea 4:7 (NKJV)
- "Their drink is rebellion, they commit harlotry continually. Her rulers dearly love dishonor." *- Hosea 4:18 (NKJV)*
- "They do not direct their deeds toward turning to their God…they do not know the LORD." *- Hosea 5:4 (NKJV)*
- "They have dealt treacherously with the LORD, for they have begotten pagan children." *- Hosea 5:7 (NKJV)*
- Israel "willingly walked by human precepts." *- Hosea 5:11b (NKJV)*
- "For your faithfulness is like a morning cloud and like early dew it goes away." *- Hosea 6:4 (NKJV)*
- "…They transgressed the covenant…they commit lewdness."
  - Hosea 6:7,9 (NKJV)
- "…They have fled from Me…they have spoken lies against Me."
  - Hosea 7:13 (NKJV)
- "For Israel has forgotten her Maker…." *- Hosea 8:14 (NKJV)*
- "Because you trusted in your own way, in the multitude of your mighty men. Therefore, tumult shall arise among your people…."
  - Hosea 10:13-14 (NKJV)
- "They were filled and their heart was exalted; therefore, they forgot Me." *- Hosea 13:6 (NKJV)*

All Scripture is given by inspiration of God and is profitable…
- 2 Timothy 3:16

Hosea's Prophetic Promises for Israel

Just as clearly as Hosea described the causes for Israel's downfall, he also prophesied God's promises in the end of time when Israel will be restored once again as God's beloved wife. God makes the following promises:

- The number of the children of Israel shall be as the sand of the sea... the children of Judah and the children of Israel shall be gathered together. - *Hosea 1:10-11 (NKJV)*
- God will "speak comfort" to Israel... "give her vineyards...she will sing there, as in the days of her youth." - *Hosea 2:14-15 (NKJV)*
- Israel will call God "My Husband." - *Hosea 2:16 (NKJV)*
- God "will make a covenant for them with the beasts...birds... creeping things...Bow and sword of battle will [be taken] from the earth." - *Hosea 2:18 (NKJV)*
- God will betroth [Israel] to Himself forever in "righteousness, justice...lovingkindness...mercy...faithfulness and [Israel] shall know the LORD.... 'In that day...I shall answer,' says the LORD." - *Hosea 2:19-23 (NKJV)*

God told Israel in Hosea 3:4 that they would be without a *king* and a *temple* where sacrifices could be offered. This has been the case since 70 A.D. Yet, there is hope.

We are told in Hosea 6:1 that Israel will return to the Lord, and He will heal them. **"After two days, He will revive us; on the third day, He will raise us up, that we may live in His sight."** – *Hosea 6:1* Could it be that the two days represent the two thousand years Israel was dead as a nation and now it is being revived on the third day to get ready for the one thousand year Millennium?

Afterwards the children of Israel shall return and seek the LORD their God and David their king. They shall fear the LORD and His goodness in the latter days.
- Hosea 3:5 (NKJV)

JUNE

For We Know That In All Things

Romans 8:28

Arlene Faith Kortright

For we know that in all things God works for the good of those who love Him, who have been called ac-cord-ing to His pur-pose Ro-mans eight twen-ty eight

LORD, I just love this verse. You've shown me where a rebuke, failure, tragedy, weakness, sickness, and even grief have turned out for my good. Help me put these times in the memory book of my mind so I will trust that everything that happens is for a reason and for my benefit because You love me. **Amen.**

Satan's Relentless Quest to Destroy the Jews (Part 1)

One of the earliest examples of the incredible fulfillment of prophecy is God's prediction in Genesis 3:15. When Adam sinned, God stated there would be enmity (*hostility, hatred*) between Satan and Christ. A careful study of biblical history shows Satan's hatred for God. His determination to destroy Christ and His seed (*the Jews*) has been relentless from the beginning of time:

Satan moved in each of the following scenarios:
- 1 John 3:12, **Cain** to kill Abel

- Exodus 1:22, **Egypt's Pharaoh** to kill all Hebrew boys

- 1 Samuel 18:10-11, **Saul** to kill David

- 2 Chronicles 22:10, **Athaliah** to destroy all the royal heirs of the house of Judah from which the Christ child would come

- Esther 3:4-9, **Haman** to plot genocide against the Jews

- Matthew 2:13-16, **Herod** to kill baby Jesus and the children two years old and under in Bethlehem and the surrounding vicinity

- John 5:16, **Wicked religious leaders** to kill Jesus before He went to the cross

Satan does everything possible to keep God's prophecies from fulfillment. Perhaps one reason is to keep mankind from trusting God's Word. In the process, Satan causes enormous sorrow and pain but never succeeds in thwarting God's divine plans.

**And I will put enmity between you (Satan) and
the woman, and between your seed and her Seed;
He shall bruise your head, and you shall bruise His heel.
- Genesis 3:15 (NKJV)**

Satan's Relentless Quest to Destroy the Jews (Part 2)

Satan's hatred for the Jewish nation did not stop with the death of Christ. His pursuit to destroy them is unparalleled. No other group of people has been so hated throughout history.

Satan's quest to destroy the Jews since the time of Christ:

- Destruction of the Jewish temple and scattering of the Jews in an attempt to contaminate the Jewish bloodline 70 A.D.

- Persecution of the early church and torture of all twelve Apostles

- Early martyrs

- Expulsion of the Jews from England 1290 A.D.

- Expulsion of the Jews from Spain 1492 A.D.

- Holocaust in Germany

- Islamic statements of a plan to wipe Israel off the map

- Growing global anti-Semitism

**And I will put enmity between you and the woman,
and between your seed and her Seed...
- Genesis 3:15 (NKJV)**

God's Final and Strategically Placed Prophecy

With the final verses of the book of Revelation, God saw fit for the Apostle John to issue *one final prophecy*. In this passage, we see a warning against changing God's Word in any way. We also see an interesting play on words. God promises to *add* plagues to those who *add* to His Word. He also promises to *subtract* one's part in the book of life, in the holy city, and in the blessings recorded in Revelation from those who *subtract* from His Word.

This is a serious warning for all who would willfully and purposely change Scripture. This warning is so serious that God recorded it not only at the *end* of His book, but also in two other strategically placed sections of His Word. We find a similar warning near the *beginning* of the Bible, in Deuteronomy 4:2 and 12:32, and another near the *center* of Scripture in Proverbs 30:5-6. We need to be very careful how we handle and teach what God's Word says!

For I testify unto every man that heareth the words of the prophecy of this book, If any man shall add unto these things, God shall add unto him the plagues that are written in this book. And if any man shall take away from the words of the book of this prophecy, God shall take away his part of the book of life, and out of the holy city, and from the things which are written in this book.
- Revelation 22:18-19

The Ark of the Covenant

The Ark of the Covenant that resided in the Holy of Holies of the Jewish Temple constituted a symbolic prophecy that pointed to the Messiah.

The *Ark* was a small box (52 inches long by 31 inches wide by 31 inches tall). It had a lid called "the mercy seat." At each end of the lid there was a statue of a cherubim (a type of guardian angel). The two cherubim faced each other with their wings thrust forward, overshadowing the mercy seat. *Inside the Ark* were three things: Aaron's rod that budded (Numbers 17:1-12), a pot of manna, and the carved stone of the Ten Commandments (Hebrews 9:4).

The Ark is referred in the Scripture as "the footstool of God" (1 Chronicles 28:2). The Shekinah Glory of God (God's earthly manifestation) resided above it. Once a year, on Yom Kippur, the High Priest would enter the Holy of Holies and sprinkle blood on the lid of the Ark as an atonement offering for the sins of the nation.

The wooden construction of the Ark pointed to the *humanity of the Messiah*. The overlay of gold inside and out signified *His deity*. The pot of manna indicated Messiah would be *the Bread of Life*. The Ten Commandments pointed to the fact that the Messiah would *perfectly obey all God's laws*. Aaron's rod was a symbol of the Messiah's *resurrection from the dead*.

Jesus fulfilled every prophetic aspect of the Ark. The Bible says when the Millennial Temple is built, there will be no Ark in the Holy of Holies (Jeremiah 3:16). **That's because Jesus is our Living Ark.**

The Messianic Birthplace Prophecy

Perhaps the best-known Messianic prophecy in the Bible is the one in Micah 5:2 which says the Messiah will be born in the town of Bethlehem Ephratah. That fact alone makes this a remarkable prophecy that clearly indicates it was a supernatural revelation from God.

But the prophecy is even more miraculous than that! That's because the passage does not simply state that the Messiah will be born in Bethlehem. Rather, it states He will be born in <u>Bethlehem Ephratah.</u> Have you ever thought about the significance of the term Ephratah? Well, if you were to ask someone where they were born, and they were to respond, "Springfield," you would have to ask another question because there is a city named Springfield in thirty-two different states.

And so it was in Israel at the time of Micah's prophecy. There were two cities named Bethlehem – one in the Galilee area up north and one located just south of Jerusalem. So, instead of just prophesying that the Messiah would be born in Bethlehem, the prophet nailed the location more specifically by stating it would be in Bethlehem Ephratah. This is not a coincidence.

But thou, Bethlehem Ephratah, though thou be
little among the thousands of Judah, yet out of thee
shall He come forth unto me that is to be ruler in Israel;
whose goings forth have been from of old, from everlasting.
- Micah 5:2

Prophetic Picture of God's "Dwelling Place"

Genesis Chapter 3 tells us God dwelled with Adam and Eve in the Garden of Eden. God walked and talked with them and had a close relationship until they chose to sin by disobeying Him. Sin put an end to their purity and ability to be in God's holy presence. However, God loved mankind so much that He initiated a very specific and tangible sacrificial system. It would temporarily cover the sins of mankind as well as demonstrate sin's serious and deadly consequences. Over time, mankind grew more and more rebellious. God then called a man named Abraham to follow Him and father a new nation, later called Israel.

At this time in history, God gave the Israelites detailed plans to build a *tabernacle* or "dwelling place" where He would reside, guide, and protect them. The Israelites were to be His witnesses to the world. The tabernacle was designed by God Himself. Each item, color, and material used in its construction, as well as its placement, had significance and pointed to God's promised Messiah. The Messiah would later fulfill the tabernacle's purpose – for God to once again dwell in the midst of His people.

An in-depth study of the tabernacle (later called temple) gives us a prophetic picture of Christ. He is the sacrifice for the sins of all who come to Him for forgiveness. He is the one who washes away our sins so we can dwell with Him forever! **His death, burial, and resurrection represent the new creations we become in Christ, allowing us to become His temple, where He dwells.** The beauty, purity, and purpose of the tabernacle was and still is an awesome example of what our body, soul, and mind should be since **we** are now His "dwelling place." What a privilege and responsibility has been given us. May we be inspired to give our utmost unto our LORD God!

**Know ye not that ye are the temple of God,
and that the Spirit of God dwelleth in you?
- 1 Corinthians 3:16**

A Spherical Earth and Innumerable Stars

Every subject addressed by the Bible reveals absolute accuracy which could only have been divinely inspired. Even 500 years ago there was the misconception among many people that the earth was flat. Yet the prophet Isaiah spoke of the earth as being a "circle." **The Hebrew word used was *khug*, which means something with "roundness or sphericity."** It does not mean flat like a platter. How did Isaiah know this?

It is he that sitteth upon the circle of the earth... - Isaiah 40:22

Jeremiah the prophet declared that the stars in the sky were countless. In Jeremiah's time (600 B.C.), only about three thousand stars could be seen on a clear night with the naked eye. Twenty-two centuries later, Galileo caught a glimpse of the vastly greater number of stars with his telescope. For the first time, humans were able to see an enormous number of stars and comprehend God's statement about the stars being countless. It was not until the last century that Sir James Jean (1930) wrote in his book *Mysterious Universe* that the *"total number of stars is roughly equal to the total number of grains of sand on all the seashores of all the world."* This scientific truth was revealed by God 2,500 years before it was discovered by man.

**As the host of the heaven cannot be numbered,
neither the sand of the sea measured....
- Jeremiah 33:22**

Moses Points to Jesus

After reading Exodus, one can't help but see what an incredible picture Moses' life paints of the coming Messiah. **Consider the following ways God used Moses' life to point us to Jesus:**

- The Egyptian Pharaoh sought to kill all baby boys at Moses' birth.
  Herod issued a decree to kill all boys under age two in his attempt to kill Jesus.
- Through Moses, God saved the Israelites from the captivity of the slavery of Egypt.
  Jesus saves us from the captivity of the slavery of sin.
- Through Moses, God brought the Israelites to the Promised Land.
  Jesus brings all who trust in Him to heaven.
- Through Moses, God performed miracles to authenticate Moses' divine appointment.
  Jesus performed miracles to authenticate His divinity.
- Through Moses, God turned the bitter water sweet to save the Israelites.
  Jesus declared Himself to be the living water that saves all who come to Him.
- The Israelites' first born were saved from death through the blood of the lamb.
  Jesus is the lamb whose blood on the cross saves us.
- The Israelites turned on Moses and falsely accused him.
  The Jews and Gentiles turned on Jesus and falsely accused Him.
- Moses offered to die in order for God to forgive the Israelites.
  Jesus did die in order for God to forgive our sins.
- Moses served as mediator between God and His people.
  Jesus is the mediator between God and His people.

For whatsoever things were written aforetime were written for our learning, that we through the patience and comfort of the Scriptures might have hope.
- Romans 15:4

Encouraging Fellow Believers

Scripture tells us to love and encourage one another as we see the *last days* approaching (Hebrews 10:24-25). Christian author Shirley McCoy observes that in the New Testament, we see many of the authors of the epistles begin and end their letters with blessings and prayers of encouragement for the believers.

In Romans, Paul wrote, **"Grace to you and peace from God our Father and the Lord Jesus Christ." -** *Romans 1:7b (NKJV)*

When writing the Corinthian believers, Paul closed by praying, **"The grace of the Lord Jesus Christ, and the love of God, and the communion of the Holy Spirit be with you all. Amen."** *- 2 Corinthians 13:14 (NKJV)*

Peter opens his book in 2 Peter 1:2 (NKJV) with, **"Grace and peace be multiplied to you in the knowledge of God and of Jesus our Lord."** He closes by lovingly requesting, **"But grow in the grace and knowledge of our Lord and Savior Jesus Christ. To Him be the glory both now and forever. Amen."** *- 2 Peter 3:18 (NKJV)*

Similar thoughts and feelings are expressed **more than 35 times** from the books of Romans through Revelation. It is a blessing to see how deeply those authors cared for and encouraged the people to whom they wrote. What an example they left us to follow, one well worth considering, especially as we head toward the End Times.

And let us consider one another in order to stir up love and good works, not forsaking the assembling of ourselves together, as is the manner of some, but exhorting one another, and so much more as you see the Day approaching. – Hebrews 10:24-25 (NKJV)

The Promise of Rewards (Part 1)

God clearly tells us that we cannot earn our way into heaven; it is a gift He offers to all who put their faith in Him. God promises us, however, that *we can earn rewards* in heaven for <u>how</u> we live on Earth and even *tells us how* in the following verses:

- And everyone who competes for the prize is <u>temperate in all</u> things. Now they do it to obtain a perishable crown, but we for an **imperishable crown.** - *1 Corinthians 9:25 (NKJV)*

- Finally, there is laid up for me the **crown of <u>righteousness,</u>** which the Lord, the righteous Judge, will give me on that Day, and not to me only but also to all who have <u>loved His appearing</u>. - *2 Timothy 4:8 (NKJV)*

- For what is our hope, or joy, or **crown of rejoicing?** Is it not even <u>you in the presence of our Lord Jesus Christ</u> at His coming? - *1 Thessalonians 2:19 (NKJV)*

- <u>Shepherd the flock of God</u> which is among you, serving as overseers, not by compulsion but <u>willingly</u>, not for dishonest gain but <u>eagerly</u>; nor as being lords over those entrusted to you, but <u>being examples to the flock</u>; and when the Chief Shepherd appears, you will receive the **crown of glory** that does not fade away. - *1 Peter 5:2-4 (NKJV)*

- Blessed is the man who <u>endures temptation</u>; for when he has been approved, he will receive the **crown of life** which the Lord has promised to those who <u>love Him.</u> - *James 1:12 (NKJV)*

For by grace you have been saved through faith, and that not of yourselves; it is the gift of God, not of works, lest anyone should boast. - Ephesians 2:8-9 (NKJV)

The Promise of Rewards (Part 2)

How we serve the Lord Jesus Christ now while we have the opportunity on Earth makes a difference. God tells us to run our race in such a way as to win the prize (I Corinthians 9:24). According to His own Word, our eternity will be affected by the following:

- How passionately we practice self control as we run our race and live for our Lord Jesus Christ. - *1 Corinthians 9:24-27*

- How faithfully we speak and behave as Christ would. How much we care about what He did for us on the cross; and how excited we are about His return. - *2 Timothy 4:7-8*

- How eagerly we share the gospel (good news) about who Jesus is and what He has done for us with others, and help them come to faith in Christ. - *1 Thessalonians 2:19-20*

- How selflessly God's people are taught and nurtured in God's truth by godly examples. - *1 Peter 5:2-4*

- How faithfully we trust and love Jesus and endure all the difficulties, discipline, troubles, heartaches, and suffering in life. - *James 1:12*

Scripture tells us in 2 Corinthians 5:10 that "we must all appear before the judgment seat of Christ" and He will closely inspect all we did for Him. *He will reward those things done in His name,* meaning we did them according to His character, authority, and honor. Everything we do for any other reason is worthless.

For we must all appear before the judgment seat of Christ, that each one may receive what is due him for the things done while in the body, whether good or bad.
– 2 Corinthians 5:10 (NIV)

Prophecy from Leviticus

The book of Leviticus is a key for understanding many later events in the Bible. It explains prophetically *how* to come back into full fellowship with God and *how* to be forgiven for our sins. The five sacrifices listed below outline what God desires from His people. All of these original sacrifices were temporary and incomplete. They all point to Jesus Christ - who would be the ultimate fulfillment of these sacrifices. When we accept Jesus Christ as the sacrifice for our sins, He enables us to be at one with God and live in His presence forever.

1. The **burnt offering** was a voluntary sacrifice to show our *complete surrender to God.*

2. The **grain offering** was a voluntary sacrifice *of thanksgiving* acknowledging God as the provider of everything we are and have. He alone is deserving of our best (first fruits).

3. The **peace offering** was a voluntary sacrifice to show our *desire for deep fellowship and peace with God.*

4. The **sin offering** was different because it was mandatory. It was a sacrifice of repentance *to purify* ourselves from any unintentional sin.

5. The **guilt offering** was also mandatory. It was a sacrifice of repentance not only to purify oneself of sin, but a serious and sincere attempt *to restore* all those that we have harmed with our sin.

Aaron (the High Priest) was a Type of Christ

The book of Leviticus goes into great detail to describe the function, dress, and responsibilities of the priests. God used Aaron as a picture of the promised Messiah hundreds of years before Christ came to Earth as Messiah. **Leviticus helps us to better understand what Christ did for us when He became the mediator between a holy God and sinful people.**

Aaron, anointed by Moses, served as the people's high priest.
Jesus, anointed by God, serves as our high priest.

Aaron served as the high priest for the nation of Israel.
Jesus was born to be the high priest for all who believe.

Aaron had to offer a sin offering to cover his and the Israelites' sin.
Jesus offered Himself, who had no sin, to cover our sins.

Aaron made sacrifices for the Israelite people.
Jesus is the sacrifice for all people who believe in Him.

Aaron served as mediator between God and the Israelites.
Jesus is the mediator between God and all who believe.

Aaron wore a consecrated garment that set him apart from others.
Jesus wears His scars that set Him apart as Messiah.

Aaron offered sacrifices that were temporary.
Jesus offered the final and permanent sacrifice.

Not with the blood of goats and calves, but with His own blood He entered the Most Holy Place once and for all, having obtained eternal redemption.
- Hebrews 9:12 NKJV

For there is one God, and one Mediator between God and men, the Man Christ Jesus, who gave Himself a ransom for all, to be testified in due time.
- 1 Timothy 2:5-6 (NKJV)

The Burnt Offering Points to Christ

God directed Moses to write the requirements for the sacrifice of burnt offering in the book of Leviticus. He prescribed this offering as a way for the Israelites to *temporarily atone* for their sins. The burnt offering also pointed to Christ, who would come around fifteen hundred years later as the perfect and final sacrifice, *made once and for all time*, in order to pay for the sins of those willing to accept this gift.

Consider the following parallels:

1. Anyone could bring an offering as an atonement for their sin. Lev. 1:2
   Anyone can accept Christ as their Savior. Revelation 3:20
2. There was only one way the burnt offering could be given. Lev. 1:1-17
   There is only one way to come to God. John 14:6; Acts 4:12
3. The burnt offering had to be without blemish. Lev.1:3
   Christ was perfect, without blemish. 1 John 3:5; 1 Peter 2:22; 2 Cor.5:21; Hebrews 7:26
4. The sacrificial animal died as a temporary substitute to appease God's wrath against sin. Lev. 1:4
   Christ gave His life as the permanent substitute to save us from God's wrath. Romans 5:8-9
5. The sacrificial animal was accepted if it met God's standards. Lev. 1:4
   Christ was accepted as the perfect sacrifice for us. Hebrews 7:22-27
6. The sacrificial animal had to be offered at the Tabernacle door. Lev. 1:3
   Christ is the door through whom all must enter. John 10:9
7. The burnt offerings were given of free will before the Lord. Lev. 1:3
   We must offer ourselves freely before the Lord. Mark 8:34
8. The entire animal had to be sacrificed in a burnt offering. Lev. 1:9
   God demands we give Him every part of ourselves. Matthew 16:24; Mark 12:30

**For by one offering he hath perfected forever
them that are sanctified.
- Hebrews 10:14**

Joseph Was a Prophetic Type of Christ

The life of Joseph is a classic example of prophecy in type since every aspect of his life was prophetic of the life of the Messiah. God gave Joseph a *message* for his kinsmen. Likewise, Jesus was sent with a message for the Jewish people. Joseph's brothers *rejected* him, just as Jesus was rejected by His people. Joseph was *symbolically killed* by his brothers when he was thrown into a pit and left for dead. Jesus was literally killed by His brethren. Joseph experienced a *symbolic resurrection* when he was pulled from the pit, pointing to the literal resurrection of Jesus from the dead.

Joseph went into a *foreign land* (Egypt) to *do a great work.* Jesus came to Earth to do an incredible work for all of mankind. Joseph took a *Gentile bride*, just as Jesus is currently taking a Gentile bride – the Church. Later, *Joseph revealed himself* to his brothers, and *they received him,* just as Jesus will soon reveal Himself once again to the Jewish people, and a great remnant of them will receive Him as their Messiah.

In fact, Jesus said He would not return until the Jewish people are ready to receive Him and proclaim, **"Blessed is He who comes in the name of the Lord"** (Matthew 23:39). According to prophecy, that will occur at the end of the Tribulation at the time of the Second Coming.

**For whatsoever things were written aforetime
were written for our learning….
- Romans 15:4**

Prophecy in the Day of Atonement (Part 1)

The Day of Atonement points to the Lord Jesus Christ. In the Old Testament, the sins of the people were temporarily covered by the blood of animals which were sacrificed by a priest for mankind's disobedience to God. Aaron was appointed as the first high priest. In the New Testament, Jesus was the more perfect sacrifice. This is made especially clear in the book of Hebrews. Jesus's death proved far superior to the Old Testament high priest's animal sacrifices by atoning for or covering the sin of all mankind once and for all. The Day of Atonement as described in Leviticus 16 is a beautiful prophetic foreshadowing of Christ, the perfect and final atonement for sin described in Hebrews 7-13. Consider the following:

Aaron introduced the *first* day of atonement.
Christ introduced the *last* day of atonement.

Aaron had to *cleanse himself* before making atonement.
Christ was *pure* and did not have to cleanse Himself.

Aaron had to put on *clothes which represented* righteousness.
Christ is the righteous one, *clothed in righteousness*.

Aaron first had to make *sin offerings for himself and his family*.
Christ was sinless. He *knew no sin*.

Aaron sacrificed an *animal's blood* for his own sin and that of the people.
Christ sacrificed His *own blood* for everyone else's sin.

Aaron's sacrifice was a *temporary* covering for sin until Christ came.
Christ's sacrifice is a *permanent* covering for our sin.

Aaron's sacrifice happened *yearly*.
Christ's sacrifice was once and for all *eternity*.

**By so much more Jesus has become
a surety of a better covenant.
- Hebrews 7:22 (NKJV)**

Prophecy in the Day of Atonement (Part 2)

Here is a continuation of the many ways Christ became the final fulfilment of the high priests who offered temporary sacrifices to cover our sins:

Aaron transferred *sins onto a scapegoat* who took them away into the wilderness.
Christ *was* the scapegoat who took our sins away.

The scapegoat took the sins *outside the camp.*
Christ was crucified, and took our sins *outside the city.*

Aaron entered the *earthly* tabernacle.
Christ entered *heaven* to appear in the presence of God.

Aaron could *not sit down* in the Holy Place.
Christ *sat down* at God's right hand, signifying the completed act of atonement.

Aaron *partially* satisfied God's wrath on sin.
Christ *totally* satisfied God's wrath on sin.

The Old Testament Israelites *could not enter* God's presence on their own.
New Testament believers *can enter* God's presence because the Holy Spirit dwells in us and Christ is our mediator.

Aaron was under the Old Testament *law.*
Christ fulfilled the law of the Old Testament. He established the New Covenant of *grace* with His sacrifice on the cross.

Through the Day of Atonement and its prophetic fulfillment in Christ, God shows us sin requires atonement because He is holy and just. God also shows us He provided atonement through His sacrificial love.

For Christ has not entered the holy places made with hands, which are copies of the true, but into heaven itself, now to appear in the presence of God for us.
- Hebrews 9:24 (NKJV)

The Deuteronomy 6 Prophecy

Deuteronomy 6 contains a prophetic promise that was given to every individual Israelite and to the nation of Israel. *This promise also applies to every person and nation on Earth.* As our Creator, God knows us better than we know ourselves. **In His Word, God tells us He knows a specific plan that will serve each one of us best (Jeremiah 29:11) and warns about what is harmful to us.** Deuteronomy 6 warns that obedience to God and His Word is key to every generation and that this can only be accomplished if parents and grandparents talk with their children about God's instruction manual and live by its commands. The Bible is our *B*asic *I*nstructions *B*efore *L*eaving *E*arth.

And these words which I command you today shall be in your heart. You shall teach them diligently to your children, and shall talk of them when you sit in your house ...walk by the way...lie down, and when you rise up.
- Deuteronomy 6:6-7 (NKJV)

God promises life, well-being, and prosperity to those who love and obey Him and guide their children to do likewise.

That you may fear the LORD your God, to keep all His statutes and His commandments which I command you, you and your son and your grandson, all the days of your life, and that your days may be prolonged. Therefore hear, O Israel, and be careful to observe it, that it may be well with you, and that you may multiply greatly....
- Deuteronomy 6:2-3 (NKJV)

The Center of the World Prophecy (Part 1)

Ezekiel 5:5 gives an interesting prophecy concerning Jerusalem. The original meaning of this Scripture would indicate that Jerusalem is at the center of the surrounding nations. But there are many other things of which it is the center:

- Jerusalem is the *geographic center* according to what God said in Ezekiel 5:5. God chose and set Jerusalem at the center of nations around her.
- Jerusalem is the *revelation center* in that this is where God's Word came from through the hand of Moses, the prophets, the apostles, and Christ.
- Jerusalem is the *spiritual center* where Jesus Christ was crucified, buried, and rose again. When Jesus returns He will set His feet on the Mount of Olives in Jerusalem (Zechariah 14:4).
- Jerusalem is the *prophecy center*. If you want to see where we are on the prophetic calendar, read and study what God is doing with the Jewish people, Israel, and Jerusalem.
- Jerusalem is the *trouble center* of the world (Zechariah 12:3).
- Jerusalem is the *peace center* of the world. God tells us that those who love Jerusalem will prosper. **Pray for the peace of Jerusalem: they shall prosper that love thee.** (*Psalm 122:6)* Although we know Christ will rule from Jerusalem in peace when He returns, a study of history will prove when countries and people loved Israel/Jerusalem and helped her, they prospered.
- Jerusalem will be the *glory center* when the Lord returns (Zechariah 8; Isaiah 2:1-3).

**Thus saith the Lord GOD; This is Jerusalem: I have set it in the midst of the nations and countries that are round about her.
- Ezekiel 5:5**

The Center of the World Prophecy (Part 2)

There are many prophecies surrounding Jerusalem which are yet to come true. Isaiah 2:3 is one such prophetic statement:

And many people shall go and say, Come ye, and let us go up to the mountain of the LORD, to the house of the God of Jacob; and he will teach us of his ways, and we will walk in his paths: for out of Zion shall go forth the law, and the word of the LORD from Jerusalem. - Isaiah 2:3

From that Scripture, we know that Jerusalem will be the center of the world during the Millennial Reign.

- Nations will go to Jerusalem to worship.

- The LORD will teach from Jerusalem.

- The law and God's Word will go forth from Jerusalem.

- Christ will reign from Jerusalem (from the throne of David). - Luke 1:32

Jesus is returning, and Jerusalem will be the seat of His worldwide kingdom.

He shall be great, and shall be called the Son of the Highest: and the Lord GOD shall give unto him the throne of his father David: and he shall reign over the house of Jacob forever; and of his kingdom there shall be no end.
- Luke 1:32-33

An Introduction to Revelation

The complete title of the last book of the Bible is "The Revelation of Jesus Christ." Its *purpose* is to *reveal the truth of Jesus*, who meant for us to understand it! The word "revelation" means a disclosure, uncovering, or revealing of something. When the word *revelation* is used in the Bible, it describes something or someone that was hidden but can now be understood. Revelation reveals who Jesus is. It uses *over 25 different titles* to describe Him to us. **It also gives us more details than any other biblical book about the End Times.**

The following is a simple outline that helps in the understanding of Revelation:

I.   The Things Which You **Have Seen** (1:1-20)
    A. The Introduction (1:1-8)
    B. The Vision of the Glorified Christ (1:9-18)
    C. John's Commission to Write (1:19-20)

II. The Things Which **Are** (2:1-3:22)
    A. The Letters to the Seven Churches:
      Ephesus, Smyrna, Pergamum, Thyatira,
      Sardis, Philadelphia, Laodicea

III. The Things Which **Will Take Place** (4:1-22:21)
    A. Worship Before God's Heavenly Throne (4:1-5:14)
    B. The Tribulation (6:1-18:24)
    C. The Second Coming of the Lord Jesus (19:1-21)
    D. The Millennium (20:1-10)
    E. The Great White Throne Judgment (20:11-15)
    F. The Eternal State (21:1-22:21)

**The Revelation of Jesus Christ, which
God gave unto him, to show unto his servants….
– Revelation 1:1**

An Amazing Insight from the Empty Tomb

Many verses of the Bible seem to be simple historical observations, but many, such as John 20:12-13, contain deep theological meaning – **if you are aware of its symbolic prophecy.** For example, what was the spiritual significance of what Mary saw in the empty tomb?

The Ark of the Covenant had a lid that was called the Mercy Seat. Statues of angelic cherubim were mounted on each end of this lid with the cherubim facing each other and their wings stretched forth, overshadowing the surface of the lid. Once a year the High Priest would enter the Holy of Holies where the Ark resided, and he would sprinkle the blood of the sacrificed animal on the lid as a sin offering for the nation.

When Mary entered the empty tomb that Sunday morning after the crucifixion, she saw two angels in the tomb. One sat at the head and one at the feet, where Jesus, the ultimate sacrifice, had been laid. His blood had been spilled as the final sin offering. Mary actually saw the amazing prophetic fulfillment of the meaning of the Ark of the Covenant.

But Mary was standing outside the tomb weeping; and so, as she wept, she stooped and looked into the tomb; and she saw two angels in white sitting, one at the head and one at the feet, where the body of Jesus had been lying.
- John 20:11-12 (NASV)

Exact Order of Jewish Return Predicted

The Bible not only predicted the regathering of the Jewish people in their homeland in the "latter days," but also the "specific order" of their regathering. Consider the following pattern we saw fulfilled in the regathering of the Jews in Israel. It was exactly as Isaiah predicted well over 2,500 years ago:

Stage 1: In 1900, Jewish people from Turkey, Jordan, Syria, Iraq, Yemen and other nations in the **Middle East** returned to Israel.

Stage 2: Between 1939 and 1948, the Jewish population in **Europe** was reduced by about six million. After the Holocaust and the birth of Israel in 1948, thousands of Jewish survivors traveled from the west to Israel to find peace and safety.

Stage 3: In 1988 under the glasnost (openness) policy of **Russia's** leader, Gorbachev, Jews were allowed to leave the country. Within two decades, about four hundred thousand Russian Jews migrated from the north and returned to Israel.

Stage 4: The final phase of returning Jews would come from the south. In 1991, approximately 14,000 black Jews (Falasha) were flown from **Ethiopia** to Israel in "Operation Solomon."

Fear not: for I am with thee: I will bring thy seed from the east, and gather thee from the west; I will say to the north, Give up; and to the south, Keep not back: bring my sons from far, and my daughters from the ends of the earth;
- Isaiah 43:5-6

Millennial Kingdom and Eternal State (Part 1)

There are many differences between the **Millennial Kingdom** and the final **Eternal State** of those who love the LORD. The Bible distinguishes between the two in the following ways.

Millennial Kingdom Revelation 20 Varied Verses	Heavenly Eternal State Revelation 21-22 and Matthew 22
Begins after the **seven year Tribulation** -*Revelation 20:3-7*	Begins after the **Millennial Kingdom and Great White Throne Judgment** - *Revelation 21:1*
1,000-year time period -*Revelation 20:3-7*	**Eternal**, there is no end -*Revelation 21:4; 22:5*
Longer life spans, but there is death -*Isaiah 65:20-23*	**No death,** sorrow, pain, or crying -*Revelation 21:4*
Sin is still **optional**, but restrained with rule of iron -*Isaiah 11:4; Zech.14:16-19*	Sin is **removed** forever -*Revelation 21:8,27*
Curse is **restrained** (Satan is bound) -*Revelation 20:1-3*	Curse is **removed** -*Revelation 22:3*
Mortals and resurrected saints live together for 1,000 years -*Revelation 20:4*	**Only those who obey God** can enter -*Revelation 22:14*
Destinies can **still be determined** by mortals -*Revelation 20:8-10*	Destinies **are sealed** -*Revelation 20:11-15*

Millennial Kingdom and Eternal State (Part 2)

The many differences between the *Millennial Kingdom* and the final *Eternal State* (continued):

Millennial Kingdom Revelation 20 and Varied Verses	Heavenly Eternal State Revelation 20-21 and Matthew 22
Judgment **will come** at the end of 1,000 years *-Revelation 20:9-15*	Judgments are **complete** *-Revelation 20:11-15*
Earth is **renovated** -Isaiah 27:6; 35	Earth is **recreated** *-Revelation 21:1, 5*
Satan is **bound** 1,000 years and temporarily loosed *-Revelation 20:1-3,7-10*	Satan is **removed forever** *-Revelation 20:10*
Rebellion occurs **one last time** *-Revelation 20:8-9*	All rebellion **ceases** *-Revelation 21:27*
Like a paradise *-Isaiah.11; 65:17-25*	**Is** paradise *-Revelation 21:1-27*
Millennial **temple will be built** in Israel *-Isaiah 2:2-4; Ezekiel 40-46*	**God and the Lamb are the temple** *-Revelation 21:22*
Children will be born *-Jeremiah 32:39; Ezek.37:26*	**No marrying**/like angels *-Matthew 22:30*
Israel will be world's **center** *-Isaiah 2:2-3; Ezekiel 5:5*	There will be **a new heaven and earth** *-Rev. 21:1-2*
There is a **sea** *-Revelation 20:13*	There is **no sea** *-Revelation 21:1*

Foreknowledge of Light Traveling in a Path

Where is the way where light dwelleth? - *Job 38:19a*

When the Lord asked Job, "Where is the way to the dwelling of the light?" God was providing us with an amazing scientific insight. The Hebrew word for "*way*" literally means a "traveled path or road."

In the seventeenth century, Sir Isaac Newton suggested that light was made of tiny particles which traveled in a straight line. Christian Huygens later proposed that light traveled as a wave. Both were correct. Scientists now know that light is a form of energy called radiant energy and that it travels in electromagnetic waves at approximately 186,000 miles per second in a straight line. **It takes about eight minutes for light to travel its "path" from the sun to the earth.** There really is a "way" or "path" of light, just as the Bible says.

It is absolutely amazing that the closer we look at each specific word used in the Bible, the more we stand in awe of its intricate detail, purposeful design, relevance across time, and perfect harmony. Only God Himself could orchestrate the writing of such a book!

As for God, His way is perfect; the word of the LORD is proven; He is a shield to all who trust in Him.
- Psalm 18:30 (NKJV)

Persecution Will Drive the Jewish People Home

Jeremiah 16:16 predicts that *persecution* would bring the Jewish people back into their land. This is not talking about the return of the Jewish people to Israel after Babylon. In that instance, God used the decree of Cyrus (2 Chronicles 36:22-23, Ezra 1) to bring them back freely, peacefully, and even with financial assistance.

The term *"fishermen"* and *"hunters that will hunt them down"* is used in Jeremiah 16:16. Both terms paint a terrifying picture of pursuit and persecution. An animal being "hunted" or "fished for" finds the process quite unpleasant! When we look at how Israel was regathered in the last century, this picture is exactly what we see happening. **Anti-Jewish persecution has been the main motivation for the Jewish people to return to the land of Israel.** God has used Czarist pogroms, Polish economic discrimination, Nazi genocide, Arab hatred, Soviet repression, and the rising of Antisemitism in Europe to drive the Jewish people back to Israel – just as Jeremiah predicted.

"Behold, I will send for many fishermen," says the LORD, "and they shall fish them; and afterward I will send for many hunters, and they shall hunt them from every mountain and every hill, and out of the holes of the rocks."
- Jeremiah 16:16 (NKJV)

Rapture and Second Coming Differences (Part 1)

The **Rapture** of the Church and the **Second Coming** of Christ are two very different events. They are such a significant part of God's plan that He talks about them in many places in the Bible. The amount of prophetic detail concerning these events deserves our attention and study.

Event	**Rapture** Jesus comes to **rescue** His followers	**Second Coming** Jesus comes to **judge** sin and set up His rule
When first mentioned	**New** Testament *(1 Cor. 15:51-52; John 14:3)*	**Old** Testament *(Ezek. 37:21-28)*
Who gathers	**Christ** gathers elect *(1Thess. 4:16-17)*	**Angels** gather elect *(Matt. 24:31)*
Time	Will happen **before** God's wrath *(1 Thess. 5:8-9)*	Will bring **end** to God's wrath *(Matt. 24:30)*
Where	Happens **above** Earth *(1 Thess. 4:15-17)*	Happens **on** Earth *(Matt. 24:30)*
Who is involved	**Believers** *(John 14:1-3)*	**Whole world** *(Matt. 24:30)*
Why	To **remove believers** from God's wrath *(1 Thess. 1:10;5:9; Rev. 3:10)*	To **judge rebellious** mankind *(Rev. 19)*
Mood	**Joy** for saints and **terror** for sinners left on Earth *(1Thess. 4:17-18; 5:3-4)*	**Death** for sinners and **relief** for saints on Earth *(Rev. 19)*
Ushers in…	**Chist opens up the seals** *(Revelation 6)*	Ends **Armageddon War** - followed by 1,000 year Millennial Reign *(Rev. 19-20)*
Who sees Christ	**Believers** *(1 Cor. 15:52-53; 1 Thess. 4:16-17)*	**Whole World** *(Matt. 24:30)*
Anticipation of	**Hope** for believers *(Titus 2:11-14)*	**Horror** for rebels *(Matt. 24:21-22)*

Rapture and Second Coming Differences (Part 2)

Event	Rapture	Second Coming
	Jesus comes to **rescue** His followers *(1 Thess. 4:14-18)*	Jesus comes to **judge** sin and set up His rule *(Matt. 24:50-51; Rev. 19)*
Events that must occur first	**Nothing** must occur first Event is **imminent** (ready to happen at any time)	**Events that must** occur first: Antichrist confirms covenant *(Dan. 9:27)* Tribulation *(Matt. 24:29-30)* Temple must exist *(Matt. 24:15)* Israel must cry out to God *(Matt. 23:39, Luke 13:35)*
Christ Will...	**Remove** peace *(2 Thess. 2:7-10)* Come in **secret** *(1 Thess. 4:16-17)* Come **alone** *(1 Thess. 4:16)* Remove **believers** *(1 Thess. 4:16-17)* **Remove the restrainer** of evil from the earth *(2 Thess. 2:7-8)* **Let Satan rule** for a time *(Rev. 12:12)* Give church **grace** *(1 Pet. 1:13)* Give living saints **glorified bodies** *(1 John 3:2)*	**Bring** peace *(Ps. 72)* Come **publicly** *(Matt. 24:30; Rev. 1:7)* Come **with saints** and **holy angels** *(Zech. 14:5; Rev. 19:11-15; Matt. 25:31)* Remove **sinners** *(Matt. 25:41,46)* **Set up God's rule forever** *(Matt. 25:34; Rev. 19:15)* **Bind Satan** for 1,000 years *(Rev. 20:1-3)* End **wrath** period *(Rev. 19:11-21)* Let living saints **enter Millennial Kingdom** *(Matt. 25:34,46)*

Thy word is true from the beginning: and every one of thy righteous judgments endureth forever.
- Psalm 119:160

Key Prophetic Covenant Promises to Israel

Thousands of years ago, God made a series of *covenants* (legal agreements) with Israel that specifically dealt with her land. **God's covenants are unconditional, irrevocable, and everlasting.**

The **Abrahamic Covenant** is the foundation for all the covenants between God and Israel. *It grants the title deed for the land of Israel* to Abraham's descendants. - *Genesis 12:1-7; 13:14-18; 17:7-8*

God's **Land Covenant** promised that Israel *will one day become the prime nation in the world.* This came close at the time of Solomon, but this will not be fully achieved until after the Tribulation. - *Deuteronomy 28:1,13; Isaiah 10:20-22; Zechariah 8:22-23*

The **Davidic Covenant** promised Israel *an eternal King who would descend from the line of David.* This was fulfilled with the birth of Christ. The remainder of the covenant promised that *Christ will rule the entire world from Jerusalem,* which has yet to be fulfilled. - *2 Samuel 7:10-16; Luke 1:31-33*

Israel has never received all the land God Himself deeded to her, nor has she become the prime nation in the world with Christ ruling the world from Jerusalem. With the Bible's one hundred percent inerrancy rate, we can know for certain God keeps His promises. We can also know from Joel 3:2 that judgment awaits those who scatter God's people and are part of dividing up her land.

**...And I will enter into judgment...on account of My people, My heritage Israel, whom they have scattered....
[T]hey have also divided up My land.
- Joel 3:2b (NKJV)**

JULY

When I Am Afraid

Psalm 56:3-4   Arlene Faith Kortright

When I am a-fraid I will trust in You, in

God whose word I praise, in

God I trust, I will not be a-fraid.

What can man do to me?

Psalm fif-ty six three and four

LORD, I love You with all of my being. Cause me to sing this praise and have it continually on my lips. I know Your Word is true because it can be tested with history, science, and prophecy and seen in Your creation and the lives You have changed. I trust You and no one can do anything to me outside of Your will. **Amen**

Prophecies of Christ in the Psalms

Christ's First and Second Comings are events referred to throughout the Old and New Testaments. These prophecies are clearly written and very specific. In Dr. Henry M. Morris' book *Sampling the Psalms,* he includes some of the many prophecies found in the book of Psalms.

Psalm 2 – The Son of God in both First and Second Comings

Psalm 9 – Christ, the Righteous Judge

Psalm 16 – The Resurrected Christ

Psalm 22 – The Crucified Christ

Psalm 23 – The Lord as the Shepherd of His sheep

Psalm 24 – The King of Glory is coming

Psalm 40 – Christ, born and rejected

Psalm 43 – Christ, the Final Conqueror

Psalm 68 – Christ sets the captives free

Psalm 69 – The Man of Sorrows is exalted

Psalm 95-99 – Christ reigns and rules

Psalm 102 – Victorious and eternal Savior

Psalm 110 – A Priest forever

Psalm 118 – The Chief Cornerstone

Psalm 119 – The Living Word of God

And he said unto them, "These are the words which I spake unto you, while I was yet with you, that all things must be fulfilled which were written in the law of Moses, and in the prophets, and in the psalms, concerning me."
- Luke 24:44

Paul's Prophetic Instructions for "Perilous Times"

In 2 Timothy 3, Paul gives a prophetic warning concerning the degeneration of society in the Last Days. He lists many very specific characteristics. Paul writes that those times would be perilous – more than just difficult. The original Greek word for perilous means "fierce or savage," which suggests violent, wild, and uncontrolled conduct.

Paul does not leave us without God's instructions for these times. It would serve us well to follow His advice, seeing that we are closer to Christ's return than ever. **The following verses in 2 Timothy tell us to:**

- Follow in the pattern of godly men and women. - *2 Timothy 3:10*
- Continue in sound biblical doctrine. - *2 Timothy 3:14*
- Understand that all Scripture is God-inspired and profitable for doctrine, reproof, correction, and instruction in righteousness in order to fully equip you to serve the Lord in every good work. - *2 Timothy 3:16-17*
- Patiently preach the word. - *2 Timothy 4:2*
- Be watchful, endure affliction, evangelize, and fulfill your ministry. - *2 Timothy 4:5*
- Fight the good fight, finish your race as a Christian, and keep focused on Christ's return because the Lord will reward you. - *2 Timothy 4:7-8*

This know also, that in the last days perilous times shall come. For men shall be lovers of their own selves, covetous, boasters, proud, blasphemers, disobedient to parents, unthankful, unholy…. - 2 Timothy 3:1-2

Israel's Return: A Frequent Prophecy

Over and over, throughout the Hebrew Scriptures, it is prophesied that **in the End Times the Jewish people will be regathered from the four corners of the world** and returned back to their homeland in Israel (Isaiah 11:10-12, Ezekiel 37:1-12, and Zechariah 10:6).

Jeremiah's prophecies about this regathering are particularly interesting. He says in two places (Jeremiah 16:14-15 and 23:7-8) that when the history of this current world comes to an end, *the Jewish people will look back on their history and conclude that their regathering in unbelief was a greater miracle than their deliverance from Egyptian captivity!* If we think about it for a moment, it means that those of us *living today* are currently witnessing one of the greatest miracles God has ever performed. Many Christians are completely unaware of the significance of what is happening among the Jewish people.

The Hebrew Scriptures also prophesy that when Jesus returns, there will be another worldwide gathering of Jews to their homeland – only it will be a regathering of those who gave their hearts to Jesus during the Tribulation (Deuteronomy 30:1-9). This remnant will then be established as the prime nation in the world (Isaiah 2:1-4) during the Millennial Kingdom.

And ye shall know that I am the LORD, when I have opened your graves, O my people, and brought you up out of your graves, and shall put my spirit in you, and ye shall live, and I shall place you in your own land: then shall ye know that I the LORD have spoken it, and performed it, saith the LORD.
- Ezekiel 37:13-14

Preparation for the Coming Deception (Part 1)

In Matthew 24, Jesus prophesied the signs that would lead up to His Second Coming. He mentions deception three times, in verses 4, 11, and 24, which highlights the importance of our not being deceived. Since the mind is where deception takes place, **may the following verses, listed in alphabetical order, prove useful in combating deception as we prepare ourselves for Christ's return.**

A	Be *ANXIOUS* for nothing,…pray and ask with thankfulness….	Philippians 4:6-7
B	Be *BLESSED* by reading, hearing, studying prophecy…. Cast your *BURDEN* on the Lord	Revelation 1:3 Psalm 55:22
C	Bring your thoughts *CAPTIVE* to the obedience of Christ. God is a God of all *COMFORT*…. God is not a God of *CONFUSION*… I have learned to be *CONTENT*….	2 Corinthians 10:5 2 Corinthians 1:3-4 1 Corinthians 14:33 Philippians 4:11
D	God is with you, don't be *DISMAYED*…. God will *DELIVER* you….	Isaiah 41:10 Psalm 91:14-15
E	Spur on, meet, and *ENCOURAGE*…. *ENDURING* trials wins us the crown of life….	Hebrews 10:24-25 James 1:12
F	God doesn't give us a spirit of *FEAR* but of power, and of love, and of a sound mind. *FORGET* what's behind and press *FORWARD*….	2 Timothy 1:7 Philippians 3:13-14

…Take heed that no man deceive you.
– Matthew 24:4

Preparation for the Coming Deception (Part 2)

G	God's *GRACE* is sufficient in weakness…. Grace is a *GIFT* of God and not earned….	2 Cor. 12:9-10 Ephesians 2:8-9
H	May the God of *HOPE* fill you with all joy and peace as you trust in Him…. Have the *HUMILITY* of Christ….	Romans 15:13 Philippians 2:3-8
I	God must *INCREASE*, but I must decrease. *I* have set the Lord always before me….	John 3:30 Psalm 16:8-9
J	In God's presence is the fullness of *JOY*….	Psalm 16:11
K	*KNOW* all things work together for good to those who love God…. You can *KNOW* that you have eternal life…through Jesus….	Romans 8:28 1 John 2:3-6 1 John 5:12-13
L	Cause me to hear Your *LOVINGKIND-NESS*…and know the way…. Gird up the *LOINS* of your mind….	Psalm 143:8 1 Peter 1:13
M	Let my words and *MEDITATION* be pleasing to You, Lord…. Oh, *MAGNIFY* the Lord with me, and let us exalt His name….	Psalm 19:14 Psalm 34:3
N	Let me meditate on You in the *NIGHT WATCHES*….	Psalm 63:6-8

And many false prophets shall rise, and deceive many.
– Matthew 24:11

Preparation for the Coming Deception (Part 3)

O	Guard what has been entrusted to you, avoiding worldly and empty chatter, and *OPPOSING ARGUMENTS* of what is falsely called knowledge....	1 Tim. 6:20-21
P	Continually offer the sacrifice of *PRAISE* to God....	Hebrews 13:15
Q	In *QUIETNESS* and confidence is your strength.	Isaiah 30:15
R	*REJOICE*, pray and give thanks....	1 Thess. 5:16-18
	Be *READY* for the Son of man is coming at an unexpected hour	Matthew 24:44
	REMEMBER the Word to your servant, it gives comfort and life....	Psalm 119:49-50
S	*SUBMIT* yourselves to God, resist the devil, he will flee....	James 4:7
	I will *SING* to the Lord as long as I live....	Psalm 104:33
T	*TEST* all things; hold fast what is good.	1 Thess. 5:21
	THINK on what is *TRUE*, honest, just, pure, lovely, virtuous, praiseworthy....	Philippians 4:8
U	Trust the Lord with all your heart and do not lean on your own *UNDERSTANDING*. In all your ways acknowledge Him....	Proverbs 3:5-6

**For there shall arise false Christs, and false prophets, and
shall show great signs and wonders; insomuch that,
if it were possible, they shall deceive the very elect.
- Matthew 24:24**

Preparation for the Coming Deception (Part 4)

V	The very hairs of your head are numbered…. you are of *VALUE*….	Matt. 10:29-31
	Let God hear your *VOICE* in the morning….	Psalm 5:3
W	If you lack *WISDOM*, ask God, He will give it liberally….	James 1:5
	For the *WORD* of the Lord is true from the beginning….	Psalm 119:160
	God *WORKS* in you both to want and to do for His good pleasure.	Phil. 2:13
X	*EXAMINE* yourselves, whether you are in the faith….	2 Corinthians 13:5
	To Him who is able to do *EXCEEDINGLY* abundantly above all we ask or think according to the power that is in us…to Him be the glory….	Eph. 3:20-21
Y	Take my *YOKE* upon you, and learn of Me; for I am meek and lowly in heart: and you will find rest for your souls.	Matthew 11:29
Z	Look for that blessed hope…. our great God and Savior Jesus Christ who gave Himself for us, to redeem…. and purify a special people *ZEALOUS* for good works….	Titus 2:13-14

**You will keep him in perfect peace, whose mind is
stayed on You, because he trusts in You.
- Isaiah 26:3 (NKJV)**

The Jeconiah Prophecy

King Jeconiah was the last descendant through David's son Solomon to rule as king of Israel before surrendering to Nebuchadnezzar in 597 B.C. **Jeremiah prophesied that none of the children of evil King Jeconiah would ever sit on the throne as king.** King Jeconiah whose shortened name was Coniah (Jeremiah 24:1; 27:20; Matthew 1:11-12) was also known as King Jehoiachin (2 Kings 24:8-16; 25:27-30).

Even though Jeconiah had seven sons, none succeeded him to the throne; nor did any of his descendants, just as Jeremiah prophesied. Jeconiah was dynastically "childless" and was the last of the Davidic kings. This is a problem because the future coming Messiah was prophesied to be a direct descendant of David. How could both prophecies be true? On the one hand, a descendant of David was to be the King of the Jews, and on the other hand, no son of this direct descendant was ever again to sit on the throne of Israel.

The "curse of Jeconiah" continued down to Joseph, the step-father of Jesus. Since Jesus was virgin-born (Matthew 1:20-21), Jesus did not come through Joseph's bloodline. Matthew 1:1-17, however, proves that Jesus inherited the throne legally. Interestingly, Luke 3:23-31 shows that Jesus' bloodline came through Mary, His actual parent, by way of David's son Nathan. **These two genealogical passages prove that the Jeconiah prophecy was fulfilled**; Jeconiah's descendants never sat on the throne of David again. They also proved the Abrahamic covenant promise and the Messianic promise to David – that Christ would come from their lineage – were true, as well. Only God could have orchestrated the fulfillment of these seemingly impossible and contradictory prophecies.

"...[F]or none of his descendants shall prosper, sitting on the throne of David, and ruling anymore in Judah."
- Jeremiah 22:30 (NKJV)

The "Almah" Prophecy

Seven hundred years before the birth of Jesus, the prophet Isaiah foretold that Immanuel (this Hebrew name means "God is with us") would be conceived by and born to a virgin. In Isaiah 7:14, the prophet used the Hebrew word *almah* (meaning virgin). The apostle Matthew wrote that Jesus' birth fulfilled this Old Testament prophecy (Matthew 1:22-23). **Matthew used the Greek word "parthenos" in translating the original Hebrew word *almah* of Isaiah 7:14.** For centuries, Bible skeptics have denied that *almah* meant virgin, but argued that it simply meant "a young woman."

The Septuagint (Greek version of the Old Testament), written 300 years before Jesus was born, also uses "parthenos" to translate almah. It is interesting that we get the word *"parthenogenesis" from parthenos, which means the development of a new individual from an unfertilized female sex cell.*

Archaeology provides additional understanding of the meaning of these words. One of the most competent Jewish scholars of this generation, Dr. Cyrus H. Gordon, has unearthed clay tablets at Ugarit in Syria which clearly use the word *almah* in the parallel/Semitic language to mean "virgin" and not "young woman." *Almah* was being used to specifically mean "virgin" long before Isaiah. The clay tablet which documents this was written even before the time of Moses (more than three thousand years ago).

**Therefore the Lord Himself shall give you a sign;
Behold, a virgin shall conceive, and bear a son,
and shall call his name Immanuel.
- Isaiah 7:14**

The Isaiah Chapter 5 Prophecy

Isaiah chapter 5 contains specific sins of which Israel was guilty. It also prophesied severe consequences. How sobering it is to read that **the LORD considered these sins as indicators of the time to call things to an end.** It is exactly what happened to the Jewish nation. We see these same sins prevalent today. It serves as a warning to us. Consider how the sins of Isaiah 5 fit our society today.

v. 8	1.	Lovers of possessions and a never-ending desire for more
v. 11-19	2.	Insatiable desire for pleasure, and a repeated lack of acknowledging and thankfulness to God
v. 20-21	3.	Denial of absolute, objective moral values; exaltation of self and one's own opinions
v. 22	4.	Frivolous life style
v. 23	5.	Collapse of justice within the nation
v. 24	6.	Total rejection and ridicule of God's Word

Scripture urges us to pay attention and realize our time is short – God's prophecies are certain! As God's people, we are called to be set apart (Psalm 4:3; Ephesians 2:10) to the Lord and His purposes. Christ tells us in Matthew 5:13-14 to be the salt and light of the world. May the urgency of the times spur us on to be both.

Therefore is the anger of the LORD kindled against his people, and he hath stretched forth his hand against them, and hath smitten them....
- Isaiah 5:25

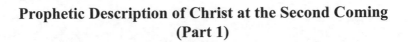
Prophetic Description of Christ at the Second Coming
(Part 1)

In the first chapter of Revelation, John gives us a prophetic look at Jesus when He returns to judge the world at His Second Coming. **In Revelation 1:13-16, John gives us ten very descriptive details about Jesus that are worth studying so they can be better understood.** They are also repeated in other places.

1. *¹³One like the Son of Man.* Christ often used this phrase to describe Himself and it is used of the Messiah in the four gospels, as well as in Daniel 7:13.

2. *¹³Clothed with a garment down to the feet.* Just as high priests wore long robes as they ministered in the temple, Jesus is our High Priest before God (Hebrew 2:17; 3:1).

3. *¹³Girded about the chest with a golden band.* In the ancient world this represented strength and authority. Christ has both (Matthew 28:18; Revelation 5:12).

4. *¹⁴His head and hair were white like wool, as white as snow.* White speaks of God's righteousness and purity (Daniel 7:9-13).

5. *¹⁴His eyes like a flame of fire.* God hates sin and is indignant over indifference and apostasy in the church.

6. *¹⁵His feet were like fine brass, as if refined in a furnace.* This phrase speaks of judgment. The brazen altar in the tabernacle is where sin was judged.

Behold, He is coming with clouds,
and every eye will see Him….
- Revelation 1:7 (NKJV)

Prophetic Description of Christ at the Second Coming
(Part 2)

This continues the list of ways Christ will be recognized when He returns (Revelation 1:15-20) :

7. *¹⁵His voice as the sound of many waters.* This statement, like in Isaiah 17:12, seems to speak of the deafening roar of turbulent waters. This also fits the way the Son of God will come on "judgment day." His voice will overpower every other!

8. *¹⁶He had in His right hand seven stars.* The Lord Himself tells us the seven stars are the angels of seven churches v. 20. The literal word for *angels* in Greek is "messengers."

9. *¹⁶Out of His mouth went a sharp two-edged sword.* Ephesians 6:17 tells us God's Word is the sword of the Spirit. Hebrews 4:12 says His Word is sharper than any two-edged sword. As Tim LaHaye writes in his *Prophecy Study Bible*, "Evidently, the spoken word of God will go forth as a sword against which there will be no defense in the day of judgment."

10. *¹⁶His countenance was like the sun shining in its strength.* This is a beautiful picture of the divine nature of our Lord Jesus Christ. It reminds us of what the disciples saw on the Mount of Transfiguration in Matthew 17:2.

Now after six days, Jesus took Peter, James, and John his brother, led them up on a high mountain by themselves; and He was transfigured before them. His face shone like the sun, and His clothes became as white as the light.
- Matthew 17:1-2 (NKJV)

The Jonah Prophecy

Jonah1:12-16 records Jonah's prediction to the sailors on the ship in which he tried to escape from obeying God. Jonah correctly prophesied that the sea would "calm" when the men picked him up and threw him into the sea. This prophetic encounter changed the lives of those sailors. It caused them to turn to and recognize the LORD, because God alone can inspire prophecy.

Jonah 1:17, however, was a prophecy destined to change the lives of millions. To this day, the event it predicted some eight hundred years before it happened has impacted our lives.

Jonah spent three days and three nights in the belly of the fish. Jesus stated that this event was a prophetic type of the three days and nights He would spend in the grave after His crucifixion. Jonah foreshadowed Jesus as the Sent One, suffering death, being buried and raised from the dead after three days, and then offering salvation to the Jews and Gentiles. Christ, Himself, verified the truth of this event with His own words – fulfilling this eight hundred-year-old prophecy.

"A wicked and adulterous generation seeks after a sign, and no sign shall be given to it except the sign of the prophet, Jonah." – Matthew 16:4 (NKJV)

Millennial Kingdom Prophecy (Isaiah 11:1-16)

The Bible predicts that Christ will return to the earth and reign for one thousand years. This is known as the "Millennial Kingdom." Isaiah 11:1-16 gives us a glimpse of what God's kingdom will be like. Isaiah wrote this book seven hundred years before Christ was born and gives us specific prophecies concerning Christ's First Coming, Second Coming, and Millennial Reign. In this passage it was written that Christ would come from the line of Jesse, which meant Christ would be both Jewish and a descendant of a man named Jesse, the future father of King David. Christ was to be born into this kingly bloodline (v. 1).

Isaiah also clearly described Christ's character (v. 2). He prophesied about the nature of Christ's rule as King during the Millennial Reign. **Christ will come to judge in absolute righteousness with perfect fairness and justice. Christ will destroy the wicked and restore the earth and nature to their original state.** The wolf will dwell with the lamb, the leopard with the goat, and the calf with the lion. Even babies will be able to play beside a cobra's hole (v. 3-9).

In the remaining verses of this section (v. 10-16), Isaiah describes God's final fulfillment of His promise to preserve a remnant of His people, the Jews, and regather them back to the land of Israel that He originally deeded to them through Abraham. Since every prophecy about Christ's First Coming came to pass, we can be sure the prophecies about the Second Coming and the Millennial Kingdom will come to pass as well.

...[T]he earth shall be full of the knowledge of the LORD....
- Isaiah 11:9

Prophecies in Lamentations

Although Lamentations is only a five-chapter book, God left His creative and prophetic fingerprint on its pages. Each chapter is a Hebraic poem. Four out of the five chapters are acrostic in style (meaning the verses begin with consecutive letters of the alphabet). Lamentations is a poetic record of the author's grief over the fall of Jerusalem and the destruction of Solomon's four hundred-year-old Temple in 586 B.C. Scripture records many prophetic warnings of this judgment which the Jewish people brought upon themselves by continuing in their wickedness and rejecting God's commands.

Within these poems, interesting prophecies can be found. For example, Lamentations 1:12 tells of *"the day of God's fierce anger."* **This refers to both the Babylonian judgment of Judah in 586 B.C. and a specific judgment day in the future.** Both Joel 2:1-11 and Zephaniah 1:14-18 spoke about this day. The Jewish people are predicted to experience the "wrath of God" during the seven-year Tribulation.

Another prophecy is found in the third chapter. It declares that the Lord will not allow the Jews to be a cast-off ancient people forever, like other ancient people groups. Against all odds, the Jewish people began moving back to their ancient homeland in the late 1800s and were once again recognized as the nation of Israel in 1948.

For the Lord will not cast off forever.
- Lamentations 3:31

The "8ᵗʰ Day Circumcision" Prophecy

Prothrombin is a chemical in our body which is absolutely critical for blood clotting. Without it, we would bleed to death from even the smallest cut. Vitamin K is vital for the production of prothrombin by the liver. Thus, both vitamin K and prothrombin are necessary for life. Newborn boys begin production of vitamin K on day five through day seven after birth. On the eighth day, a newborn male child reaches his lifetime maximum level of prothrombin. Therefore, **on the eighth day after birth, a male baby has the highest clotting rate** of any time in his life. If a male baby is going to be circumcised, the eighth day after birth would be the safest day for this to take place.

Isn't it interesting that over four thousand years ago God told Abraham to have newborn males circumcised on the eighth day! Before God told Abraham to undergo this procedure, there was no trial-and-error testing to find the best day on which to circumcise a baby. Only our Creator could have known this biological fact and made sure that this fact was included in the Bible.

And he that is eight days old shall be circumcised among you, every male child in your generations....
- Genesis 17:12

The Tabernacle Transfer (Part 1)

When Moses brought the Israelites out of Egypt, God designed a special place to meet with His people. God's desire was to dwell with them and bless their lives. He promised prosperity, protection, and happiness. God wanted the Israelites to be witnesses to the surrounding nations that He alone was the one true and faithful God.

In order to set the Israelites apart as His chosen people, God gave Moses detailed instructions on how to build His dwelling place, the Tabernacle (Exodus 25-28). It would serve as the central focus of their lives and be a visible reminder that God was holy, just, and righteous. God could and would not tolerate sin. A relationship with Him required perfect obedience. Since God knew mankind could not attain this in their sinful state, God showed the people how to atone for their sin through sacrifices. *Everything* about the Tabernacle pointed to the coming Savior. This includes the design, size, furniture, materials used, colors, utensils, priestly clothing, types of sacrifices, strategic placement of things and specific procedures to follow. This coming Savior would be the perfect and final sacrifice and atonement for their sin, enabling God to permanently dwell with not only the Israelites, but *all* those who accept Him as their Lord and Savior.

The original *Tabernacle* was portable since the Israelites were on a journey to the land God promised them. Once the Israelites entered their land they built God a more permanent structure in Jerusalem called the *Temple*.

And let them make me a sanctuary; that I may dwell among them. According to all that I show thee, after the pattern of the tabernacle, and the pattern of all the instruments thereof, even so shall ye make it.
- Exodus 25:8-9

The Tabernacle Transfer (Part 2)

Christ, as both God and man, came to Earth as the promised Messiah. He went to the Temple and presented Himself as King but was rejected and crucified. Christ fulfilled every requirement for any perfect sacrifice for sin that was to be offered at the first Tabernacle in the wilderness. More importantly, He put an end to the sacrificial system by paying for the sins of all those who put their trust in Him as their Lord and Savior.

Christ now makes His dwelling place in each of us as believers. *We* have become *His temple.*

As God resided in the center of the Israelite camp, so should He reside at the center of our lives. Great care was taken to build the desert Tabernacle under Moses (Exodus 36-39) and the Temple under Solomon (1 Kings 7). So, too, should we take good care of our bodies, which are His temple, His dwelling place. **Since collectively all Christians constitute the temple (1 Cor. 3:16) we are to take care of unity and holiness in our relationships.**

The high priest served as mediator for the Israelites; we have Christ Himself. Doesn't this warrant giving our utmost for Jesus Christ?

Know ye not that ye are the temple of God, and that the Spirit of God dwelleth in you? - 1 Corinthians 3:16

Pattern of Escaping God's Judgment

Noah, Lot, Rahab and some Jewish people were given a way of escape from the judgment mankind brought upon themselves.

- **Noah** was given clear directions to build and get on the Ark before God would destroy the earth with the worldwide Flood. *Genesis 6:14-22*

- **Lot** was told to leave everything behind and was pulled out of the corrupt city of Sodom before God destroyed it with fire. *Genesis 19:12-29*

- **Rahab** and her family followed specific instructions to ensure that they would be spared from the complete destruction of Jericho when the city's walls collapsed and all the people inside the walls were killed. *Joshua 2;6:22-25*

- **Jews** who remembered and listened to Jesus' warning that the Temple and Jerusalem would be destroyed within one generation were able to escape before the destruction took place in 70 A.D. *Matthew 24:1-2*

In each case, those who obeyed God and put their trust in Him escaped His judgment. God has warned us throughout His Word of His coming judgment, as well. We all have a choice to make. We can *ignore* God or trust and *obey* Him.

For God hath not appointed us to wrath, but to obtain salvation by our Lord Jesus Christ, who died for us, that, whether we wake or sleep, we should live together with Him.
- 1 Thessalonians 5:9-10

Prophecy in Isaiah 7:16

The Old and New Testaments have *hundreds of detailed prophecies* that have been fulfilled. Common sense alone dictates that the authenticity of the Bible is beyond doubt. Many prophecies continue to be validated when we take a closer look at the original wording and study history.

One example can be found in Isaiah 7:16, which Isaiah wrote *seven hundred years before its fulfillment*:

> **For before the Child shall know to refuse the evil and choose the good, the land that you dread will be forsaken by both her kings. - Isaiah 7:16 (NKJV)**

This prophecy predicts that Syria and Ephraim, called Syria and Samaria in Jesus' lifetime, would be forsaken by their kings. The prophecy also states this would happen *before* Jesus "shall know to refuse the evil and choose the good" – which was known to be a child's "Bar Mitzvah." God is always true to every last detail of His Word. Not only was this prophecy fulfilled within four years of Christ's Bar Mitzvah, but also Syria and Samaria, although populated, had ceased to exist as nations with kings or armies.

**For prophecy never came by the will of man, but holy men of God spoke as they were moved by the Holy Spirit.
- 2 Peter 1:21 (NKJV)**

Uniqueness of Every Star

There are more than 10^{22} stars in the universe, but each one is unique. No two stars have exactly the same properties. This may sound like guesswork since we have analyzed very few stars in detail; but the conclusion is a certainty. **A star has so many variables that the probability of two identical stars is essentially zero.** These variables include the total number of atoms, the exact composition of elements, its size, and its temperature. Some stars show obvious color and brightness differences. Others require spectroscopic study to detect each star's particular identity or fingerprint.

The Bible states in 1 Corinthians 15:41 that "star differs from star in glory." How could ancient man have known this? The Creator of the stars chose to tell man to include this in the Bible. In Psalm 147:4 the Bible also says that God "determines the number of stars and calls each by name." Truly, God's abilities have no limit.

There is one <u>glory</u> of the sun, and another glory of the moon, and another glory of the stars: for one star <u>differeth</u> from another in glory. - 1 Corinthians 15:41

The "Tyre" Prophecy (Part 1)

Specific predictions were made against the ancient city of Tyre. The prophecy in Ezekiel stated that this city would be destroyed by Nebuchadnezzar, and many nations would come against it. It was predicted that Tyre would be made bare as the top of a flat rock and fishermen would spread their nets over the site. The walls and the towers would be destroyed, the debris would be scraped clean, and Tyre would be left barren. **This prediction was made at the height of Tyre's power and importance.** Imagine a similar statement being made about New York City!

A few years after the prophecy was given, Nebuchadnezzar began a thirteen-year siege on the mainland city of Tyre. When he finally entered the city, he found that most of the people had fled by boat to an island half of a mile off the coast. They had fortified a city on this island with powerful walls that reached to the very edge of the sea. The original city had fallen, but the people remained. Only part of this prophecy was fulfilled.

Some claim that Ezekiel wrote this prophecy after the events happened, but that is impossible, because in Ezekiel's lifetime the original city of Tyre still had ruins standing and tons of rock, rubble and timber from the destruction. In addition, God had said their city would be *"scraped clean like the top of a bare rock"* and *"fishermen would spread their nets over the site."* - Ezekiel 26:4-5

I am against you, O Tyre, and will cause many nations to come up against you …[T]hey shall destroy the walls…towers… [H]e will heap up a siege mound… will direct battering rams against your walls.…[T]hey will lay your stones, your timber, and your soil in the midst of the water.… [Y]ou shall be a place for spreading nets, and you shall never be rebuilt, for I the LORD have spoken. - Ezekiel 26:3-4, 8-9, 12, 14 (NKJV)

The "Tyre" Prophecy (Part 2)

About two hundred and fifty years after Ezekiel wrote the prophecy quoted in Part 1, Alexander the Great laid siege to the island of Tyre. These people must have laughed at his command for them to surrender! But Alexander and his chief engineer, Diades, came up with an incredible plan. They built a two hundred-foot-wide causeway across the Mediterranean Sea to the island of Tyre using the rubble from the original city. Alexander issued the order, "Tear down the walls of Tyre, take the timbers and the stones, the rubble and the logs, and cast them into the sea." As the army obeyed, they fulfilled the Word of God.

History records that Tyre was leveled and scraped clean of everything to make this causeway. Alexander was able to move his army across the land bridge and utterly destroy the island city. The prophecy doesn't end here. Many subsequent attempts were made to rebuild Tyre, but sieges always destroyed the city. **Today, both the original city and the island city are bare rocks where fishermen can be seen drying their nets.** The accuracy of biblical prophecy is stunning and undeniable evidence for the Bible's authenticity.

**The entirety of Your word is truth, and every one of Your righteous judgments endures forever.
- Psalm 119:160 (NKJV)**

Foreknowledge of Cleanliness

Moses was a prince of Egypt brought up in Pharaoh's palace. Acts 7:22 states, "Moses was learned in all the wisdom of the Egyptians...." Yet, Egyptian medical practices included such remedies as:

- Smearing the blood of worms mixed with donkey dung into open wounds.
- Applying the fat from horses, crocodiles, and snakes mixed with donkey teeth and honey to the scalp in order to grow hair.
- Pouring drinking water over stone idols in order to cure snake bites.

Even nineteenth-century doctors were woefully ignorant in certain areas of hygiene. They routinely caused the death of patients by going from dissecting dead bodies to examining live patients without washing their hands. They also bled people to the point of death to remove "bad blood." George Washington was killed in this manner. However, three thousand years before mankind discovered the existence of bacteria and viruses, the Holy Spirit inspired Moses to institute modern methods of cleanliness. Here are just a few insights God gave him:

- Leviticus 11:35 warns against touching or bringing any **cooking utensil in contact with dead animals**.
- Leviticus chapter 13 details the first **procedures for medical quarantine** in order to prevent the spread of contagious diseases.
- Leviticus 15:13 calls for the prevention of disease by the **washing of the body and clothes under "running water."**
- In Deuteronomy 23:12-13, Moses even writes of the need for **proper sewage disposal**.

How could a man trained in Egyptian medical nonsense have written about such *modern procedures* unless he was inspired by God?

Now unto the King eternal, immortal, invisible, the only wise God, be honor and glory for ever and ever. Amen.
- 1 Timothy 1:17

Similarities Between the TWO Visits of Christ

We know much about both the predictions and events surrounding Christ's First Coming because it already happened, over two thousand years ago. But there are also many clear statements in Scripture about His guaranteed return. Although the purpose of each of Christ's appearances is vastly different, there are some similarities which are meant to inform, warn, and prepare us.

Consider these similarities between the first and second physical visits of Jesus to Earth. Note that both...

- were **predicted** thousands of years beforehand.

- happen during a time of **political unrest.**

- happen during a time of **spiritual darkness.**

- happen at a time when the **Scripture is ignored.**

- **reveal Christ** so mankind can see Him.

- give **many specific prophetic signs** to assure us that Christ is the one and only true God.

- **bless** those who are prepared for His coming.

**For whatsoever things were written aforetime
were written for our learning, that we through patience
and comfort of the scriptures might have hope.
- Romans 15:4**

Prophetic Pattern of True Worship (Part 1)

A careful study of the sacrificial system God instituted for the Israelites in Leviticus is a prophetic pattern for true worship. Close analysis and adherence to this pattern safeguards us from the dangers of false worship – which our holy Lord God detests. Consider the following model He set forth in Leviticus chapters 1 through 10. In the bullet points below: OT refers to Old Testament practices and NT refers to New Testament worship understanding.

- **There is divine order in worship; there is no confusion.** (OT – Moses wrote all God commanded in designing the Tabernacle, priestly garments, sacrificial offerings, etc. NT – Order in worship as commanded in 1 Corinthians 14:33.)
- **Repentance** (admission and turning from sin) **is first and foremost in importance.** (OT – Sin offering came before self-sacrifice and thanksgiving. NT – The order is the same.)
- **Sin requires a payment of death before a holy God.** Blood must be shed for our sins so we can come before God with a pure heart. (OT – animal sacrifice. NT – Jesus' shed blood, sacrificed once and for all.)
- **Sinful man requires a mediator.** (OT – priesthood. NT – Jesus Christ.)
- **God desires our complete surrender.** (OT – total animal sacrifice was burned. NT – We surrender all to God.)
- **Total exposure of our sin confessed and laid out before God.** (OT – offering laid out on an altar before God. NT – we are reminded that God sees the heart, nothing is hidden.)
- **Acknowledgement of who God is and thanksgiving to Him enables us to dwell at peace with Him.** (OT – grain and peace offering. NT – confession and repentance of sin brings us peace.)

For God is not the author of confusion, but of peace, as in all churches of the saints.
- 1 Corinthians 14:33

A Prophetic Pattern of True Worship (Part 2)

The interesting parallels between the *Old Testament* worship commands and our *New Testament* understanding continues:

- **God requires our first and best offering.** (OT – Unblemished and domesticated animals (which had special value) were offered. NT – pure worship from the heart.)
- **God demands awesome respect.** (OT – Priest wore special garments, to set them apart to do specific priestly duties. NT – Believers are to be a special "set apart" people in their attitudes, words, and actions. – 1 Peter 2:9)
- **God only has only one way to come to Him.** (OT – in total obedience to His commands. NT – through Jesus Christ alone. John 14:6)
- **God is always available for confession and repentance of sin.** (OT – the altar's fire never went out. NT – the Holy Spirit is always with us.)
- **Through our obedience, God grants direct access into His presence.** (OT – the high priest followed precise directions to enter the holy of holies. NT – Christ followers are a holy priesthood and have access to God. 1 Peter 2:5)
- **God desires to dwell in a pure and holy temple.** (OT – God dwelt in the Tabernacle and Temple. NT – the believer's body is God's temple. 1 Corinthians 3:16-17; 6:19)
- **God reveals Himself to and communicates with His children.** (OT – He came in smoke, fire, miracles. NT – Bible and answered prayer.)
- **Anything less than serious holy worship angers God.** (OT – Nadab and Abihu, Leviticus 10. NT – Ananias and Sapphira, Acts 5:1)
- **Religious leaders are held accountable.** (OT – Priests had to atone for their own sins first. NT – teachers will be more accountable. (James 3:1)
- **Understanding God's holiness and power lead to our rejoicing and falling on our faces before Him.** (OT – Leviticus 9:24, NT – Revelation 4:10-11)

**But ye are a chosen generation, a royal priesthood,
a holy nation, a peculiar people; that ye should shew forth
the praises of him who hath called you out of darkness
into his marvellous light;
– 1 Peter 2:9**

The Jewish Wedding (Part 1)

Dr. Billy Crone sets forth interesting parallels between the Jewish wedding and the relationship Christ has with His true followers. In his book, *The Rapture, Don't be Deceived*, Dr. Crone describes the seven basic phases of the Jewish wedding for the reader to consider.

1. "Shiddukhin" (the match) – Marriages were arranged by the fathers.

> Scripture tells us that God chose us and we will see Him face to face. This parallels how the groom's father chooses the bride whom the groom often does not meet until the wedding day.
> **You did not choose Me, but I chose you....**
> *- John 15:16 (NKJV)*
> **All that the Father gives Me will come to Me....**
> *- John 6:37 (NKJV)*

2. "Mohar" (the bride price) – Right after the "match" was made, a mohar or "price" for the value of the bride was agreed on by both parties.

> The Bible tells us that Jesus agreed to pay an extremely high price for us – He died for us. Just like in the case of a Jewish bride, the bride has no part in determining her value.
> **...You were not redeemed with corruptible things, like silver or gold...but with the precious blood of Christ.**
> *- 1 Peter 1:18-19 (NKJV)*

3. "Mattan" (the love gift) – The groom can voluntarily offer gifts to the bride as an expression of his love before the wedding.

> Just as the groom brought gifts, Christ showers us with His gifts of love *(John 3:16)*, peace *(John 14:27)*, joy *(John 15:11)*, forgiveness *(1 John 1:9)*, grace and protection *(Hebrews 13:5-6)*, etc. before we see Him.

The Jewish Wedding (Part 2)

4. "Shiluhim" (the dowry) – The father of the bride gives the bride gifts to help equip her for her new life with the groom.

> God gives us gifts to equip us for our life in Christ.
>
> **And I will pray the Father, and He will give you another Helper, that He may abide with you forever–the Spirit of truth... - *John 14:16-17a (NKJV)***
>
> **Having then gifts differing according to the grace that is given us…. - *Romans 12:6 (NKJV)***

5. "Ketubah" (the marriage contract) – The marriage is legally finalized by a written marriage contract or covenant. It records the bride price, the groom's promises and the rights of the bride.

> Christ finalized His new covenant with the Lord's Supper *(1 Corinthians 11:24-25)*. Just like the Jewish wedding contract, Scripture records the price Christ paid for His bride, His promises to us, and the new-found freedoms or rights we, the bride, have in Jesus.

6. "Kiddushin" (the betrothal) – After the contract is signed, the couple is considered legally married. The marriage, however, is not yet consummated nor does the couple live together. The bride has to demonstrate her purity. She undergoes a ritual cleansing bath called the "Mikvah."

> Christ cleanses us when we repent and ask Him for forgiveness. Without this, we cannot be His bride.

If we confess our sins, He is faithful and just to forgive us our sins, and to cleanse us from all unrighteousness.
- *1 John 1:9 (NKJV)*

The Jewish Wedding (Part 3)

The <u>bride</u> also has to demonstrate she has been faithful before the marriage is allowed to proceed. The veil she wears when she steps out of her house shows she is "out of circulation" and set apart for marriage to a certain person. It lets other men know she is not available and she will resist any other offers as she waits for her true love, who bought and paid for her. The bride is called a "mkudeshet," which means *"one who is betrothed"* or joined to another. The bride is dedicated to her husband.

> Christ expects us (as His bride) to set ourselves apart from the world as we await His return. If we love the Lord, we will resist the devil (James 4:7) and set ourselves apart from sin by continually living in obedience to His Word.
> **...For I have betrothed you to one husband, that I may present you as a chaste virgin to Christ. - *2 Corinthians 11:2 (NKJV)***

The <u>groom</u> makes preparations for his bride as well. He has to go back to his father's house and start building an addition to the house, called the "bridal chamber." It is here the couple will consummate the marriage and live together as a family.

> Jesus promised His followers He was going to prepare a place for them, so they could be with Him forever.

In My Father's house are many mansions; if it were not so, I would have told you. I go to prepare a place for you. And if I go and prepare a place for you, I will come again and receive you to Myself; that where I am, there you may be also.
- John 14:2-3 (NKJV)

The Jewish Wedding (Part 4)

7. "Nissun" (the taking) – Once the new dwelling place is ready, the groom's father inspects it and tells his son to go get his bride. The Jewish bride has no idea when her groom is coming. It could be at any time, so she always had to be ready for his unannounced arrival. It was often at night. Right before the groom gets to the bride's house, the groom and his attendants make their way by torchlight through the dark streets of the town to the house of the bride. The bride has to have a "lamp" and "oil" to be ready to go (like the parable Christ told in Matthew 25:1-13). The groom brings a group with him to the bride's house who announces the groom's arrival with a shout, *"Behold the bridegroom cometh."* The shofar (traditional Hebrew trumpet made from a ram's horn), is blown and the groom literally whisks his bride away.

Christ describes His return in *1 Thessalonians 4:16-18*:

1. Christ will return when He finishes preparing our dwelling places (John 14:1-3) and God the Father tells Him to go get His bride.

2. A loud shout will be given and the trumpet blown.

3. Christ's bride (the Church) will be raptured (snatched away or caught up) and meet Christ in the air.

Once the couple returns to the father of the groom's house, they consummate their marriage and celebrate their wedding feast for the next seven days (during which the bride stays closeted in her bridal chamber).

Scripture tells us Christ's bride likewise will be whisked away and closeted in her "bridal chamber" with Him in heaven, implying she will be in heaven for seven years during the Tribulation.

AUGUST

Never Will I Leave You

Hebrews 13:5-6

Arlene Faith Kortright

Never will I leave you, I never will forsake you,

We can say with confidence The Lord is my helper, I

1. will not be afraid

2. will not be afraid

He-brews thir-teen five and six.

LORD, thank You for this incredible promise. Give me a thankful heart. Help me not to focus on or feel sorry for myself, feel lonely or be afraid, especially when I know You promised to be with me. **Amen**

The "Chalepos" Prophecy (Part 1)

Chalepos is an interesting Greek word which means *perilous, dangerous, fierce, or savage.* Paul used this word to describe what it would be like in the "last days."

> **This know also, that in the last days <u>perilous</u> times shall come.** - *2 Timothy 3:1*

The word "chalepos" can be found in one other place in Scripture. Matthew used it to describe the two demon-possessed men Christ met in the country of the Gergesenes.

> **And when he was come to the other side into the country of the Gergesenes, there met him two possessed with devils, coming out of the tombs, exceeding fierce so that no man might pass by that way.** - *Matthew 8:28*

Matthew's reference to the demoniacs as exceedingly fierce and Paul's singular choice of the same word tells us Paul was purposeful in his description of the "last days" and very specific that it *shall* come. The question is, how close is the world today to fitting this description?

One only has to consider the increase of wars, abortions, violent crimes, mass shootings, drug use, interest in the occult, suicide bombings, road rage, child abuse, suicides, religious persecution, and technological, biological, chemical and nuclear weapons to answer this question.

The "Chalepos" Prophecy (Part 2)

Just as the behavior of the demoniacs can be seen as "crazed," so does the world around us become crazier as we near the End Times. **Here are a few of the absurdities which result from rejecting the Bible as a source of absolute truth:**

- Teaching that humans came from aliens while ignoring where these supposed aliens came from
- Spending more time talking to machines than humans
- Knowing people drink and drive causing thousands of accidents yearly, yet promoting recreational marijuana and believing this will not make things worse
- Relying on the internet or news media known to contain errors and bias, but denying truth in the Bible, which is verifiable by historical, archeological, scientific, and prophetical evidence
- Making treaties with countries whose worldview denies the possibility that truth and honesty exist
- Throwing our borders open to immigrants, yet not expecting their help, support, and loyalty to their new country
- Spending millions on luxuries for pets while ignoring human poverty
- Spending money we don't have on things we don't truly need
- Expecting to raise "good kids" with poor parenting
- Confiscating guns while promoting violent movies, video/internet games, songs, and television programming
- Severely penalizing people for destroying the eggs of endangered animals but approving of killing babies in the womb
- Demanding that the government provide for all our needs, while ignoring where the money will come from
- Denying the biological gender written on our DNA and replacing it with desires and emotions
- Spending billions to cure AIDS while rejecting the most cost-effective cure – abstaining from multiple sex partners

For whatever things were written before were written for our learning, that we through the patience and comfort of the Scriptures might have hope.
- Romans 15:4 (NKJV)

Why Crucifixion Instead of Stoning?

King David wrote Psalm 22 one thousand years before Jesus was born. It describes in detail what would happen at the time of the Messiah's death. Most miraculously, it prophesies in verse 16 that the Messiah would die by having His hands and feet pierced. We must keep in mind this prophecy was written one thousand years *before Jesus was killed* and seven hundred years *before the Romans perfected crucifixion* as a form of execution. **At the time David wrote this psalm, there was only one way the Jews carried out executions, and that was by stoning.**

One thousand years later, this was still true. In the time of Jesus, however, the land of Israel was under Roman rule and the Jewish leaders did not have the power to execute anyone. That power resided with their Roman rulers. As a result, the Jewish leaders were forced to go to the Roman authorities to request the execution of Jesus, and the Roman method was crucifixion instead of stoning – thus fulfilling prophecy. By fulfilling this prophecy, the Romans confirmed Jesus was the Messiah and the Bible is the Word of God.

...[T]he congregation of the wicked has enclosed Me.
They pierced My hands and My feet;
– Psalm 22:16 (NKJV)

Enoch's Prophecy (Part 1)

Enoch was a godly man who made it into the list of faith-filled men included in Hebrews 11. Scripture gives us Enoch's lineage in two separate places (1 Chronicles 1:3; Luke 3:37-38). We are told Enoch was the seventh generation from Adam (who was still alive when Enoch was born). Scripture tells us in Genesis 5:18-24 that Enoch "walked" with God. The word translated "walked" (halak) means to walk along with, follow, and talk to or communicate with. Hebrews 11:5 adds that Enoch "pleased" God.

When Enoch was sixty-five years old, he had a son whom he named Methuselah. God evidently gave Enoch a prophecy that would take place at Methuselah's death. **The prophecy was contained in Methuselah's very name - which means "his death shall bring."** When Methuselah died, the worldwide Flood took place. Interestingly, Methuselah lived longer than any man on earth. How like God to extend His mercy as long as possible before reluctantly bringing judgment. God is repeatedly referred to as "longsuffering." Genesis 6 records, however, that judgment could wait no longer, and the world-covering Flood began at Methuselah's death.

**Surely the LORD God does nothing, unless He reveals His secret to His servants the prophets.
- Amos 3:7 (NKJV)**

Enoch's Prophecy (Part 2)

In Jude 14-15, Jesus' half brother recorded a second prophecy of Enoch. He mentioned that Enoch was the seventh generation from Adam. Jude not only lets the reader know *which* of the five Enochs in the Bible gave this prophecy, but also provided us with a way to determine the approximate date of the prophecy. Using Old Testament birth and death records, we can determine this prophecy was given around 3382 B.C. In verse 4, Jude tells us that Enoch gave this prophecy to the ungodly people of his day, as well as ours. They were guilty of:

1. Turning the grace (*benefits, graciousness*) of God into lewdness (*obscenity, vulgarity*)
2. Denying (*contradicting, rejecting*) the only LORD God and LORD Jesus Christ

Enoch prophesied that the Lord would come with ten thousand of His saints to execute judgment on everyone and would convict all who are ungodly in what they did and said against Him. Since every past prophecy has been fulfilled, we can be certain this prophecy will be, as well.

Now Enoch, the seventh from Adam, prophesied about these men also, saying, "Behold, the Lord comes with ten thousands of His saints, to execute judgment on all, to convict all who are ungodly among them of all their ungodly deeds which they have committed in an ungodly way, and of all the harsh things which ungodly sinners have spoken against Him."
- Jude 14-15 (NKJV)

The "Peace" Prophecy Explained (Part 1)

The prophet Isaiah gave us a remarkable prophecy of peace:

You will keep him in perfect peace, whose mind is stayed on You, because he trusts in You. - Isaiah 26:3 (NKJV)

"Shalom" is the Hebrew word for perfect peace. It comes from the root word "salam" which means to be safe (in mind, body), to make good again, to restore. It is a completeness, a friendship with God, especially, in a covenant relationship. In other words, we can totally trust God.

Isaiah continues to explain that in order to receive this predicted promise of peace or being safe with God, our mind is stayed on Him. The Hebrew word for stay, "samak," is defined as leaning on or resting ourselves on God. Isaiah tells us that those who lean on God do so because they trust in Him. They put their complete confidence in Him. They are sure of and secure in the fact that God is all He says He is.

Christ repeats this prophetic promise in the New Testament and adds to it. In John 14:27 and 16:33, He assures His followers that He *will* give them His peace (quiet rest and oneness with Him), reason to be cheerful, and they do not have to be afraid.

Peace I leave with you, my peace I give unto you: not as the world giveth, give I unto you. Let not your heart be troubled, neither let it be afraid.
– John 14:27

These things I have spoken unto you, that in me ye might have peace. In the world ye shall have tribulation: but be of good cheer; I have overcome the world.
– John 16:33

The "Peace" Prophecy Explained (Part 2)

Peace, or quiet rest and oneness with God, can only come through Jesus Christ. **God said He reveals Himself to everyone through His creation.** No one will have an excuse for not believing who He is (Romans 1:19-20).

> **Jesus said to him, I am the way, the truth, and the life. No one comes to the Father except through Me.** *- John 14:6 (NKJV)*

Our trust in the fact that Jesus is God and that He came to Earth as a man to die in our place for our sins and rose from the grave to conquer death *is the only way we can be saved*. It is the only way we can have peace and be at one with God.

To have peace with God is the most important decision we will ever make. It alone determines our destiny.

- It is the result of faith in God and, with His help, obeying Him in doing what is right. *- Romans 5:1; Isaiah 32:17*
- It removes our fear. *- John 14:27*
- It sees us through trials. *- John 16:33*
- It guards our hearts and minds. *- Philippians 4:6-7*
- It gives us security. *- Psalm 4:8; 119:165; John 16:33*

As for God, His way is perfect; the Word of the LORD is proven; He is a shield to all who trust in Him.
- Psalm 18:30 (NKJV)

Lazarus' Resurrection Foreshadows Christ's (Part 1)

John 11 is an interesting chapter that records the miraculous account of Lazarus' resurrection from the dead. Christ raised him after four days in the tomb, something the Jewish people *knew* could *only* be done by the "Messiah." The Jews thought a person's spirit (nephesh) stayed around the body until the third day when the body began to decay.

Christ had already resurrected the only son of the widow of Nain (Luke 7:11-17) and Jairus' daughter (Luke 8:40-56) shortly after they died – before decay had set in. Because of this, these resurrections could be explained away by the leaders and unbelievers. Lazarus' resurrection, however, was different. When a messenger was sent to Jesus by Mary and Martha, urgently informing Him that their brother, Lazarus, was *very* sick, Jesus' response was unexpected.

We are told Jesus stayed in town two more days before going to help them. In John 11:14-15, Jesus tells the disciples that Lazarus is dead and **He is glad for their sakes that He was not there when it happened so they would believe.** When Jesus does finally arrive in Bethany, He goes to Lazarus' tomb and asks for the stone to be rolled away. Martha responds with a logical statement found in John 11:39.

**...Lord, by this time he stinketh,
for he hath been dead four days.
- John 11:39.**

Lazarus' Resurrection Foreshadows Christ's (Part 2)

Once the stone at Lazarus' tomb was rolled away, Christ prayed and said the specific purpose of raising Lazarus from the dead after four days was **"that they may believe that You sent me" - John 11:42 (NKJV).** The next verse tells us Jesus called, "Lazarus, come forth," and he did, grave wrapping and all. John 11:45 states that because of seeing the things Jesus did, many Jews believed in Him.

Lazarus was undeniable proof that Jesus was the "promised Messiah," and disbelief was a deliberate and willful rejection of that fact. From that point on, the religious leaders began to plot Christ's death (John 11:53) and the death of Lazarus who was the living evidence of Christ's deity (John 12:10).

The resurrection of Lazarus was a foreshadowing of the resurrection of Jesus. Luke 24:46 records that Christ arose on the third day just as He had predicted in Luke 18:31-33. He would be beaten, would be put to death, and on the third day would rise again. Christ's resurrection proved He was the Messiah and the fulfillment of Old Testament prophecy (Psalm 22; Isaiah 25:8-9; 53).

When Christ returns, mankind will seek to kill Him again at the battle of Armageddon, just as they sought to kill Lazarus after he was resurrected. We know, however, Christ *will* end the battle with the spoken Word and *will be victorious*.

...[A]nd all things that are written by the prophets concerning the Son of man shall be accomplished.
- Luke 18:31

The Isaiah 9:10 Parallel

Isaiah 9:10 shows how Israel responded to a national calamity when the Assyrians invaded in 732 B.C. The Jewish people did not see the invasion as a warning judgment for turning away from God. Instead, they responded in arrogance by vowing to build bigger and better defenses. Judgment came, and the nation fell.

In his book, *The Harbinger*, Jonathan Cahn notes that the 9/11 attack on America brought a response which also could have been described by Isaiah 9:10 – one of defiance, not repentance. For several months "God Bless America" signs appeared everywhere. Then, political leaders even quoted Isaiah 9:10, bragging America would rebuild bigger and better. **Like Israel, America is not heeding the warning and turning back to God.** Instead, America is bent on sexual perversion: violence throughout television, movies, and gaming; and increasing desensitization toward widespread pornography. Abortion, the mockery of God and marriage, a lack of respect for authority, a greed for power and money, and an obsession with self and entertainment are all on the increase.

Romans 15:4 tells us Scripture was written for our instruction so that through it we can have hope. Personal and national repentance (turning back to God) is our only hope.

The bricks are fallen down, but we will build with hewn stones: the sycamores are cut down, but we will change them into cedars.
- Isaiah 9:10

Jesus as Prophet

In Acts 3:22-26, Luke wrote that Jesus was the prophet Moses foretold would rise up from the Jewish nation (Deuteronomy 18:15). As a prophet, Jesus referred to, quoted, or drew parallel truths from at least 125 passages in twenty-four of the thirty-nine Old Testament books. **He spoke the words God gave Him (John 3:34) and obeyed His Father in all He did (John 17:4).** He authenticated Scripture throughout His teaching. Jesus prophesied His own death, burial, and resurrection. He also prophesied about this present age, His Second Coming, and His ultimate reign. But Jesus is far more than a prophet.

Jesus is the Word of God in the flesh (John 1:14). He is the way, the truth, and the life, and no one comes to the Father except through Him (John 14:6). Jesus would declare truth and enable all who heeded His Word to turn from their sins. He was fully God and fully man (Colossians 2:8-9). He came to Earth to fulfill God's law (Matthew 5:17) and did so perfectly. Jesus Christ alone was able to take away the sins of the world with His willing sacrifice of Himself on the cross (Hebrews 9:14-15).

Revelation 19:10 is a summary statement of God's final endorsements of Jesus' true nature. *Testimony* (martyria) means record, witness, or report. *Spirit* (pneuma) is the word for breath, the rational soul or mind, and *prophecy* (propheteia) means divinely inspired conversation that declares the purposes of God. In other words, the record or witness of Jesus *is* the breath of God, declaring God's purposes.

**...[F]or the testimony of Jesus is the spirit of prophecy.
- Revelation 19:10**

The Diaspora – Scattering of the Jews

But it shall come to pass, if you do not obey the voice of the LORD your God, to observe carefully all His commandments and His statutes which I command you today, that all these curses will come upon you and overtake you. *- Deuteronomy 28:15 (NKJV)*

Moses gave the prophecy found in Deuteronomy 28:15-68 to Israel about 1,500 years *before* its fulfillment. He warned that if Israel departed from God's laws and covenants, she would experience the following consequences: loss of livestock, decreased rain, famine, horrible sickness, confusion and violence would abound. The land would be ravaged, enemies would overtake them, their cities be torn down, and they would even resort to eating their own children. The people would eventually be driven from their land and scattered all over the world. In Matthew 24:2 and Luke 19:43-44, Jesus prophesied that Jerusalem and the Temple would also be destroyed. Forty years later, in 70 A.D., the predictions of Moses and Jesus came to fulfillment.

First century historian Josephus left us his detailed writings which prove these prophecies true. This was the beginning of the age of Jewish dispersion into all the nations, known as the Diaspora. The prophecy does not end here, however. The Old Testament predicted that the Jews would return to their land. Even in the New Testament, Jesus predicted Jerusalem would NOT be trodden down by the Gentiles (non-Jews) *forever*; the Jewish people would return (Luke 21:24).

...[A]nd Jerusalem shall be trodden down of the Gentiles, until the times of the Gentiles be fulfilled.
– Luke 21:24

The Gifts of the Holy Spirit (Part 1)

In 1 Corinthians chapters 12-14, Paul addresses the spiritual gifts God promises to those who accept and obey Christ as their Lord and Savior. A careful reading of these chapters teaches us that God selects specific gifts for each of His children. The Holy Spirit then empowers us to use these gifts to build up and encourage one another. **When God's people work together, all using the gifts they are given, the "Church" or "body of Christ" becomes most effective.**

In 1 Corinthians 12, we learn about some of the specific gifts God assigns. It is clear that all gifts are important and necessary. Ranking their importance, or using God's spiritual gifts for selfish reasons, is contrary to the will of God.

Love is described in 1 Corinthians 13 as being the most necessary element in the use of our spiritual gifts. Since Scripture tells us "God is love" (1 John 4:8), we can begin to recognize who God is by looking at Paul's description of love in the chapter. *As the return of Christ approaches*, we need to increase our understanding of God and His love in order to reach others before it is too late.

If I speak in the tongues of men or of angels, but have not love, I am only a resounding gong or a clanging cymbal. If I have the gift of prophecy and can fathom all mysteries and all knowledge, and if I have a faith that can move mountains, but have not love, I am nothing. If I give all I possess to the poor and surrender my body to the flames, but have not love, I gain nothing. Love is patient, love is kind. It does not envy, it does not boast, it is not proud. It is not rude, it is not self-seeking, it is not easily angered, it keeps no record of wrongs. Love does not delight in evil but rejoices with the truth. It always protects, always trusts, always hopes, always perseveres. Love never fails.
– 1 Corinthians 13: 1-8 (NIV)

The Gifts of the Holy Spirit (Part 2)

In the original Greek, the word *prophesy* can mean to foretell events or speak under the inspiration of God, as well as praise, teach, admonish, and comfort others under God's inspiration. Verse 3 of 1 Corinthians chapter 14 helps clarify the word *prophesy*.

But he who prophesies speaks edification and exhortation and comfort to men. - 1 Corinthians 14:3 (NKJV)

Revelation 22:18-19 clearly warns us *not* to *add* or *subtract* anything from the Scripture lest we be removed from God's book of life and eternity with Him. Due to this statement, we know that no one can add *new* revelation from God. We are, however, encouraged to speak *edification* (build up and help promote Christian growth), *exhort* (urgently advise, warn), and *comfort* others.

In light of the ever-darkening world (which was foretold by Christ Himself in Matthew 24), as we approach the End Times we have a positive and encouraging directive. We are to *desire* to be used by God to promote Christian growth, to urgently tell others about Christ and His Word, and to help calm and comfort others with the hope of our Lord and Savior.

Pursue love, and desire spiritual gifts, but especially that you may prophesy. - 1 Corinthians 14:1 (NKJV)

Prophecies Fulfilled in 1948

Over 50 biblical prophecies were fulfilled between the years 1948 and 2008! A complete list of them, with their explanations, can be found in Ken Johnson's book *Ancient Prophecies Revealed*. In 1948 alone, the year Israel became a nation, about twenty Old Testament prophecies came to pass. A partial list of those prophecies and their Scriptural references are listed below.

Prophetic Fulfillments	References
Israel is established as a nation	Isaiah 11:11-12
British ships first to bring Jews home	Isaiah 60:9
Israel returns as one nation, not two	Hosea 1:11; Ezekiel 37:18-22
Israel is born in one day	Isaiah 66:8
Israel is reestablished in ancient land	Jeremiah 30:2-3
Hebrew language is revived	Jeremiah 31:23
Jordan occupies West Bank	Zephaniah 2:8; Zechariah 12:1-7
Israel is initially restored without Jerusalem	Zechariah 12:1-7
Discovery of the Dead Sea Scrolls	Isaiah 29:1-4
Jewish people return in unbelief	Ezekiel 37:7-14

The Bible is the only book on Earth with hundreds and hundreds of prophecies that have come true. Their fulfillment extends from the past into the future.

**The LORD of hosts hath sworn, saying,
Surely as I have thought, so it shall come to pass;
and as I have purposed, so it shall stand.
- Isaiah 14:24**

How Not to Interpret a Prophecy

The Apostle Paul gave a warning in 1 Thessalonians 5:20: **"Do not despise prophecies."** The original word for despise means to have contempt or hatred for, as well as to consider something worthless. The word prophecies in this verse is the Greek word *propheteia,* meaning prediction. God's Word clearly tells us we are not to hate what God tells us about the future or consider it without merit.

False teachers throughout history did not like what was predicted in Scripture so they denied or twisted them to mean something else. 1 Thessalonians 5:21 tells us to test all things and to hold tightly onto the truth. In order to do this, we need to understand how Scripture is being twisted. Some examples are:

1. **Changing a specific statement to mean a vague one.** i.e., *distorting the clear statement of "six days of creation" to mean millions of years.* (Exodus 20:9-11)
2. **Looking for things that are not in Scripture.** i.e., *changing the statements about salvation as "a gift of God" to the belief that good works will qualify us for heaven.* (Ephesians 2:8)
3. **Mixing symbolic prophecies with literal prophecies.** i.e., *the historic heresy that the Jewish people are "the serpent's seed".* (1 John 3:9-10)
4. **Taking a prophecy out of context.** i.e., *the misbelief that all prophecies for Israel apply to the "church" today.* (Romans 11)
5. **Adding or subtracting from a prophecy.** i.e., *trying to determine the day of Christ's return when we are clearly told no one can know this.* (Matthew 24:36)

Watch therefore, for ye know neither the day nor the hour wherein the Son of man cometh.
- Matthew 25:13

The Israeli Flag Prophecy

The prophet Isaiah lived about seven hundred years before Christ. God inspired him to record a prophecy about the flag of Israel thousands of years before it existed.

The Hebrew word for flag is "ensign." Isaiah 11:10 states that in "that day," Israel will have a specific ensign or flag to represent it. What future day is so significant it should be designated as "that day"? Isaiah chapter 11 describes that day when the Creator of the universe will choose to physically return to Earth to judge mankind for their sinfulness and return all creation to its original perfection. Isaiah tells us the "root of Jesse" will be on the flag of Israel at this time.

Jesse was the father of King David. The six-pointed star was the crest or symbol of his household. Today we know this to be the Star of David, which is the symbol for Israel and is on the modern Israeli flag. Once again, we see God's Word proven true by fulfilled prophecy which came to pass well over twenty-five hundred years after it was given. We can also see that we must be drawing very close to "that day."

And in that day there shall be a root of Jesse, which shall stand for an ensign of the people...
- Isaiah 11:10

The Timeline of the Major and Minor Prophets

Many individuals were called to speak for God as His prophets during the writing of the entire Bible. The last seventeen books of the Old Testament, however, are divided into the *Major* and *Minor Prophets*. These terms were used to refer to the *length,* not the importance, of the books. On average the books of the Major Prophets Isaiah, Jeremiah, Lamentations (written by Jeremiah), Ezekiel, and Daniel were much longer books than the twelve that follow. The books are not in the order written, so it helps to know their approximate dates. The following major and minor prophets reported on events during these approximate chronological times:

800-700 B.C.	Joel, Jonah, Amos, Isaiah, Hosea, Micah
700-500 B.C.	Nahum, Jeremiah, Zephaniah, Daniel, Ezekiel, Habakkuk, Obadiah, Zechariah, Haggai
500-400 B.C.	Malachi
400 B.C. to the birth of Christ were the *"silent years"* between the Old and New Testaments.	

Many books claiming to be prophetical were written during the "silent years." They not only *contain errors*, but were also *not authenticated* as Scripture by Christ, the apostles, and early church fathers.

Surely the Lord GOD does nothing, unless He reveals His secret to His servants the prophets.
- Amos 3:7 (NKJV)

Who Is Zechariah the Prophet?

At least twenty-seven Old Testament men had the name Zechariah. Only one, however, was called by God to be a prophet and encourage the Jewish people, even into the future, with God's Word and inspired writing. Zechariah's message was for the people to return to God, repent of their sins, and commit to finish the rebuilding of the Temple in Jerusalem. Zechariah was born and raised in Babylon and was one of the Jewish returnees to Judah. He was also given prophetic visions to help explain God's future promises of both the First and Second Comings of the Messiah, Jesus Christ.

Within the three generations listed in Zechariah 1:1, God ordained a remarkable prophecy. In Hebrew, the grandfather's name *Iddo,* means **His time**; the son's name *Berechiah* means **Jehovah blesses**; and the grandson's name *Zechariah* means **he who Jehovah remembers**. Together they create a unique prophetic statement: **"In His time, Jehovah blesses who He remembers."** God had predicted Judah's fall and captivity to the Babylonians for their rejection of Him. He promised, however, He would not forget them and He would bring them back to their homeland after seventy years of captivity. God fulfilled His promise in every detail.

In the eighth month, in the second year of Darius, came the word of the LORD unto Zechariah, the son of Berechiah, the son of Iddo the prophet, ...
- Zechariah 1:1

The 70-Year Babylonian Captivity Prophecy

In Leviticus chapter 25, God commanded Moses to allow the land He promised to Israel to "rest" every seventh year. Israel failed to obey God's command to Moses. Instead, the people planted crops for 490 years without allowing any years of "rest." Thus, they "owed" God and the land seventy years of rest.

Jeremiah prophesied they would be taken captive by Babylon for exactly seventy years. *The land would be given its rest.* **At the end of the seventy years, God would then punish Babylon (Jeremiah 25:11-12).** Although the harsh Babylonian captivity was the result of the Israelites' idolatry (Deuteronomy 31:16-18), God would not allow the Babylonians to go unpunished for their own sins against Him and His people.

Daniel records the fulfillment of this seventy-year prophecy. He lived through the captivity and knew the seventy years were coming to an end (Daniel 9:1-3). He saw God bring every word to pass. God blessed Daniel by using dreams and the gift of interpreting dreams to outline not only the fall of Babylon, but also coming successive world empires. Daniel 11 details the period between 537 B.C. and 1948 A.D.

And the LORD spoke to Moses on Mount Sinai, saying "Speak to the children of Israel, and say...'Six years you shall sow your field, and six years you shall prune your vineyards, and gather its fruit; but in the seventh year there shall be a sabbath of solemn rest for the land, a sabbath to the LORD. You shall neither sow your field nor prune your vineyard.' "
- Leviticus 25:1-4 (NKJV)

Persia and the Four Kings Prophecy

In 536 B.C., the *prophet Daniel predicted* there would be four kings after Darius the Mede. The fourth would be the richest, most powerful, and would arouse the whole Persian Empire against Greece.

History informs us that there were exactly four kings of Persia after Darius the Mede: Cambyses (530-522 B.C.); Pseudo-Smerdis (522 B.C.); Darius (522-486 B.C.); and Xerxes I (486-465 B.C.). The fourth king, Xerxes I, grew exceedingly strong and rich, just as Daniel had prophesied. He attacked Greece at Sardis of Asia Minor with sixty thousand men and twelve hundred ships in 480 B.C. This was the largest invasion force the world had ever seen up to that time. Eighty-four years after Daniel gave this prophecy, a battle took place. It looked as if the Greeks were doomed, but they were able to stand their ground, and the Persians lost the war.

Also, in the first year of Darius the Mede, I, even I, stood up to confirm and strengthen him. And now I will tell you the truth: Behold, three more kings will arise in Persia, and the fourth shall be far richer than them all; by his strength, through his riches, he shall stir up all against the realm of Greece.
- Daniel 11:1-2 (NKJV)

Alexander the Great in Prophecy

Daniel gives us another very specific and unusual prophecy in Daniel 11:3-4 concerning the Greeks' rise to power.

Alexander the Great was born in Pella in 356 B.C. When he took the throne of Greece, he started a campaign against the Persian Empire. When he was twenty-two years old, Alexander entered Asia with thirty-four thousand men against Darius' four hundred thousand and within one year gained control of Syria. During the next nine years, Alexander the Great gained control of the known world. But three years later, in 323 B.C., Alexander died.

None of his children took the throne. Instead, the kingdom was split into four parts between his four leading generals. Seleucus Nicator took Syria; Cassander took Macedonia (Greece); Lysimachus took Thrace (Turkey); and Ptolemy took Egypt. **Historical records verify that Alexander the Great is the mighty king who fits Daniel's more than 200-year-old prophecy.**

And a mighty king will arise, and he will rule with great authority and do as he pleases. But as soon as he has arisen, his kingdom will be broken up and parceled out toward the four points of the compass, though not to his own descendants, nor according to his authority which he wielded; for his sovereignty will be uprooted and given to others besides them.
- Daniel 11:3-4 (NASV)

The Cyrus Prophecy

Hundreds of years before its conqueror was even born, the fall of Babylon was predicted. The prophet Isaiah wrote specific prophecies, not only naming the conqueror Cyrus, but also predicting the details of how he would capture Babylon.

Babylon was a fortified city with outer walls three hundred feet high and seventy feet thick. It had more than 250 watchtowers along the walls with moats and other defenses. The city could withstand a siege indefinitely because it sat on the Euphrates River, giving it access to all the food and water the inhabitants needed. **Scripture records the following predictions concerning Cyrus. History confirms their total fulfillment (Isaiah 44:26-28; 45:1-6).**

- With the use of careful engineering, the **river was diverted,** allowing Cyrus' troops to march under the walls of the city.

- The underground **gates were left open.**

- The **Babylonian Empire was destroyed.**

- The **Jews were freed to go back to their land.**

- **Cities of Judah were rebuilt and Jerusalem was inhabited** again.

- The **Temple foundation was laid.**

- **Sacred vessels from Solomon's Temple were returned** to the Jews.

Thus says the LORD to Cyrus His anointed..."For the sake of Jacob My servant and Israel My chosen one, I have also called you by your name; I have given you a title of honor.... I will gird you, though you have not known Me; that men may know...I am the LORD, and there is no other."
- Isaiah 45:1,4-6 (NASB)

The "Joy" Prophecy

The Hebrew and Greek words translated as "joy" in the Bible are used over 170 times. In almost every case, "joy" is defined as gladness, great delight, or a sense of cheerfulness. In Scripture, we are commanded to be joyful because it is God's will (1 Thessalonians 5:16-18). We are told *what joy will do* for us. *God's delight in our thoughts, words, and actions is our strength (defense, force, protection).*

For the joy of the LORD is your strength. - Nehemiah 8:10b

We are even told *how to have joy* – by obeying God (John 15:10-11). Joy, however, is also a *prophetic promise*. God tells us in both the Old and New Testaments that in God's presence we will have fullness of joy. We get a taste of this joy here on Earth when we enter into God's presence as we pray, read, obey His Word, and sing to Him. One can't even imagine the fullness of joy we will experience when we see our Lord face-to-face.

**You will show me the path of life;
in Your presence is fullness of joy….
- Psalm 16:11 (NKJV)**

**You have made known to me the ways of life;
you will make me full of joy in Your presence.
- Acts 2:28 (NKJV)**

The Crown of Life

The *"crown of life"* is used twice in the Bible. **A crown is an emblem of glory, and both times the term is used it is in regard to the reward given to those who persevere through life's difficulties and prove faithful to the Lord God until the end.** A closer look at the meaning of the two verses talking about this crown demonstrates the love and care God has for His followers.

God knows *exactly* what we are going through. Going through hard times, enduring temptations, being provoked, being rejected, and even being disciplined have a purpose. We are told in both the Old and New Testaments that God has His eyes on the righteous and He hears our prayers (Psalm 34:15; 1 Peter 3:12). Although we may not always understand the trials we go through, we have *God's promise* that He *will award us* the "crown of life" if we persevere in our love for Him to the end.

Blessed is the man who endures temptation; for when he has been approved, he will receive the crown of life which the Lord has promised to those who love Him.
- James 1:12 (NKJV)

Do not fear any of those things which you are about to suffer....
Be faithful until death, and I will give you the crown of life.
- Revelation 2:10 (NKJV)

Balaam's Prophecies (Part 1)

Balaam was a soothsayer – which means he was involved in the occult. His story is detailed in Numbers 22-24 and is so significant that he is mentioned in eight other books of the Bible (always in a negative way). Both Peter and Jude went so far as to say Balaam had a place reserved for him in the *"blackness of darkness forever"* (2 Peter 2:15-17; Jude 11-13). **What makes the account of Balaam so unusual is that this wicked man was given important prophecies by God for both the near and distant future.**

Numbers 22 tells us Balaam was hired by Balak, the king of one of Israel's enemies, the Moabites. Balaam would be paid well to come and use his abilities to curse Israel so she could not remain a strong and forceful threat to the surrounding heathen nations.

God warned Balaam not to go to Balak because He had blessed Israel (Numbers 22:12), but Balaam disobeyed. God even warned and protected Balaam three times from His wrath, using Balaam's donkey (Numbers 23:31). Balaam, however, desperately wanted the money offered him (2 Peter 2:15). God finally permitted Balaam to go see King Balak but told him that he would only be able to say what God allowed him to speak. King Balak took Balaam to three different locations trying to get a curse on Israel. Even at Balaam's own admission that he *had* to say what God told him, King Balak still insisted that Balaam try to curse Israel.

"Did I not tell you, saying, 'All that the
LORD speaks, that I must do'?"
- Numbers 23:26 (NKJV)

Balaam's Prophecies (Part 2)

Numbers 23 and 24 contain the four prophecies God directed Balaam to speak. God used Balaam to get His message across to people then and also to us today. The main message from each of the prophecies is as follows:

Prophecy 1: God allows no one to go against His decrees.

> **How shall I curse whom God has not cursed? And how shall I denounce whom the LORD has not denounced?**
> **- Numbers 23:8 (NKJV)**

The Bible tells us the world will come against Israel (Zechariah 14:1-3). Today many nations threaten Israel's annihilation, yet we have the prophetic promise that God will protect His people (Ezekiel 36).

Prophecy 2: God will bless Israel. The world will be forced to see God's hand on Israel in the end.

> **...It now must be said of Jacob and of Israel, "Oh, what God has done!" Look, a people rises like a lioness, and lifts itself up like a lion.... - Numbers 23:23-24 (NKJV)**

Even after almost two thousand years of being scattered and non-existent as a nation, we can see Israel is rising economically, militarily, technologically and agriculturally. This prophecy will come to its complete fulfillment in the Millennial Kingdom, just like the Bible predicts.

Balaam's Prophecies (Part 3)

Prophecy 3: Balaam's third prophecy was given to magnify the LORD God and demonstrate His deep love for and commitment to His people Israel. Balaam states that just as God brought Israel out from under the bondage of Egypt, He will consume and destroy Israel's enemies in the end. This prophecy also opened up an opportunity for the whole world to receive God's blessings (Numbers 24:3-9) if they blessed Israel.

Blessed is he who blesses you,
and cursed is he who curses you.
- Numbers 24:9b (NKJV)

A study of the history of nations that cursed or blessed Israel proves the undeniable truth of this statement.

Prophecy 4: In this prophecy, Balaam predicted the First Coming of the Messiah. This Messiah would come out of the lineage of Jacob and would be a King - Numbers 24:17-24.

"I see Him, but not now; I behold Him, but not near;
A Star shall come out of Jacob;
a Scepter shall rise out of Israel …."
- Numbers 24:17 (NKJV)

The first part of this prophecy came to pass at the birth of the Lord Jesus Christ. He was born out of the lineage of Jacob, just as the prophecy had predicted well over a thousand years earlier. He is the King out of Israel and will rule on Earth in the future Millennial Kingdom.

Rebirth in Christ Reserves an Inheritance for Us

The verses in 1 Peter 1:3-5 record a remarkable prophetic promise. It is for anyone and everyone who trusts in the fact that Jesus Christ died for their sins. When we put our trust in Christ, we die to our selfishness. We are born into a new life centered on what Christ wants. But it is up to us to yield to the new Spirit of the Lord who dwells within us.

Christ promises that we will receive an inheritance from Him and that it is reserved for us in heaven. He also said our inheritance is imperishable (*can't be destroyed*). It is undefiled (*pure, clean*) and will not fade away (*lose its magnificence*). Our faith guarantees our protection by God's power. We will get our full salvation (*rescue, deliverance*) in the end of time!

Blessed be the God and Father of our Lord Jesus Christ, who according to His great mercy has caused us to be born again to a living hope through the resurrection of Jesus Christ from the dead, to obtain an inheritance which is imperishable and undefiled and will not fade away, reserved in heaven for you, who are protected by the power of God through faith for a salvation ready to be revealed in the last time.
- 1 Peter 1:3-5 (NASB)

Increase of Religious Deceivers (Part 1)

Matthew's gospel tells us the disciples asked Christ what the signs would be of His coming and the end of the age. The very first thing Christ mentions (Matthew 24:4-5) is that there would be "many deceivers" (*wanderers from the truth, those who persuade others to disobedience and disloyalty*). He stated that these deceivers would come in His name (*authority, character*). Christ is specifically talking about religious deceivers. He warns His disciples to take heed (*beware, see, discern*). Peter mentions the rise of the religious deceivers in 2 Peter 2:1. He says there would also be "many false prophets" (*pretended foretellers, religious imposters*) and adds that many would be deceived.

2 Peter 2:1-19 gives us a clear description of the religious deceivers which Christ warned about. It was meant to help us know what to watch for so we do not become part of the "many" Christ said would be led astray. In the *Jeremiah Study Bible*, Dr. David Jeremiah lists twenty-two attributes of these religious deceivers:

1.   They infiltrate the church (2:1).
2.   They come in secret (2:1).
3.   They deny the work of Jesus (2:1).
4.   They blaspheme the truth (2:2).
5.   They are greedy (2:3, 14)
6.   They use words that sound remarkably close to the truth (2:3).

But there were also false prophets among the people, just as there will be false teachers among you. They will secretly introduce destructive heresies, even denying the sovereign Lord....
- 2 Peter 2:1 (NIV)

Increase of Religious Deceivers (Part 2)

The continuation of the characteristics of false teachers found in 2 Peter 2:10-19:

7. They follow the flesh (2:10).
8. They are presumptuous and self-willed (2:10).
9. They do not want to be under anyone's authority (2:10, 11).
10. They exhibit peace on the outside but are like untamed beasts on the inside (2:12).
11. They speak more evil than good (2:12).
12. They are ignorant (2:12).
13. They love to deceive others (2:13).
14. They are full of adultery (2:14).
15. They cannot cease from sinning (2:14).
16. They prey on unstable new believers (2:14).
17. They intentionally speak lies (2:15).
18. They are out for monetary gain (2:15).
19. They talk a lot, but say nothing (2:16, 18).
20. They make grandiose promises but never deliver (2:17).
21. They use alluring thoughts to provoke the attention of their audience (2:18).
22. They make promises they cannot deliver (2:19).

God does not want His children to be deceived. Not only does He warn us not to be deceived throughout Scripture (Luke 21:8, 1 Corinthians 6:9; 1 Corinthians 15:33; Galatians 6:7; 2 Timothy 3:13), but He also tells us *exactly what to watch for.*

And Jesus answered and said unto them, Take heed that no man deceive you. For many shall come in my name, saying, I am Christ; and shall deceive many.
- Matthew 24:4-5

SEPTEMBER

He Shall Not Be Afraid

Psalm 112:7

Arlene Faith Kortright

He shall not be a - fraid of e - vil tid - ings His heart is fixed trust - ing in the Lord He shall not be a - fraid of e - vil tid - ings His heart is fixed trust - ing in the Lord Lord Psalm one hun - dred twelve sev - en

LORD, help me to meditate on and trust this verse when I watch the news or hear evil tidings. Give me a joyful heart and passion to share You with others. **Amen**

The Seven-Sealed Book Prophecy (Part 1)

The *"seven-sealed scroll prophecy"* is found in Revelation 5. It deals with a scroll which will be opened up in heaven at the beginning of the Tribulation. According to the Bible, this scroll is a legal document, the *"title deed"* to planet Earth. Originally, God gave this land deed to Adam - who lost it to Satan when Adam sinned. Satan has been given temporary control over much that happens here on the earth because we forfeited this privilege. Throughout the last six thousand years, evil has eventually overwhelmed every civilzation. However, Scripture tells us that this will only be allowed to repeat in cycles for a limited time because Christ will return and take back the title to the earth (which He rightly owns).

According to this prophecy, Christ will open the "seven-sealed" scroll in heaven. **Christ is both able to open and worthy of opening this scroll because He alone meets the criteria to access the scroll.** Christ is entitled to the deed because He is of the *right tribe and lineage.* He alone has the *ability to redeem the land* lost to Satan with the sacrifice of His sinless life. Christ is also *willing to redeem the entire world.*

To fully understand the seven-sealed scroll mystery, one needs to understand the laws of the kinsman redeemer given to us in Leviticus 25:1-55, Jeremiah 32:6-15, and the book of Ruth.

> **And I saw in the right hand of Him who sat on the throne a scroll written inside and on the back, sealed with the seven seals. Then I saw a strong angel proclaiming with a loud voice, "Who is worthy to open the scroll and to loose its seals?"...I wept much, because no one was found worthy.... but one of the elders said to me, "Do not weep. Behold, the Lion of the tribe of Judah, the Root of David, has prevailed to open the scroll...."**
> **- Revelation 5: 1, 2, 4, 5 (NKJV)**

The Seven-Sealed Book Prophecy (Part 2)

Land in the Middle East was given to the Israelite nation almost four thousand years ago through God's promise to Abraham, Isaac, and Jacob. It was never to be permanently sold. It was to remain with this people group forever. In specific dire circumstances, land could be sold temporarily, but it had to revert back to the original tribe every fiftieth year, which was called the Year of Jubilee. It could also be purchased back by a kinsman (relative) and be redeemed for the family.

This law was the foreshadowing of what Christ was prophesied to do for mankind. Christ fulfilled all these criteria. The only thing we are waiting for is His timing. Christ was prophesied to come to Earth in His First Coming, which He fulfilled at His birth. After the Rapture, Christ is prophesied to come a second time to reclaim the ownership title for the Earth. This prophecy will be fulfilled as well.

Between His First Coming and Second Coming, people have the opportunity to turn to Christ for forgiveness of their sins and accept Him as their Lord and Savior. When *Christ returns and sets His feet on Earth*, the opportunity to accept Him is over. The time to accept Christ is now. (*2 Corinthians 6:2*)

"In an acceptable time I have heard you,
and in the day of salvation I have helped you."
Behold, now is the accepted time of salvation.
- 2 Corinthians 6:2 (NKJV)

"Common Sense" Prophecy

During Israel's seventy-year captivity in Babylon, some of the Israelites repented (Daniel 9:1-19). They admitted that God's judgment was deserved because the warnings of the prophets had been ignored and they had continued in their sinful ways. God's judgment on His people is always based on their attitudes and behaviors. Acknowledgment of and obedience to God always bring blessings. Rejection and disobedience inevitably bring discontentment, chaos, and grief. A careful reading of Israel's history is not only a prophetic picture of what happens to nations who reject God, but also a picture of hope when they return to Him.

In other cultures, these same results happen whenever God's moral commands are ignored. Romans 1:18-32 reveals the inevitable downward spiral of nations which reject God as Creator and then place their reverence and enjoyment of the creation above acknowledgement and obedience to their Creator. **Common sense tells us that rejection of God's guidelines dooms any culture to these consequences:**

- When marriage guidelines are rejected – families fall apart.
- If justice is ignored – evil and corruption run rampant.
- When children have no discipline – they become rebellious.
- Without placing Jesus in control of our lives – we drift toward hopelessness, selfishness, and greed.
- Without moral boundaries – we have drugs, abortion, violence, sexual perversion, and chaos.
- Without responsibilities – we have laziness, unemployment and wastefulness.
- Rejection of God – leads to worship of self, materialism, pleasure, and the occult.

"...Return to Me," says the LORD of hosts,
"and I will return to you" ….
- Zechariah 1:3 (NKJV)

Jerusalem's Future Glory

Zechariah chapter two records a vision which the prophet Zechariah received from the Lord. It prophesies the rebuilding of Jerusalem after the Babylonian Captivity, but it also foreshadows reconstruction of Jerusalem for the Millennial Kingdom.

This timely prophecy came when the returning Israelites were struggling to rebuild Jerusalem and the Temple. It contained four promises:

1. Jerusalem will experience **prosperity** and will be much larger because of its increased population and material wealth. *Zechariah 2:4b*
2. Jerusalem will be **protected by God.** He will dwell there. *Zechariah 2: 5, 10*
3. Jerusalem's **population will be multiplied** greatly when God calls them home. *Zechariah 2:6-7*
4. **God will punish the nations** who reject Israel (which includes Jerusalem). *Zechariah 2:8-9*

Zechariah saw the prophecy partially fulfilled in his day. We can be assured it will be completely fulfilled when the Lord comes to dwell in Jerusalem during His Millennial Reign.

"…Jerusalem shall be inhabited as towns without walls, because of the multitude of men and livestock in it. 'For I,' says the LORD, 'will be a wall of fire all around her, and I will be the glory in her midst.' "
- Zechariah 2:4b-5 (NKJV)

Time and Prophecy

Albert Einstein made the following statement once he came to understand the nature of time, "People like us, who believe in physics, know that the distinction between the past, present, and future is only a stubbornly persistent illusion."

Space is measured in three dimensions – length, width, and depth. All physical objects are measured in these three dimensions. Time has been called the "fourth dimension" and has been found to be part of, not independent from, the physical universe. Einstein, and multiple experiments since his time, have shown that the rate at which time moves is affected by the amount of matter in its immediate vicinity, and by the speed and acceleration with which any object is traveling through space. This modern understanding of time leads to some interesting conclusions about the nature of God.

God is the Creator of the universe, and time is part of that creation. Thus, **God is totally and completely outside of time as we know it.** This is why He is both the "beginning and the end." Our Lord and Maker simultaneously sees everything which has ever happened, is happening, and will ever happen. Prophecies in the Bible show the timeless nature of God. Bible prophecies assure us that the Bible is indeed authored by the One who created the universe; therefore, He is outside of time and knows the future.

I am Alpha and Omega, the beginning and the ending, saith the Lord, which is, and which was, and which is to come, the Almighty."
- Revelation 1:8

Resurrection Prophecies

Salvation, or the saving of one's soul, depends on both the death and the resurrection of Christ. The Bible is full of prophecies about Christ's death. Each one came true. Without the resurrection, however, Christ would not have accomplished God's plan. Christ had to rise from the dead to show mankind that He conquered death once and for all. Christ made a way for us to have eternal life with Him by giving us reason to put our full trust and obedience in Him. **Christ proved to be the risen Lord God and Savior.**

God's plan for the resurrection is prophesied throughout the Bible. For instance, the book of Psalms informs us that after His death on the cross, He (Christ the Messiah) would *not undergo decay* (Psalm 16:10), and that God the Father *would receive Him* (Psalm 49:15). In Acts we are told *death could not hold Him.*

And God raised Him up again, putting an end to the agony of death, since it was impossible for Him to be held in its power.
- Acts 2:24 (NASB)

In Ephesians 4, Paul refers to Psalm 68:18 as proof that Jesus indeed *was resurrected, ascended, and provided salvation* for all who believed. Acts 1:1-11 recounts the actual event. Again the emphasis is the prophecy that after Christ died *and rose again,* He would *ascend back to heaven* and sit at the right hand of God the Father until it was time for His final return at the Second Coming.

...He was lifted up while they were looking on,
and a cloud received Him out of their sight.
- Acts 1:9 (NASB)

Jerusalem's Call to Sing

The "daughter of Zion" (another name for Jerusalem) is told to praise God and rejoice over her future. A closer look at the prophecy in Zechariah 2:10-12 tells us why. The people of Jerusalem will sing and rejoice because:

- God will dwell in their midst (v. 10).

- Believers who trust in the Lord from many nations will be joined to the Lord and become His people (v. 11).

- Jerusalem will have the privilege of being uniquely chosen by God (v. 12).

Zechariah 2:12 is the only place the phrase "holy land" is used in the Bible. The land of Israel will only become "holy" when her sin is removed on the day of Christ's Second Coming (Zechariah 3:9; 13:1). Only then, during the Millennial Reign, will the people become the "Holy People" (Isaiah 62:12) and be made Christ's priests and servants (Isaiah 61:6).

"Sing and rejoice, O daughter of Zion! For behold, I am coming and I will dwell in your midst," says the LORD. "Many nations shall be joined to the LORD in that day, and they shall become My people. And I will dwell in your midst. Then you will know that the LORD of hosts has sent Me to you. "And the LORD will take possession of Judah as His inheritance in the Holy Land and will again choose Jerusalem."
- Zechariah 2:10-12 (NKJV)

A Better Understanding of End Time Prophecy (Part 1)

Daniel wrote prophecies he did not understand. We are told in this passage they would be closed, or "kept secret," until it was time for them to be understood. As we approach the final days, we can understand prophecies as never before.

Consider the following prophecies:

- **The End-Time existence of Israel as a nation before Christ's return (*Isaiah 11:10-12*).** For almost two thousand years, the Jews were scattered all over the world. On May 14, 1948, Israel was re-established as a nation.

- **The Jews will reoccupy Jerusalem (*Luke 21:24*).** The Jewish reoccupation of Jerusalem occurred on June 7, 1967. The complete fulfillment is yet in the future.

- **Jerusalem will be the world's trouble spot (*Zechariah 12:1-3*).** There is continual fighting over Jerusalem. The world's uproar at the move of the U.S. Embassy to Jerusalem in 2018 bears this out.

- **Christ said in Matthew 24:37-38 that it would be "like the days of Noah" before He returns in the End Times.** An in-depth study of Genesis 6:1-12 implies the possibility that satanic genetic manipulation was happening. Could this be part of what Christ was referring to? Genetic manipulation is going on today. DNA can be altered and plant, animal, and human genes are being mixed. Experiments altering humans using molecular machines and artifical intelligence are also being conducted.

> And I heard, but I understood not: then said I,
> O my Lord, what shall be the end of these things?
> And he said, Go thy way, Daniel: for the words
> are closed up and sealed till the time of the end.
> - Daniel 12:8-9

A Better Understanding of End Time Prophecy (Part 2)

Like no time in history, we are able to understand ancient prophetic statements of the Bible:

- **The magnitude of the slaughter of people in the Tribulation (*Revelation 6-9*).** One-fourth of the world's population will die during the initial Tribulation judgments. The development of nuclear weapons (1945) and intercontinental ballistic missiles (in the 1960s) makes this unprecedented slaughter possible for the first time in history.

- **The two witnesses in Jerusalem (*Revelation 11:3-12*).** The Bible tells us God will send two witnesses who will serve as prophets to the world in the Tribulation. The Antichrist will not only kill them but will allow *the entire world* to see them as they lie in the streets for three and one-half days. Not only has technology made this possible, but there are cameras set up in Jerusalem enabling the world to watch the streets twenty-four hours a day.

- **The three-and-one-half day world-wide distribution of gifts (*Revelation 11:9-10*).** There is no time in history when packages could have been distributed to every place on earth within three and one-half days, until the invention of airplanes and drones.

- **The mark of the beast (*Revelation 13:16-17*).** In Revelation 13 we are told the Antichrist will control all of the buying and selling worldwide through a mark on the right hand or forehead. The invention of computer technology and artificial intelligence has now made this possible for the first time in history.

The "Branch" Prophecies

Isaiah 11:1-2 and Jeremiah 33:15-16 identify the Messiah as "The Branch." In Zechariah 6:12-15, we find some very interesting prophecies about **"The Branch"** spoken by the LORD of hosts. The following prophecies were given to Zechariah not only to encourage the rebuilding of the Second Temple, but also to serve as an encouragement to the Jewish people – leading up to final fulfillment in the Millennial Kingdom. According to the prophecies, Messiah (The Branch) would:

- **"Branch out"** (*Zechariah 6:12*). The Messiah came as a "tender plant, as a root out of dry ground" (Isaiah 53:2). He would come to Earth as a humble servant, grow strong, and be elevated to great heights (Isaiah 53:2-12).

- **"Bear the glory"** (*Zechariah 6:13*). In the Millennial Kingdom, Messiah will finally receive the honor, majesty, and glory He is due when He reigns as both King and Priest.

- **"Sit and rule on His throne"** (*Zechariah 6:13*). Messiah will rule the earth and reign from Jerusalem.

- **"Be a priest on His throne"** (*Zechariah 6:13*). As both King and Priest, Messiah will bring peace.

- **"Build the temple of the LORD"** (*Zechariah 6:13*). With gifts from many nations, the Messiah will build the Millennial Temple.

What is said about "The Branch" is consistent with what we are told about Christ in the New Testament. In Matthew, Messiah is seen as a *King*, in Mark as a *Servant*, in Luke as *Fully Man,* and in John as *Fully God.*

> **...Thus speaketh the LORD of hosts, saying,**
> **Behold the man whose name is The BRANCH.**
> **- Zechariah 6:12**

The Retribution Prophecy

God's retribution (or punishment) came upon Israel because of her disobedience. In His mercy, God gave Israel chance after chance to repent. God responded with loving patience. But finally, He did not respond to their cry for help because they refused to hear the prophets' message. God scattered the Israelites *"among the nations which they did not know"* (Zechariah 7:14): Assyria (722 B.C.) Babylon (586 B.C.), Rome (70 A.D.), and then the world (135 A.D.) The land of Israel, which was once pleasant and said to *"flow with milk and honey"* (Exodus 3:8), was made a wasteland and lay in ruins.

Isn't it interesting that during the last 1,900 years, when Israel ceased to be a nation and the Jewish people were scattered, the land itself became desolate and undeveloped. The only time the land blooms is when the Jewish people are in it! In 1948, when Israel became a state and her people returned to the land, it began to bloom once again and continues to become more and more productive.

"Therefore it happened, that just as He proclaimed and they would not hear, so they called out and I would not listen," says the LORD of hosts. "But I scattered them with a whirlwind among all the nations which they had not known. Thus the land became desolate after them, so that no one passed through or returned; for they made the pleasant land desolate."
- Zechariah 7:13-14 (NKJV)

The Passover Lamb (Part 1)

Passover was instituted by God around 1440 B.C. **This event provides a prophecy of the coming crucifixion of Christ, the Lamb, and how we are saved through Him alone.**

The Passover took place at the time of "the Exodus," an actual historical event when the Israelites were about to be released from their cruel slave bondage to Egypt. Just before the people were miraculously freed, God gave His people specific instructions that would protect them from the final forthcoming plague upon Egypt (Exodus 12:1-13). God's final warning was that if the Egyptian Pharaoh did not let the Israelites go, God would take the lives of all first-born people and animals.

In order to avoid this punishment, God mercifully ordained the Passover. He orchestrated this event to authenticate Himself to the entire world. The Passover serves as a model of Christ, who would come to save all who believe and put their trust in Him.

For the Passover, the Israelite people were told to choose an unblemished male lamb on the tenth of Nisan (which is in the spring on the Jewish calendar). On the fourteenth of Nisan, at twilight, they were to sacrifice this perfect lamb and put its blood on their doorposts and their lintel (the piece across the top of the door opening). The firstborn of all those who obeyed God were "passed over" and spared.

...The blood shall be to you for a token upon the houses where ye are; and when I see the blood, I will pass over you.
- Exodus 12:13

The Passover Lamb (Part 2)

The "Passover" happened only one time in history, when God judged the land of Egypt (Exodus 12). Only one time did the Israelites apply the Passover lamb's blood to their homes. **Every Passover since then has been a memorial of what happened on the first Passover.** This Passover foreshadowed the future when Christ became the sacrificial Lamb for the world. Once and for all, Christ's death made it possible for God to "pass over" our sins by placing them on His sinless Son, Jesus, who took our punishment for us. Christ fulfilled the prophecy pictured by the Passover lamb.

Christ and the Passover lambs:

- Were examined on the tenth of Nisan.

- Were male and unblemished.

- Were killed publicly and were silent before those who slaughtered them.

- Were killed on Passover as an atonement (covering) for sin.

- Had their blood put on wooden beams.

- Their blood protected those who put their faith in God.

- Were not allowed to have any broken bones.

- Were requested by God to be remembered with a specially designated meal (Passover meal/ Lord's Supper).

- Underwent God's fiery wrath. (The lamb had to be roasted. Christ had God's wrath poured on Him for the sins of the world.)

Knowing that you were not redeemed with corruptible things as silver and gold, from your aimless conduct received by tradition from your fathers, but with the precious blood of Christ, as of a lamb without blemish and without spot.
- 1 Peter 1:18-19 (NKJV)

The Psalm 23 Prophecy (Part 1)

Psalm 23 is a six-verse psalm (or poem), originally set to music. It was written by King David of Israel over three thousand years ago. Due to the fact that David spent most of his youth tending sheep, he was an expert at shepherding.

In this psalm, David sees himself as a sheep under the care of his Shepherd – the Lord God. The first three verses are written as if David is speaking to his fellow sheep. He tells them Who his Shepherd is, with the Hebraic definition of "shepherd" being one's friend and companion, who rules with deep care and concern. In the first half of the psalm, David explains what his Shepherd did for him and can do for us:

- The Lord, as our Shepherd, provides for our complete satisfaction (v. 1).
- He gives rest and guides us as we meet with Him in quiet places, feed on His Word, and have a relationship with Him (v. 2). (Jesus claimed to be our drink and food in John 4:10-14, 6:35.)
- He also restores or fixes the souls of all who follow Him and guides us to do the right thing for His own name or character's sake (v. 3).

Why would anyone not want such a Shepherd to be in control of his life?

**The LORD is my shepherd; I shall not want.
He makes me to lie down in green pastures;
He leads me beside the still waters,
He restores my soul; He leads me in the paths of
righteousness for His name's sake.
- Psalm 23:1-3 (NKJV)**

Psalm 23 Prophecy (Part 2)

David includes prophecy in his song, but first he identifies additional benefits (gifts) given to us by the LORD our Shepherd:

- The Lord our Shepherd gives us *comfort* (a change of mind to turn from sin) with His loving *rod* (individualized discipline and guidance) and *staff* (support) (v. 4).
- He prepares our *table* (what we eat or go through in life) in the midst of all the distresses and suffering (v. 5a).
- He soaks us with His presence and fills us to overflowing (v. 5).

Within the closing verses of Psalm 23, the Lord gives us three prophetic promises:

- Because the Lord is our Shepherd and He is with us, *we will fear no evil.*
- God's *goodness and mercy will accompany us all of our life* on Earth.
- *We will go to live with Him forever* when we die.

What awesome prophetic promises for everyone who claims Christ as his Shepherd and follows Him as one of His sheep.

Yea, though I walk through the valley of the shadow of death, I will fear no evil; for You are with me; Your rod and Your staff, they comfort me. You prepare a table before me in the presence of my enemies; You anoint my head with oil; my cup runs over. Surely goodness and mercy shall follow me all the days of my life; and I will dwell in the house of the LORD forever.
- Psalm 23:4-6 (NKJV)

A Most Serious Biblical Prophecy

The Bible contains around two thousand prophecies throughout the Old and New Testaments. Some are warnings, some are promises, *all will happen.* This is based on the one hundred percent accuracy of every area the Bible addresses, from history, geography, health, and the sciences to ethics and prophecy. Scripture's many prophetic warnings about eternal judgment and hell are terrifying. Whether or not people ignore, deny, or choose to believe them is beside the point. The predictions will come to pass since God "cannot lie" (Titus 1:2; Hebrews 6:18).

Perhaps most frightening is the prophecy that comes from Christ. He addresses His warning to those who think they will go to heaven because they are good. Christ even specifies those who claim to have prophesied, cast out demons, and done wonderful works in His name. Christ will say He *"does not know them."* Their actions were for their edification, not the Father's will. This should cause us to examine ourselves to see if our actions flow from a desire to obey, serve and glorify God or to glorify or benefit ourselves.

Not everyone that saith unto me, Lord, Lord, shall enter into the kingdom of heaven; but he that doeth the will of my Father which is in heaven. Many will say to me in that day, Lord, Lord, have we not prophesied in thy name? and in thy name have cast out devils? and in thy name done many wonderful works? And then will I profess unto them, I never knew you: depart from me, ye that work iniquity.
- Matthew 7:21-23

The Adding and Subtracting Prophecy (Part 1)

The Bible gives us clear prophetic warning that *no one* is to *"add to or take away from"* God's Word in any way. The word "add" means to exceed or go beyond what God actually said in Scripture. **No one is to add laws, make additional demands, or twist God's Word like we so often see done in many religions.** Nor are we to claim added revelations from God. "Taking away" from Scripture means *to remove or cut away the parts* one may not like or understand. True believers should never tamper with or adjust God's Word in any way. However, this doesn't mean that true Christ followers won't ever make mistakes in judgment or mistakenly interpret the Bible incorrectly or inadequately. We are to diligently seek God's guidance and be open to correction.

God is so serious about this command that He repeated this prophetic warning at least four times in Scripture and had it strategically placed throughout the Bible. The warning is found at the *beginning* of the Old Testament when God's laws were first given (Deuteronomy 4:2 and 12:32) and at the *center* of the Bible (Proverbs 30:5-6). The final and most detailed warning is recorded in the *closing chapter* of the Bible (Revelation 22:18-19).

This is why Paul so emphatically stressed the importance of studying and teaching God's Word correctly.

**Study to show thyself approved unto God,
a workman that needeth not to be ashamed,
rightly dividing the word of truth.
- 2 Timothy 2:15**

The Adding and Subtracting Prophecy (Part 2)

The following verses repeat God's prophetic warning quite clearly. The final warning is the most passionate and adds crucial details. It tells us that intentionally adding or taking away from God's Word will result in an eternal punishment with no possibility of entering into God's presence when we die.

You shall not add to the word which I commanded you, nor take from it, that you may keep the commandments of the LORD your God which I command you.
- Deuteronomy 4:2 (NKJV)

Whatever I command you, be careful to observe it; you shall not add to it nor take away from it.
- Deuteronomy 12:32 (NKJV)

Every word of God is pure; He is a shield to those who put their trust in Him. Do not add to His words, lest He rebuke you, and you be found a liar.
- Proverbs 30:5-6 (NKJV)

For I testify to everyone who hears the words of the prophecy of this book: If anyone adds to these things, God will add to him the plagues that are written in this book; and if anyone takes away from the words of the book of this prophecy, God shall take away his part from the Book of Life, from the holy city, and from the things that are written in this book. - Revelation 22:18-19 (NKJV)

Israel and the Jerusalem Restoration Prophecy (Part 1)

Zechariah chapter 8 focuses its prophecies on the Millennial Kingdom when Israel will be restored and renewed – enjoying peace and prosperity. The fasting Israel did in her past will finally turn to joyful feasting, and her relationship with the Lord will be restored (Zechariah 8:19).

"The LORD of hosts" is used eighteen times in Zechariah chapter 8, emphasizing the absolute certainty that God will fulfill His promises to restore Israel and His special city of Jerusalem. Even though the following promises are yet to be fulfilled in the Millennial Kingdom, Zechariah and the Jewish returnees were blessed and encouraged. Jewish people throughout history (even to today) yearn for these prophecies to be fulfilled.

Verse	Prophetic Promises from Zechariah 8
3	The LORD will return to Zion.
	The LORD will dwell in the midst of Jerusalem.
	Jerusalem will be called the City of Truth.
4	Old men and women of great age will sit in the streets of Jerusalem.
5	The streets of Jerusalem will be filled with playing children.
7-8	The LORD will save His people and bring them back to live in Jerusalem. They will be His people, and He will be their God.

Thus saith the LORD; I am returned unto Zion,
and will dwell in the midst of Jerusalem:
and Jerusalem shall be called a city of truth;
and the mountain of the LORD of hosts the holy mountain.
- Zechariah 8:3

Israel and the Jerusalem Restoration Prophecy (Part 2)

In the last two verses of Zechariah 8, the prophet Zechariah predicted that the Gentiles (non-Jews) would seek the Lord during the Millennial Kingdom. People from many nations will come to Jerusalem seeking the Lord because God will be there. Scripture tells us the Millennial Kingdom will be an incredible period of time. In Revelation 20:2-7, we learn that this period will last 1000 years.

Verse	Prophetic Promises from Zechariah 8
12	Israel's seed shall be prosperous.
	The vine shall give its fruit.
	The ground shall give her increase.
	The heavens shall give their dew.
	The LORD will cause the remnant of this people to possess all of the above.
13	The LORD will save Israel.
	Israel will be a blessing.
15	The LORD will do good to Jerusalem and Israel.
19	Israel's fasts will be joyful, glad, and cheerful feasts.
20-22	People from many cities will go to Jerusalem and pray before the LORD.
23	People from all nations will want to go with the Jewish people.
	People from the different nations will hear that God is with the Jewish people.

Thus saith the LORD of hosts: In those days it shall come to pass that ten men shall take hold out of all languages of the nations, even shall take hold of the skirt of him that is a Jew, saying, 'We will go with you: for we have heard that God is with you.'
– Zachariah 8:23

The One-Way-Only Prophecy

In the biblical account in 2 Samuel 6, we are told King David wanted to move the "Ark of God" to Jerusalem. He made the serious mistake of putting it on a "new cart." Moses had carefully recorded God's detailed instruction on how the Ark of God was to be made, moved, and handled (Exodus 25, Numbers 4, 1 Chronicles 15:15). The consequence for Uzzah's incorrect way of moving and handling the Ark of God proved fatal (2 Samuel 6:1-7).

God's command in both the Old and New Testaments is clear even back to Cain, Adam's son, who offered a sacrifice to God "his way." **In every case throughout the Bible, God's way cannot be compromised.** The same is true with the way back into fellowship with God. He created us and gives us the only way to eternal life with Him. We must admit the fact that we sin (miss the mark of God's required perfection) and are disqualified from entering His presence. However, if we accept Jesus' gift of paying for the punishment of our sins on the cross, His death and resurrection assure us He will forgive our sins and take us to heaven. Out of deep gratitude and trust in Jesus alone, we turn the control of our thoughts, desires, words, actions, and emotions to Him and prove our love by obeying His Word.

Rejecting or ignoring God's ways is always detrimental and deserves our utmost attention. With regards to eternity, trying to come to God "our way" is fatal. We are given this profound prophetic warning in both 2 Samuel 6 and by what Jesus stressed in John 14:6.

Jesus saith unto him, "I am the way, the truth, and the life: no man cometh unto the Father, but by me."
- John 14:6

Gospel Ordained Within Patriarchs' Names

The Gospel message was prophesied in a very unusual way within the Hebrew language. Only God could have planned and brought this to pass. It is found in the *meanings* of the *names* of the first ten generations, which covered a period of over 1,600 years.

> **Adam means "*man.*"**
> **Seth means "*appointed.*"**
> **Enosh means "*mortal.*"**
> **Kenan means "*sorrow.*"**
> **Mahalalel means "*the blessed God.*"**
> **Jared means "*shall come down.*"**
> **Enoch means "*teaching.*"**
> **Methuselah means "*his death shall bring.*"**
> **Lamech means "*the despairing.*"**
> **Noah means "*comfort (or rest).*"**

Putting it all together, we find that the very names of the first ten generations of mankind form the promise of our coming Savior. **"Man [is] appointed mortal sorrow; [but] the Blessed God shall come down, teaching that His death shall bring the despairing comfort (or rest)."**
Could this be a coincidence, or can we see that the Holy Spirit truly directed both history and the writing of every detail of Scripture?

...Who hath declared this from ancient time?
Who had told it from that time? Have not I the LORD?
And there is no God else beside me;
a just God and a Saviour; there is none beside me.
- Isaiah 45:21

Prophecies Fulfilled During Christ's Ministry

In his book, *Ancient Prophecies Revealed*, Dr. Ken Johnson
documents over forty prophecies that happened within Christ's three-
and-a-half-year ministry. The prophecies are very specific, some
of which were given many hundreds of years prior. *The statistical
probability of all of them happening in one individual is virtually
impossible.*

OT Prediction	Prophecy	NT Fulfillment
Malachi 3:1	Preceded by a messenger	Matthew 11:7-11
Psalm 110:4	Will be a priest	Hebrews 5:5-6
Isaiah 11:2	Anointed by the Holy Spirit	Matthew 3:16
Psalm 2:7	Declared "God's Son"	Matthew 3:16-17
Isaiah 9:1-2	Ministry starts in Galilee	Matthew 4:13-17
Isaiah 35:5-6; Isaiah 29:18	Will heal blind/deaf/lame/dumb	Matthew 11:5
Isaiah 8:14-17	Stumbling stone to Israel	1 Peter 2:8
Zechariah 9:9	Enter Jerusalem as a king	Matthew 21:5
Haggai 2:6-9; Malachi 3:1	Will come to the Temple before it is destroyed	Matthew 21:12-15
Zechariah 13:7	Disciples will fall away	Matthew 26:31-32
Psalm 41:9; 55:12-14	Betrayed by friend	Matthew 26:21-25
Zechariah 11:12	Sold for 30 pieces of silver	Matthew 26:15
Psalm 27:12; 35:11	Accused by false witnesses	Matthew 26:60
Psalm 35:19; 69:4	Hated without cause	John 15:25
Isaiah 53:3; Psalm 118:22-23	Rejected/ despised by His own	Matthew 21:42 John 1:11-12

Moses' Prophetic Outline of Israel's Future

Shortly before Moses' death (around 1400 B.C.), he spoke to the people of Israel and gave them a prophetic warning. It predicted what would happen to them over the next three thousand years – if they did not heed God's Word.

A careful reading of Deuteronomy 4:25-31 will reveal this following outline:

- When Israel and her descendants grew old "in the land" they were given by God, they would act corruptly and become idolatrous (v. 25).

- Israel would be forced out of the promised land (v. 26-27).

- The LORD **"will scatter you among the peoples, and you will be left few in number among the nations where the LORD will drive you"** (v. 27).

- While in other lands, the Israelites (Jewish people) would worship and serve other gods (v. 28).

- In their dispersion, the people would seek the LORD their God and would find Him if they would **"seek Him with all your heart and all your soul"** (v. 29).

- The Jewish people would be in distress (especially in the latter days) (v. 30).

- When in distress, they would turn to the LORD their God: **"He will not forsake you nor destroy you, nor forget the covenant of your Fathers which He swore to them"** (v. 31).

All of these prophecies have been fulfilled except for the last three, which are heading toward their final fulfillment.

Prophetic Warning from King David

King David's life gives us a prophetic peek into what our lives will be like when we choose to follow and not to follow God's biblical counsel. David's biography is found in 1 and 2 Samuel. Every time David *sought* the counsel of God, he was blessed. For example, when David heeded God's advice through Abigail (1 Samuel 25), he was kept from unnecessary bloodshed. When he waited for God to hand him the kingdom of Israel instead of grabbing it for himself (2 Samuel 5:1-12), David won the support and earned the respect of all the people. When David sought God's direction in his wars with the Philistines (2 Samuel 5:19-25), he was victorious.

On the other hand, each time David *ignored or rejected* God's counsel, he failed grievously. David sought no counsel in choosing a wife and controlling his desires for women (2 Samuel 11). As a result, his home life was full of heartaches and disasters – from jealousies, rape, and murder, to rebellious children (2 Samuel 13-18). His refusal to obey God by taking a census cost thousands of lives (2 Samuel 24).

David lived a prophetic picture of a life with and without God's counsel. Although he fully repented of his sins, David had to pay heartbreaking consequences, some of which we are warned of by his own writings in the book of Psalms.

Thy word have I hid in my heart,
that I might not sin against thee.
- Psalm 119:11

The Last Prophecy of Malachi

Malachi was the last of the Old Testament prophets. A hundred years had passed since the Jewish people had returned to Jerusalem after the Babylonian captivity. The Temple had been rebuilt, and there was a brief spiritual revival under Ezra and Nehemiah, but Israel fell into empty religious hypocrisy. The priests had become apathetic and sacrilegious. They set a terrible example, so corruption ran rampant. Believers in God married non-believers, marriage vows were ignored, and godly children were not being raised. God was not honored with tithes and offerings; injustice and corruption were everywhere. God's name was despised.

Malachi meticulously laid out God's complaints against the wayward people and warned them to turn from their sins. He also recorded God's promise of present blessings and the future hope of the coming Messiah. Malachi then prophesied about End Times and the great day of the LORD.

It is interesting that Malachi, whose name means "messenger," prophesied of two messengers. One would announce Christ at His First Coming (*to provide salvation*) and the other would announce Christ at His Second Coming (*to judge the earth*). After Malachi's prophecy, God was silent toward Israel for the next four hundred years. The first messenger, John the Baptist, came to announce the arrival of Jesus Christ. The second messenger is yet to come. Malachi's warnings are being fulfilled right on schedule and are worth both reading and hearing.

Behold, I will send you Elijah the prophet before the coming of the great and dreadful day of the LORD.
- Malachi 4:5

The Nineveh Prophecy

Nineveh was the capital of Assyria. The prophet Nahum predicted how Nineveh would be destroyed for its wickedness. This city had already been warned by the prophet Jonah over one hundred years earlier, at which time it repented and turned away from evil. Over the years, however, Nineveh went back to its evil ways. Its destruction was inevitable because a just God does not allow sin to go unpunished.

Nahum predicted the destruction of Nineveh by the Babylonians. Just as Nahum wrote, Nineveh was taken easily at night while the *guards were drunk* and the *city burned with fire.* The historian Diodorus of Sicily (30 B.C.) recorded that the Assyrian king gave his soldiers too much wine. Archaeological records show evidence of fire dating back to the destruction of the city in 612 B.C., after which *the city ceased to be important,* just as God's Word predicted.

"...He will make a complete end of its site....Like tangled thorns, and like those who are drunken with their drink, they are consumed as stubble completely withered....The LORD has issued a command concerning you: your name will no longer be perpetuated. I will cut off idol and image from the house of your gods. I will prepare your grave, for you are contemptible....There fire will consume you, the sword will cut you down; it will consume you as the locust does."
- Nahum 1:8, 10, 14; 3:15 (NASB)

God Knows Us Better Than We Know Ourselves

As fallen human beings, in rebellion against our Creator, we are constantly deceiving ourselves about our motivation and goodness. Only God can clearly see who we truly are and what we need. Our hearts (a biblical term for feelings, will, and intellect) *"are deceitful above all things and desperately wicked."* (Jeremiah 17:9). The rhetorical question at the end of the verse implies the answer – **God knows our thoughts, our true motivation, and the future outcomes of our choices.** This is why understanding this prophetic statement ("who can know our hearts?") and trusting the moral guidelines and warnings of the Bible are so critical.

God's Word is not a list of rules to keep us from enjoying life. It is guidance to keep us from deceiving and harming ourselves and others. It is because God knows the future that we must trust Him with our actions in the present.

**The heart is deceitful above all things,
and desperately wicked: who can know it?
- Jeremiah 17:9**

Jeremiah's Three Generation Prophecy

The prophet Isaiah predicted that the Babylonian Empire would be destroyed by the Medes and Persians more than three hundred years before it happened (Isaiah 13:17; 21:2,9). Jeremiah, however, added some interesting details about the Babylonian Empire that preceded Babylon's downfall. **Jeremiah predicted the Babylonian Empire would end after three generations.**

Nabopolasser defeated the Assyrian Empire as prophesied. He handed the kingdom over to his son *Nebuchadnezzar* who ruled for 45 years. Nebuchadnezzar's son, the *Evilmerodach,* ruled for twenty-three years. During Evilmerodach's last three years, Nebuchadnezzar's grandson, *Belshazzar,* co-ruled with his father. The Babylonian kingdom fell to the Medo-Persians in 537 B.C., after only three generations, just as Jeremiah predicted.

And now I have given all these lands into the hand of Nebuchadnezzar the king of Babylon...so all nations shall serve him and his son and his son's son, until the time of his land comes; and then many nations and great kings shall make him serve them. - Jeremiah 27:6, 7 (NKJV)

Zechariah's Six Promise Prophecy

An interesting prophecy is recorded in Zechariah 1:16-17. The prophecy came at the end of the seventy-year captivity of the Israelite people. They had been transported from Judah into Babylon and *were now finally returned* to their own land. **God had the young prophet Zechariah write the following six prophetic promises:**

1. God would return to Jerusalem with mercy. v. 16

2. God's temple would be rebuilt in Jerusalem. v. 16

3. Jerusalem's boundaries would be reestablished. v. 16

4. God would restore Judah's cities and make them prosper. v. 17

5. God would comfort it. v. 17

6. Although God had **to reject Israel (Hosea 1:9) and chasten her because of her sin, her election would stand secure.** God would again choose Jerusalem. v. 17

These promises were partially fulfilled in Zechariah's day. Over two thousand years later, a greater fulfillment still lies ahead. We know it will come to pass because God said it will when He comes to judge Israel's enemies at His Second Coming.

> **Therefore thus says the LORD: "I am returning to Jerusalem with mercy; My house shall be built in it," says the LORD of hosts, "And a surveyor's line shall be stretched out over Jerusalem." Again proclaim, saying, "Thus says the LORD of hosts: 'My cities shall again spread out through prosperity; the LORD will again comfort Zion, and will again choose Jerusalem.'"**
> **- Zechariah 1:16-17 (NKJV)**

OCTOBER

Be Anxious For Nothing

Philippians 4:6-7

Arlene Faith Kortright

Be an- xious for noth- ing

but in ev - ery thing by prayer and sup - pli -

ca - tion with thanks - giv - ing let your re -

quest be known to God and the

peace of God which sur -pass - es all un - der - stand - ing

will guard your hearts and minds through Je - sus

Christ Phil - ip - pi - ans fo - ur

six and sev - en

Lord, thank You for reminding me to come to You for help with everything and fully trust Your promise to take my worries, guard my mind and give me Your peace. Amen

Prophetic Promise of Justice

Peter warns us in 2 Peter of the false prophets and teachers that bring in damnable heresies, even denying that as believers we are purchased by Christ's death on the cross. Peter tells us these deceivers will speak evil of the truth (v. 2) and will use and abuse us (v. 3).

It may seem like evil goes unpunished and godliness unrewarded, but 2 Peter 2:4-6 reminds us that God overlooked neither in the past. He brought either horrific judgment or deliverance on angels, people, and/or entire cities. Peter goes on to recall specific incidents in history where God's justice on evil needed to be remembered: the *angels that sinned* (Genesis 6:1-8), *the cataclysmic worldwide Flood of Noah's day* (Genesis 6:9-9:17), and the *obliteration of Sodom and Gomorrah* (Genesis 19). Peter pointed out that God is faithful to His holy nature and will deal with both the wicked and the righteous with perfect justice.

We are reminded throughout Scripture that wickedness and evil will increase whenever God is ignored, rejected, or denied. We are not to lose heart. God is in *absolute control* (Isaiah 14:24) and *does not change* (Malachi 3:6). He will work all things out for the good of those who truly love Him (Romans 8:28). Since God was faithful in His promise of justice in the past, we can be assured that He can be trusted in the present and future as well.

The Lord knoweth how to deliver the godly out of temptations, and reserve the unjust unto the day of judgment to be punished.
- 2 Peter 2:

Israel's Agriculture Is Fulfilling Prophecy

Over fifty percent of Israel's saline soil is arid or semi-dry. Only twenty percent is fit for growing crops. In spite of this, Israel has almost tripled the land area used for farming since 1948, and production is almost twenty times greater than in 1948.

Israel is the world leader in agro-technologies and agricultural research. Nations all over the world use and benefit from her developments and discoveries. Cooperation between farmers, the agro-industry and technological research is encouraged. Israel's *technological successes* include computer-controlled drip irrigation, computerized early-warning systems for leaks, thermal imaging for crop water stress detection, biological pest control, extensive water reuse (eighty-six percent), and desalinization plants.

Israel has also generated *unique software* to help grow fruits and vegetables, raise poultry and dairy cows, manage vineyards, and make olive oil. *New strains of potatoes* that thrive in hot, dry climates and can be irrigated by saltwater have been developed, along with *new varieties* of tomatoes and other unique and unusual crops.

Algae harvesting has been advanced for use as fodder algae, dietary supplements, veterinary pharmaceuticals, cosmetics, bio-plastics and fertilizers. *Post-harvest technologies* include modified atmosphere packaging (using biodegradable materials), non-chemical hot water rinsing, and biocontrol against disease-causing agents.

**Seeing that Abraham shall surely become
a great and mighty nation, and all the nations
of the earth shall be blessed in him.
- Genesis 18:18**

A Lamentations Prophecy (Part 1)

For over forty years, the prophet Jeremiah warned about the coming destruction of Jerusalem and Solomon's beautiful Temple. **Jeremiah saw first-hand how Judah offended God's holiness with her open rebellion and rejection of Him. Because of this, he predicted God would have no choice but to judge His chosen people.** In the book of Jeremiah, we are told how this prophet was scorned for preaching doom and gloom. Lamentations describes the partial fulfillment of Jeremiah's predictions. It also completes the prophecies given by Moses about nine hundred years prior, in Leviticus 26:14-39 and Deuteronomy 28:15-68.

Lamentations describes the fall of Jerusalem and destruction of the Temple of Solomon in 586 B.C. These passages also foreshadow the fall of Jerusalem, the second Temple (Herod's) in 70 A.D., and ultimately the two thousand-year period after Christ's death into the Tribulation (still ahead). Both the Leviticus and Deuteronomy passages paint a horrific picture of rebellion against God and sin without restraint.

In God's divine purpose to bring Judah back to Himself, He used Nebuchadnezzar and the Babylonian army in the prophesied destruction of Jerusalem. Jeremiah was an eyewitness to this destruction and wrote Lamentations. The destruction was so critical that four Old Testament chapters recorded the facts of the event (2 Kings 25; 2 Chronicles 36:11-21; Jeremiah 39:1-12; Jeremiah 52).

...For the LORD hath afflicted her for the multitude of her transgressions: her children are gone into captivity before the enemy.
- Lamentations 1:5

A Lamentations Prophecy (Part 2)

Jeremiah wrote Lamentations when the destruction of Jerusalem was still fresh in his memory. As he witnessed the nation of Judah's judgment by the Babylonians, Jeremiah reacted in compassion and deep sorrow toward the suffering and stubborn people. In Lamentations, he describes his anguish over the judgment of God for their unrepentant sins.

Jeremiah's tears foreshadowed those of Jesus, who would weep over the sins of this same city almost six hundred years later. The Jewish people rebelled against God once again, only this time they rejected *"God among us"* (Jesus Christ). **Even though Christ will be both Judge and Executioner, like Jeremiah, it broke His heart to foresee both the coming destruction of Jerusalem in 70 A.D. and of the Tribulation of the Last Days.**

Lamentations is one of the Old Testament books read in the Synagogue on special occasions. It is read on the Ninth of Av to commemorate the day of Jerusalem's destruction by Nebuchadnezzar. This is also the exact day of the destruction of the second Temple by Herod. Since God did not hesitate to judge His beloved people (Deuteronomy 32), what will He do to all the other nations in the world that reject Him?

In all their affliction, He [God] was afflicted....
- Isaiah 63:9

Israel Was Prophesied to Buy Its Land Back

The Jews started to return to their homeland in the early 1900s. **They paid exorbitant prices for a desolate wasteland filled with malaria-infested swamps.** The Arabs who lived there sold them land to which they often did not have clear titles to – so the Jews had to pay the full price a *second* time.

In 1901, the Jewish National Fund (JNF) was established at the Fifth Zionist Congress in Basel, Switzerland. Its single purpose was to acquire and develop land for the Jewish people. Between World War 1 and World War 2, the Jewish National Fund distributed about one million collection boxes to Jewish homes throughout the world. The Jewish National Fund also sold stamps from 1902 to the late 1940s to raise additional money. In 1903, the Jewish National Fund bought fifty acres about twenty-five miles north of Tel Aviv. By 1927, they had purchased over fifty thousand acres of land, and by May 14, 1948, the Jewish National Fund had acquired 231,290 acres of land. The Jews started living on the land only *after* it was legally purchased, just as Jeremiah prophesied.

And fields shall be <u>bought</u> in this land, whereof ye say, it is desolate without man or beast; it is given into the hand of the Chaldeans. Men shall <u>buy</u> fields for money, and subscribe evidences, and seal them, and take witnesses in the land of Benjamin, and in the places about Jerusalem, and in the cities of Judah, and in the cities of the mountains, and in the cities of the valley, and in the cities of the south: for I will cause their captivity to return," saith the LORD.
- Jeremiah 32:43-44

Egypt in Prophecy

Over 2,600 years ago, Ezekiel proclaimed that Egypt would no longer rule the nations. For many centuries, she had dominated many nations. At times even Judah was under her rule. With this prophecy, Egypt's status, however, was about to change forever. In about 605 B.C., the Babylonians defeated both the Egyptian and Assyrian armies at Carchemish (which is near the border of Turkey and Syria).

History confirms what Ezekiel prophesied. Egypt has been ruled by other nations since that battle. The last Egyptian Pharaoh was King Nectanebo II, who was defeated by the Persians in 343 B.C. Later, Egypt fell to the Greeks, the Romans, the Ottomans, and finally the British. It took almost 2,300 years for Egypt to regain her sovereignty, but she never regained her prominence in world leadership, just as Ezekiel had predicted.

And I will bring again the captivity of Egypt, and will cause them to return into the land of Pathros, into the land of their habitation; and they shall be there a base kingdom. It shall be the basest of the kingdoms; neither shall it exalt itself any more above the nations: for I will diminish them, that they shall no more rule over the nations.
- Ezekiel 29:14-15

Christ in the Book of Numbers (Part 1)

A careful study of Scripture will reveal symbols, pictures, and patterns of Jesus Christ in *every* Old Testament book. The book of Numbers, written almost fifteen hundred years before Christ was even born, contains many such prophetic types. Jesus can be found in the book of Numbers as:

- The **Creator of law, order, and justice,** who can be seen in the *census, the ordering* of the tribes, and *the laws* given to the Israelites (throughout Numbers).

- The **Standard (banner, flag)** that Christ's followers are to be known and live by as seen in *the standards of each tribe* which had to be put up by their campsite (Numbers 1:52).

- Our **Living Sacrifice**, who can be seen in the *Passover* as the Israelites were reminded of God passing over them and sparing the lives of their firstborn children and cattle (Numbers 9:1-5). This is a beautiful example of God passing over our condemnation for our sins when we accept Christ as our Savior.

- Our **Shepherd,** who can be seen in the *cloud by day and fire by night* (Numbers 9:15-23) as the Israelites traveled. They were both protected and guided by "Christ the light."

- The symbol of **One who calls us** to Himself as seen in the *silver trumpets,* which were used to call the congregation (Numbers 10:1-10) and lead them.

Let them praise the name of the LORD: for his name alone is excellent; his glory is above the earth and heaven.
– Psalm 148:13

Christ in the Book of Numbers (Part 2)

Jesus Christ can be seen in the book of Numbers as:

- The **Bread of Life** (John 6:32-35, 48-51) in the *manna* coming down from heaven that would be rejected by the people (Numbers 11).

- Our **Mediator,** who covers our sins with His sacrifice and pleads our case before God as *Moses mediated* for the Israelites in the wilderness and their lives were spared (Numbers 14).

- Our **Resurrected Savior,** who went from death on the cross to life. He can be seen in *Aaron's rod, a dead stick that budded*, blossomed, and yielded fruit before the other rods. God authenticates Himself. He alone is God (Numbers 17).

- **Our Perfect Redeemer,** who can be seen in the symbol of the *red heifer* which had to be perfect in order to qualify for the sacrifice. Its ashes were used in the purification of the people (Numbers 19), as Christ's death on the cross purifies those who believe on Him.

- Our **Living Water** (John 4:10-14) and our **Rock**. We can see this in the symbol of the *rock* which Moses struck to bring the *water* that sustained the Israelites (Numbers 20:1-11). Christ is our unmoveable, unchanging rock – our "living water."

- Our only **Way, Truth, and Life**. Only Christ, who was *lifted up on the cross*, can save us, just as only those who looked up to the bronze serpent on the pole lived (Numbers 21:9).

In the beginning was the Word, and the Word was with God, and the Word was God.
– John 1:1

The Temple Stones Prophecy

The context of Matthew 24:2 is Jesus' disciples wanting to show Him the magnificence of the Temple buildings. When Jesus' disciples asked Him *when* the End Times would happen, Christ gave a specific list of End Times events (Matthew 24:3-51). These End Times events actually started shortly after Christ's death. **A little over thirty-five years after Jesus predicted the destruction of the Temple, the "Temple stones" prophecy came to pass.**

The Jewish people rebelled not only against God, but also against the Roman authority, so a vast Roman army was sent to put down the rebellion at Jerusalem in 70 A.D. Due to this siege, food supplies ran so low, that people even resorted to cannibalism. The rebellious people turned on each other instead of uniting against their common enemy. Nearly one-and-a-half million people lost their lives. Jerusalem was set on fire, and the gold from the Temple melted into the rocks and crevices. In order to recover the lost gold, scavengers threw down every stone of the Temple. Christ's *exact words* were fulfilled – not one stone was left upon another!

And Jesus said unto them, See ye not all these things? Verily I say unto you, There shall not be left here one stone upon another, that shall not be thrown down.
– Matthew 24:2

Prophecies with More Than One Fulfillment

Prophecy is often meant for more than one specific time in history. When prophecy was given and fulfilled within a short time span, God's Word proved its authenticity to people living at the time. When it has a future fulfillment, it also assures people living in the future that Scripture does not change. Since prophecies were fulfilled in the past, it is certain they will be fulfilled in the future.

In 2 Samuel 7:10-16, we see an example of such prophecies. They contain both present and future implications. They were given and fulfilled in King David's lifetime and were also meant to be fulfilled by Christ during His Millennial Reign.

1. Israel was given land; a kingdom was established and there was peace (temporarily). v. 10

   Christ will reign from Jerusalem in Israel in perfect peace.

2. David was given temporary peace from his enemies. v. 10

   Christ will bring in eternal peace from enemies.

3. Solomon built the first Temple. v. 13

   Christ is building us as His Temple and will build the final Millennial Temple.

4. David had a Father/son relationship with God. v. 14

   Christ has a perfect Father/Son relationship with God.

5. David was given a temporary house, kingdom, and throne. v. 16
   Christ has an eternal house, kingdom, and throne.

**Thy word is true from the beginning....
- Psalm 119:160**

The Jeremiah 29:11 Prophecy

Judgment fell upon Israel in 586 B.C. It seemed like God's plans for Israel were finished, yet He gave a commonly repeated prophetic promise to His people through Jeremiah 29:11. The Hebrew word for "thoughts" is *makhashabah*. This word is translated as "intention or plan, a curious work." It actually describes a skillful, careful, intricate weaving. In other words, God had a specifically designed plan for Israel.

Throughout the Bible, God gives us glimpses of how His plans for those who love Him are far greater than they could possibly imagine. We see this truth as God made *Abraham* the father of the Jewish nation. God chose *Esther* to save her people from extinction and made *David*, a mere shepherd boy, into the king through whom the Messiah would come. In the New Testament, we see God using *Paul* to evangelize the Gentiles and *John* to reveal God's specific plan for the latter days.

Not only can we see how God's prophetic plan for Israel is unfolding before our eyes today, but God's plan also works within the lives of individuals. The Jeremiah 29:11 prophecy gives us hope that *our future in Christ* is also part of an intricately woven plan. We may not fully understand it, but we can be certain it will be revealed in the future. May we submit to the Master Weaver as He works this prophecy out in our lives.

For I know the thoughts that I think toward you, says the LORD, thoughts of peace and not of evil, to give you a future and a hope.
- Jeremiah 29:11 (NKJV)

Israel's Desert Prophecy

A prophecy in Isaiah 35 tells us that Israel's desert shall "blossom as a rose." The Negev Desert covers over one-half of Israel. Where the rest of the world is battling the expansion of its deserts, Israel's Negev Desert is shrinking. Israel is implementing her agricultural expertise and turning the desert sand into green fields by irrigation, using the Negev's vast underground supply of brackish (slightly salty) water. **Consider the following evidences of a blossoming desert:**

- Desert agriculture is one of Israel's greatest successes.
- Drip irrigation technologies allow desert crops to grow with extreme limits of water.
- Cherry tomatoes grown in the Negev are two to three times sweeter due to monitored watering and unique mineral quality. Tomato yields are also three to four times greater than anywhere else.
- Water conservation techniques save most of the desert's sparse rainfall.
- Potatoes have been developed to grow in the desert climate with brackish water.
- In Israel's Judean desert, farmers use minerals found in the Dead Sea, sand, and soil. As a result, onions are especially strong tasting, dates are outstanding, and Israeli basil is considered the world's best.
- Israel has over ten thousand brackish water specialists who are training agronomists and farmers in fifty-four countries.
- The United Nations declared Israel the most agriculturally efficient land in the world.

Although complete fulfillment of this prophecy will be reached in the Millennial Kingdom, God is not only *giving us a foretaste* of what is to come, but *building our faith* in His Word.

The wilderness and the solitary place shall be glad for them; and the desert shall rejoice, and blossom as the rose.
- Isaiah 35:1

Preparing for Christ's Return (Part 1)

In order to prepare ourselves for Christ's return, the following verses help us stay focused. Memorizing these verses keeps us looking up with joy and a fervent desire to redeem the time!

<u>Submit to God and direct our focus on Him.</u>

- **Therefore submit to God. Resist the devil and he will flee from you.** *- James 4:7 (NKJV)*

- **For it is God who works in you both to will and to do for His good pleasure.** *- Philippians 2:13 (NKJV)*

- **But I discipline my body and bring it into subjection, lest, when I have preached to others, I myself should become disqualified.** *- 1 Corinthians 9:27 (NKJV)*

<u>Give God our attitude, mind, and mouth.</u>

- **Let nothing be done through selfish ambition or conceit, but in lowliness of mind let each esteem others better than himself.** *- Philippians 2:3 (NKJV)*

- **Set your mind on things above, not on things on the earth. For you died, and your life is hidden with Christ in God.** *- Colossians 3:2-3 (NKJV)*

- **Do not let any unwholesome talk come out of your mouths, but only what is helpful in building others up according to their needs, that it may benefit those who listen.** *- Ephesians 4:29 (NIV)*

Preparing for Christ's Return (Part 2)

Prepare, trust and encourage.

- But sanctify the Lord God in your hearts, and always be ready to give a defense to everyone who asks you a reason for the hope that is in you, with meekness and fear. - *1 Peter 3:15 (NKJV)*

- "My grace is sufficient for you, for My strength is made perfect in weakness"...Therefore I take pleasure in infirmities, in reproaches, in needs, in persecutions, in distresses, for Christ's sake. For when I am weak, then I am strong. - *2 Corinthians 12:9a,10*

- And let us consider one another in order to stir up love and good works, not forsaking the assembling of ourselves together, as is the manner of some, but exhorting one another, and so much the more as you see the Day approaching. - *Hebrews 10:24-25 (NKJV)*

Persevere; stay joyful, thankful, prayerful, alert, and look up!

- Be joyful always; pray continually; give thanks in all circumstances, for this is God's will for you in Christ Jesus. - *1 Thessalonians 5:16-18 (NIV)*

- Therefore, preparing your minds for action, and being sober-minded, set your hope fully on the grace that will be brought to you at the revelation of Jesus Christ. - *1 Peter 1:13 (ESV)*

- Looking for the blessed hope and glorious appearing of our great God and Savior Jesus Christ, who gave Himself for us, that He might redeem us from every lawless deed and purify for Himself His own special people, zealous for good works. - *Titus 2:13-14 (NKJV)*

Patterns in Psalm 119

The late scientist and theologian Dr. Henry M. Morris stated that *"all of God's physical creation is filled with evidence of design and order, capable of being described and analyzed mathematically."* **It should not surprise us, then, that God's written revelation also shows evidences of design, order, and structure.** Consider the uniqueness of Psalm 119:

1. It is the longest chapter in the Bible with its 176 verses; almost every verse points to the importance of God's Word.

2. Each of the twenty-two stanzas is headed by a consecutive letter of the twenty-two letter Hebrew alphabet.

3. Each stanza has eight lines, and each line within the twenty-two stanzas starts with the same Hebrew letter.

4. Psalm 119 uses eight different words to describe God's Word:
   Torah = Law
   Edah = Testimony
   Dabar = Word
   Chuggah = Statute
   Imrah = Word
   Mishpat = Judgment
   Piqqu = Precept
   Mitzvah = Commandment

5. The total number of verses in Psalm 119 is divisible by eight, and the total number of references to the Bible in this psalm is 2x88.

Perhaps this incredible pattern is the result of an early poetic genius, but it is more likely inspired by God. From the beginning, God's design, order, and structure were planned to authenticate His Word!

Forever, O LORD, thy word is settled in heaven.
- Psalm 119:89

Israel's United, Then Divided, Prophecies

Israel was united as a nation under King David. David was succeeded by his son Solomon. During Solomon's reign, the prophet Ahijah predicted the united kingdom of Israel would break into two because of Israel's unfaithfulness to God. **After Solomon's son Rehoboam became king, the northern part of Israel broke away and formed a new kingdom.** That kingdom retained the name Israel and was made up of ten of the twelve tribes. Isaiah prophesied this Northern Kingdom (*sometimes referred to as Ephraim or Israel*) would come to an end. Around 722 B.C., this prophecy came to pass with the Northern Kingdom's defeat by the Assyrians.

Isaiah also prophesied about the destruction of the remaining two tribes of the Southern Kingdom (*which was referred to as Judah*). They also turned from God and were warned of their coming destruction. This destruction came in two stages. First, they were taken captive by Babylon in 586 B.C., and both Jerusalem and the Temple were destroyed. After the predicted seventy years of Babylonian captivity, some of the Jewish people returned from exile, helped rebuild Jerusalem and the Temple, but quickly fell into apostasy. The second stage of total destruction came by the Romans after many warnings from the prophets. In 135 A.D., Jerusalem and the rebuilt Temple were totally destroyed, and the Jewish people were scattered to the ends of the earth. Scripture prophesied, however, that the Jews would be regathered to Israel in the End Times as one nation, not two. This was fulfilled in 1948, as predicted (Hosea 1:11; Ezekiel 37:18,19,22).

> **...[W]ithin threescore and five years shall Ephraim be broken, that it be not a people.**
> **- Isaiah 7:8**

> **Then shall the children of Judah and the children of Israel be gathered together, and appoint themselves one head...**
> **- Hosea 1:11**

A Key Prophetic Chapter (Part 1)

God's covenant promise to Israel's King David makes 2 Samuel 7 one of the most important prophetic chapters in the Bible. The Gospel rests on this promise God made to David. **God would send a special "King" through David's lineage who would reign forever.** This prophecy could only be fulfilled in Jesus Christ.

In addition to the many references to 2 Samuel 7 in the Old Testament, the New Testament opens with Christ as that special *"King"* from David's lineage who would reign forever. The angel Gabriel gave this prophecy to Mary in Luke 1:30-32. Peter refers to it at Pentecost in Acts 2:29-30, and Paul affirms it in Romans 1:1-3. Christ Himself declares to be the fulfillment of this prophecy in Revelation 22:16 when He says, *"I am the root, the offspring of David, the bright and morning star."*

2 Samuel 7 also has other extraordinary prophetic promises to King David. David was told God appointed Israel to a permanent place forever. History shows us the people were temporarily removed for their disobedience, but the Bible says the land of Israel was appointed to them forever.

"Moreover I will appoint a place for My people Israel, and will plant them, that they may dwell in a place of their own and move no more; nor shall the sons of wickedness oppress them anymore, as previously....And your house and your kingdom shall be established forever before you. Your throne shall be established forever."
- 2 Samuel 7:10, 16 (NKJV)

A Key Prophetic Chapter (Part 2)

Throughout history, Israel has continually been oppressed. The prophets told us this would be a consequence for refusing to obey God. **But Israel's oppression will come to an end.** God promised this, and God cannot lie (Titus 1:2, Hebrews 6:18). David was told not only that Israel would dwell in a place of their own, but that the sons of wickedness or people who try to destroy them will never oppress them again in the future. This prophecy remains unfulfilled. God's prophetic promise in 2 Samuel 7 also states the Davidic house (lineage), kingdom, and throne would be established forever. This will only be possible when Christ returns to reign.

Every one of the over one hundred different prophecies concerning Christ's *First Coming* came to pass. Isn't it both wise and logical to believe every prophecy concerning the *Second Coming* will also be fulfilled?

In hope of eternal life, which God, that cannot lie, promised before the world began;...
- Titus 1:2

Revelation Is God's Last Words on Our Future

Every one of the Bible's sixty-six books is unique and demonstrates "Divine design" in its perfect accuracy, order, and purpose. **The prophetic book of Revelation is no exception; it is unique in the following ways:**

- Its name in Greek, "apokalypsis," means disclosure, an unveiling or revealing of something.

- It is the final book in the Bible and was written by the last living disciple.

- It offers a blessing to all who **read** (*know accurately, acknowledge*) it, **hear** (*give audience, understand*) the prophecy, and **keep** (*guard, keep the eye upon, watch*) those things written in it. *Revelation 1:3*

- It pulls all the Old and New Testament prophecies together. (*Psalm 119:160*)

- It is a fulfillment of God's promise that the Holy Spirit would show the things to come. *John 16:13*

- It warns of severe consequences to anyone who would add or subtract from the Bible. *Revelation 22:18-19*

- Its purpose is to bless readers and unveil the future to them.

- It records the restoring of all things to God's perfect creation.

The Revelation of Jesus Christ, which God gave unto him, to show unto his servants things which must shortly come to pass....
- Revelation 1:1

Biblical Prediction of Increased Evil (Part 1)

In 2 Timothy 3, Paul warns Timothy of the perilous times in the last days. One of the warnings Paul gives Timothy is that there will be a tremendous increase of evil men and imposters. The Greek word translated "evil" in this text is *poneros*. It refers to people who are hurtful in their effect and influence. It carries the implication of morally obscene, vulgar, malicious, and wicked, causing pain and trouble to Christian faith or steadfastness. The Greek word translated "imposters" is *goes* and is linked to wizards or the occult.

Scripturally and historically, the church has always acknowledged the reality of Satan's existence. However, in recent generations, liberal theologians have ridiculed this belief. Satan has used this shift in thinking to gain acceptance for the perversions he promotes. As a result, Satanism is growing globally at a feverish pace.

The Bible declares:

For rebellion is as the sin of witchcraft....
- 1 Samuel 15:23.

It is obvious that we are living in an age that is saturated with the spirit of rebellion. This was also predicted by Christ (Matthew 24:7, Mark 13:8, Luke 21:10). It logically follows that rebellion is a natural breeding ground for allegiance to Satan.

But evil men and imposters will grow
worse and worse, deceiving and being deceived.
- 2 Timothy 3:13 (NKJV)

Biblical Prediction of Increased Evil (Part 2)

There is verification for the truth of 2 Timothy 3:13 that states **there will be a continual worsening of evil and deception as we head toward the End Times.** If we pay attention, it can readily be seen in the compromise and increase of evil in the following areas:

- Obscene books and magazine articles and illustrations
- Ungodly internet websites and social media conversations
- Classroom behavior and education – elementary through college
- Vulgarity on radio, television, and in movies
- Increased and accepted irreverent use of the word "God" and "Jesus Christ"
- Compromises on doctrinal issues within many churches
- Vulgarity in song lyrics and entertainment
- Bible versions that have been added to or subtracted from
- Redefinition of terms meant to confuse and deceive
- Organizations and special interest groups promoting immorality, violence, and rebellion
- Political corruption
- Vulgar fashions, consumer goods, and advertisements
- Occult practices
- Violent toys and games

As we see evil growing on a worldwide scale, we find that God encourages His children in the midst of it through the writings of Paul to Timothy. We are told that as believers in Christ we should *remain steadfast* in the *things we have learned and are assured of in Holy Scripture.* We are not to lose hope.

But evil men and imposters will grow worse...but you must continue in the things you have learned and been assured of....[Y]ou have known the Holy Scriptures, which are able to make you wise for salvation through faith which is in Jesus Christ. All Scripture... is profitable...that the man of God may be complete, thoroughly equipped for every good work.
- 2 Timothy 3:13-17 (NKJV)

Naomi, a Type of Israel

The Old Testament book of *Ruth* is full of prophecies that find their fulfillment in the New Testament and on into the future. Naomi is an example of a prophetic type of Israel. **Just as Naomi extended her love to her Gentile daughter-in-law, Ruth, God extended His love to the Gentiles, with the intent of using Gentile believers to bring the Jewish believers back to Himself.** The following additional comparisons are striking:

Naomi was joined to Elimelech, whose name means "My God is King," in a covenant of marriage.	Israel was in a covenant of marriage to God, her King.
Naomi found herself with no husband, living in exile from her homeland.	Israel found herself living in exile from her homeland for almost 2,000 years.
Naomi's pain and sorrow drove her back to her homeland.	Israel's pain and sorrow, especially after World War II, drove her back to her homeland.
Ruth represents the Gentile (non-Jewish) nations. She came to know God through the Jewish woman Naomi.	The Gentile "Church" (true believers in Christ) came to know Jesus through the Jews (Israel).
Ruth became Naomi's adopted daughter.	The Church became God's adopted children.
Ruth's baby brought blessings to Naomi.	The Church (those who bless Israel as God commanded in Genesis 12:2-3) brought blessings to the Jews.
Ruth was grateful to Naomi for helping her to be redeemed through Boaz.	The Church is grateful to Israel for her redemption through Jesus Christ.

Ancient Names and Locations of Israel's Cities Revived

Today we associate the cities of Israel with their biblical names and locations. Archaeological discoveries have confirmed this more than 2,500 year-old prophecy. It is amazing how this prophecy was fulfilled in just the last hundred years – after thousands of years of foreign occupation.

In 70 A.D., Jerusalem was destroyed. The **Romans** took control, reassigning cities with Roman names. When the **Muslims** seized control, they renamed many cities with Muslim or Arabic names. The **Crusaders** came and stayed in the land for two hundred years, followed by the **Byzantines** and **Turks,** who lost the land to the **British Empire**. The British designated the land as belonging to the Jews.

God promised the Jewish people throughout Scripture that in the End Times they would be regathered into the land He had promised Abraham. **God said the cities would be named and settled according to their "former estates" or old biblical names and locations.** A visit to Israel today will show the tourist original names and locations of ancient cities, just like the Bible prophesied.

And I will multiply upon you man and beast; and they shall increase and bring fruit: and I will settle you after your old estates, and will do better unto you than at your beginnings: and ye shall know that I am the LORD.
- Ezekiel 36:11

...Thou shalt be inhabited; and to the cities of Judah, Ye shall be built, and I will raise the decayed places thereof.
- Isaiah 44:26

A Hope That Changes Us

Paul wrote the book of Colossians to the Christians at Colosse. He told the people he had heard of their faith in Jesus Christ and their love for all the saints. In this passage, Paul mentions the reason these Christians had such faith in Christ and love for others. They had hope in what was laid up for them in heaven.

The Greek word for "hope" does not mean a wishful thought. It means a "confident expectation." **The people had a joyful and confident expectation of eternal salvation.** They knew they would go to be with Christ in heaven. This hope changed their lives. Their strong faith in Christ and love for each other was evident!

We should ask ourselves, *"Is our hope of heaven so certain that it motivates us to live an obvious and observable life of faith in Christ and love for others?"*

**Since we heard of your faith in Christ Jesus
and of your love for all the saints; because of the hope
which is laid up for you in heaven...
- Colossians 1:4-5a (NKJV)**

Worldwide Impact Predicted

About 2,700 years ago, the prophets Micah and Isaiah predicted the Messiah would be known throughout the world and would be a light to all. About seven hundred years after these prophecies, Jesus Christ was born in Israel. He began His ministry around the age of thirty and taught for about three years. **All of the Old Testament prophecies concerning His life on Earth were fulfilled.** The New Testament was written after Christ died, but contains Christ's own words predicting that He would be known worldwide.

> **...[Y]e shall be witnesses unto me both in Jerusalem, and in all Judea, and in Samaria, and unto the uttermost part of the earth. - Acts 1:8**

Of all the religious leaders of all faiths throughout history, Jesus is the *only one* who not only predicted, but also fulfilled and continues to fulfill this prophecy through His followers. Christ has had the most widespread impact of any human being in history. His teachings (i.e. the Bible) are the most verifiable, sold, circulated, and written about on Earth. This in itself should warrant our attention.

> **...[F]or now shall he be great unto the ends of the earth. - Micah 5:4**

> **...I will also give thee for a light to the Gentiles, that thou mayest be my salvation unto the end of the earth. - Isaiah 49:6**

Isaac: A Prophetic Type of Jesus

The Bible includes an interesting prophetic type in the *father-son relationship* of Abraham and Isaac that points to God the Father and Jesus Christ.

Consider the following:

• Abraham offered his beloved son Isaac.	• God so loved the world He gave His only begotten Son.
• Abraham brought Isaac to the place of sacrifice on a donkey.	• Jesus rode to Jerusalem on a donkey, just before His crucifixion.
• Abraham had Isaac carry the wood he was to be sacrificed on.	• Jesus carried the cross on which He would be crucified (sacrificed).
• Isaac willingly submitted to Abraham.	• Jesus willingly submitted to His Father's will.
• Isaac was bound to the wood.	• Jesus was bound to a wooden cross.
• Abraham told his servants that he and Isaac would return.	• Jesus told His disciples He would return.
• A ram took Isaac's place.	• Jesus took our place.

The entire Bible is about Jesus Christ. The Old Testament accurately predicts future New Testament events which the life of Jesus fulfills. **By studying the Old Testament, we see the fulfillment in the New, often hundreds and even thousands of years later.** The perfect accuracy rate of fulfilled biblical prophecy proves the authenticity of Scripture and that it was God inspired.

And so we have the prophetic word confirmed, which you do well to heed as a light that shines in a dark place, until the day dawns and the morning star rises in your hearts.
- 2 Peter 1:19 (NKJV)

Solomon's Prophecy (Part 1)

Over 930 years before Christ was born, King Solomon wrote a very thought-provoking passage in his book of Ecclesiastes. Solomon stated, *"There is nothing new under the sun."* This is hard to believe in light of our present-day technologies. There are a few facts, however, we must consider.

No civilization in history has failed to deteriorate, given enough time. First, we know that **conquering people destroy the cities and cultures of those they attack,** so we do not know all the knowledge that was lost. A perfect example would be the destruction of the over 2,000-year-old library at Alexandria, Egypt, which held over a million books (in scroll form). A more recent example is the murder of tens of millions of educated people in the "Killing Fields" of Cambodia in the 1970s.

Second, **natural disasters, starting with the worldwide Flood and continuing to this day, have destroyed technology, records, and cultures.** Earthquakes, mudslides, volcanoes, fires, etc. have caused massive destruction. We do not know all that was lost in Noah's Flood, Sodom and Gomorrah, Pompey, or other ancient civilizations. Thus, it is entirely possible that significant knowledge of the past has been lost and the principles of modern science were known to people long ago.

That which has been is what will be, that which is done is what will be done, and there is nothing new under the sun. Is there anything of which it may be said, "See, this is new"? It has already been in ancient times before us. There is no remembrance of former things, nor will there be any remembrance of things that are to come by those who will come after.
- Ecclesiastes 1:9-11 (NKJV)

Solomon's Prophecy (Part 2)

Specific examples of the *truth* of King Solomon's prediction are listed below. These are just a few of many examples of "modern technology" which are much older than commonly believed:

- In the Minoan Palace site at Phaistos on Crete, a clay disk was discovered with a series of impressed symbols produced by using hardened clay "type sets" fifteen hundred years before the Gutenberg press of 1440.
- Brain surgery was performed in Peru well over one thousand years ago. Paper manufacturing was started twenty-five hundred years ago in China, and a Chinese seismometer (detecting earthquakes) has also been discovered dating back nineteen hundred years.
- In Egypt, iron tools were used thirty-five hundred years ago to build pyramids, and sophisticated technologies were developed for embalming.
- Ancients of over four thousand years ago were using a unique superglue to adhere stone spearheads to wooden shafts.
- Pure aluminum was found in an ancient tomb dated from the Jin Dynasty. Yet pure aluminum can only be obtained using a complex chemical or electromagentic processing only recently "discovered." Since the Chinese are one of the earliest civilizations, dating back to the time of Noah, this find could conceivably have been passed down from before the Flood of Noah over five thousand years ago.
- Over two thousand years ago, people in the Middle East were producing and using electric batteries.

Solomon's prophecy about the future "discoveries" certainly gives us something to think about.

**Is there anything of which it may be said, "See, this is new"?
- Ecclesiasties 1:10 (NKJV)**

Prophecies of Jeremiah 31

Jeremiah 31 is a major prophetic passage which describes **God's future blessings to the Jewish remnant who survives the Tribulation.** The following are very specific promises which God gave to His people in Jeremiah 31 (NKJV). These predictions are yet to be fulfilled and will be in the future.

V. 1 - "I will be the God of all the families of Israel, and they shall be My people."

V. 4 - "Again I will build you, and you shall be rebuilt…."

V. 10 - "Hear the word of the LORD, O nations….He who scattered Israel will gather him, and keep him as a shepherd does his flock."

V. 12 - "And they shall sorrow no more at all."

V. 14 - "And My people shall be satisfied with My goodness," says the Lord.

V. 19, 20 - "Surely, after my turning, I (Jewish people) repented…. I was ashamed, yes, even humiliated…I will surely have mercy on him", says the LORD.

V. 31 - "Behold, the days are coming, says the LORD, when I will make a new covenant with the house of Israel and with the house of Judah."

V. 33 - "But this is the covenant that I will make with the house of Israel after those days, says the LORD: I will put My law in their minds, and write it on their hearts; and I will be their God, and they shall be My people."

V. 38, 40 - "Behold, the days are coming", says the LORD, "that the city shall be built for the LORD….It shall not be plucked up or thrown down anymore forever."

God's Word on Hell (Part 1)

There is a lot of confusion about hell. Is hell real? Is it eternal? Who will go there? What is it like? How can hell be avoided? Since Christ created hell for Satan and his angels (Matthew 25:41), He knows more and spoke more about hell than anyone in Scripture. The Bible alone can be trusted with the truth. **God wants us to know about hell so we can avoid it.**

1. Christ created hell (*John 1:1-3*). He spoke about it throughout Scripture. Hell is real.
2. Christ warns us about hell and tells us to fear it. *Luke 12:5, Matthew 10:28*
3. Hell was prepared for Satan and his angels. *Matthew 25:41*
4. Christ has the keys of hell and death. *Revelation 1:18*
5. Hell is for:
   a. the wicked and all nations that forget God. *Psalm 9:17*
   b. those who do not bring forth good fruit. *Luke 3:8-9; John 15:1-6*
   c. the Devil and his angels. *Matthew 25:41*
   d. all who worship the beast and take his mark. *Revelation 14:11*
   e. all who reject and disobey God and His Word. *John 12:48; 2 Thessalonians 1:8*
6. Hell is everlasting punishment. *Matthew 25:46; 2 Thessalonians 1:9*
7. Hell is separation from the LORD and the glory of His power. *2 Thessalonians 1:8-9*

**And fear not them that which kill the body,
but are not able to kill the soul: but rather fear him
which is able to destroy both soul and body in hell.
– Matthew 10:28**

God's Word on Hell (Part 2)

Denying hell does not mean it does not exist. God warns us about it. He does not want anyone to go to hell. The choice is ours to accept Him and spend eternity with Him in heaven or reject Him and spend eternity without Him in hell. The following are some additional specific truths in Scripture about hell:

8. Hell is <u>permanent</u>. No one can leave. *Luke 16:19-31*
9. Hell is <u>eternal</u>. *Matt. 25:41-46; 2 Thess. 1:8-9; Jude 7; Mark 9:43-48; Rev. 14:11*
10. Hell is <u>certain</u> for those who reject God and Jesus Christ. *2 Thess. 1:8-9*
11. <u>Only God has the power</u> to cast someone into hell. *Luke 12:5*
12. God testifies that <u>both soul and body go</u> to hell. *Matt. 10:28*
13. Hell is <u>marked by fire</u>. *Jude 7; Rev. 14:10; Rev. 19:19-20; Matt. 13:42*
14. God committed <u>all judgment for sending</u> one to heaven or hell to His Son. *John 5:22; 2 Tim. 4:1*
15. There are <u>degrees</u> of hell. *Matt. 10:14-15; 11:21-24; Mark 12:38-40*
16. <u>No one</u> will be able to <u>call hell unfair</u> or <u>have an excuse</u> for not knowing God. *Rom. 1:20; Matt. 12:36-37*
17. Heaven and hell are our <u>only two choices</u>. *Matt 25:46*
18. Hell is a place of:
    - <u>Misery, pain, torment</u> and <u>no rest</u> *Rev. 14:10-11*
    - <u>Weeping, wailing</u>, and <u>anger</u> *Matt. 13:41-42; 24:51*
    - <u>Remembering</u> and <u>remorse</u> *Luke 16:19-31*
19. Hell is <u>avoidable</u> if we repent and believe in Jesus Christ. *John 3:16; 5:24*
20. There is <u>only one way</u> to avoid hell. It is through Jesus alone. *John 14:6; 1 John 5:12; Acts 4:12*

The LORD is not slow to fulfill His promise as some count slowness, but is patient toward you, not wishing that any should perish, but that all should reach repentance.
- 2 Peter 3:9 (ESV)

NOVEMBER

God Is Our Refuge

Psalm 46: 1-2

Arlene Faith Kortright

God is our ref - uge and strength in times of trou - ble There - fore we will not fear though the earth be re - moved and though the moun - tains be car - ried in - to the midst of the sea Psalm for - ty six one and two

LORD, You are my Rock. Thank You for being my refuge and strength. You've seen me through all my troubles, so I know I can fully trust You for everything ahead of me. **Amen**

Prophecy from a Woman

God included a beautiful prophecy in Proverbs chapter 31. The mother of King Lemuel taught this prophecy to her son, who recorded it. This section of Scripture predicts what characteristics will make the most wonderful wife for a man and how this wife will be blessed.

Character traits the prophecy includes:	
v. 11	Trustworthiness brings prosperity to the husband
v. 12	Treats her husband well his entire life
v. 13-14	Willingly works with her hands
v. 15, 20	Provides for her household, helps others
v. 16, 24	Manages her money well, is enterprising
v. 17, 22	Takes care of herself
v. 18, 19, 27	Hard-working
v. 21, 27	Plans for and watches over her family
v. 23	Adds honor to her husband's reputation
v. 25-26	Strong, honorable, wise, speaks with kindness
v. 30	Fears (reveres & honors) the Lord God

The predicted rewards for such a woman:	
v. 10	She will be valued far above rubies.
v. 11	Her husband will trust her completely.
v. 28, 30	Her husband and children will call her "blessed," and she will be praised.
v. 31	Her works will be honored and speak to all of her character.

...but a woman who feareth the LORD, she shall be praised.
- Proverbs 31:30

Israel's Past, Present, and Future (Part 1)

God's Word reveals His plan for mankind. God tells us He chose Israel to be the witness that He is God (Isaiah 43:10). By looking at the history of the Jewish people, we can see a timeline bringing us closer and closer to the end of time.

An Outline of Israel's Past Before Christ:

- Abrahamic Covenant, Genesis 12:1-7

- Mosaic Covenant, Exodus 19:5; 24:3-8

- Land Covenant, Deuteronomy 29:1-30; 30:1-20

- Davidic Covenant, 2 Samuel 7:8-17; 1 Chronicles 17:3-15

- New Covenant, Jeremiah 31:31-40; Hebrews 8:8-13

- Israel (ten Northern Tribes) destroyed by Assyria, 722 B.C.

- Judah (two Southern Tribes) destroyed by Babylon, 586 B.C.

- Jewish remnant returned to Jerusalem from exile, 536 B.C.

- Silent years between the Old and New Testaments, around 400 B.C.

**Surely the Lord GOD does nothing, unless He reveals His secret to His servants the prophets.
- Amos 3:7 (NKJV)**

Israel's Past, Present, and Future (Part 2)

After Israel rejected Christ, God turned to the Gentiles to spread His Word. However, He continues to deal with the Jewish people. God is bringing events to fulfillment, step-by-step.

Outline of Israel's Past from the Time of Christ into the Present

- Israel rejected the Messiah, who was crucified in 33 A.D.

- Israel is destroyed by Rome in 70 A.D.

- Israel ceased to be a nation and the Jewish people scattered, from 70 A.D. to 1948.

- World War II Holocaust drove masses of Jewish people home to Israel.

- Israel became a nation on May 14, 1948.

- Israel captured Jerusalem in the 1967 Six-Day War.

- Jerusalem is recognized as Israel's capital by the United States on December 6, 2017.

- United States Embassy was moved to Jerusalem on May 14, 2018, exactly 70 years after Israel became a nation.

The LORD of hosts has sworn, saying, "Surely, as I have thought, so it shall come to pass, and as I have purposed, so it shall stand." - Isaiah 14:24 (NKJV)

Israel's Past, Present, and Future (Part 3)

God tells us He will deal with Israel and bring her back to Himself during a seven-year time period called the "Tribulation." His purpose is to bring the Jewish people to recognize Him as Christ, their promised Messiah.

Outline of the future Tribulation (Time of Jacob's Trouble)

- Covenant with the Antichrist is confirmed. *Daniel 9:27*

- Christ opens the scroll and unleashes the Seal Judgments upon the earth. *Revelation 6:1-17*

- 144,000 Jewish Witnesses are assigned to evangelize the earth. *Matthew 24:14; Revelation 7:1-8*

- Two witnesses in Jerusalem will evangelize, perform miracles, be killed, and be resurrected. *Revelation 11:3-13*

- Trumpet Judgments. *Revelation 8:6-11:19*

- Antichrist sets himself up as "God" in the Temple. *Revelation 13:1-18; Daniel 11:36-45*

- Perscuted Jews flee. *Matthew 24:15-20*

- Bowl Judgments. *Revelation 15-16*

- War of Armageddon. *Revelation 16:12-16; Zechariah 12*

- Christ returns to the Mount of Olives in Israel. *Revelation 19:11-16; Zechariah 14:3-4*

- Believing Jews are saved. *Zechariah 12:10; Romans 11:26*

After the Tribulation, all Jews and Gentiles who survived and accepted Christ will enter the Millennial Kingdom in their physical bodies.

...Behold, the tabernacle of God is with men, and he will dwell with them, and they shall be His people....
- Revelation 21:3

Israel's Birth Precedes Her Birth Pains

Isaiah 66:7-8 holds two very unusual prophecies. **Israel would be born as a nation and her birth would come** *before* **her birth pains began.** These prophecies, given over 2, 500 years earlier, accurately describe Israel's rebirth on May 14, 1948. On this date, the Jewish people declared independence for the united and sovereign nation of Israel.

Only hours earlier, the United Nations mandate ended British control of the land. During a twenty-four-hour period, both foreign control of Israel ceased and Israel declared its independence. The United States, under President Harry Truman, issued a statement recognizing Israel's sovereignty. Other nations acknowledged Israel's independence, as well.

The prophet Isaiah said the labor pains would come *after* the birth. This, too, is exactly what took place. Within hours of Israel's birth as an independent nation, Israel was attacked by the neighboring countries of Egypt, Transjordan, Iraq, Syria, and Lebanon. Israel wasn't born *because* of a painful war; she was the *cause* of one.

"Before she was in labor, she gave birth; before her pain came, she delivered a male child. Who has heard such a thing? Who has seen such things? Shall the earth be made to give birth in one day? Or shall a nation be born at once? For as soon as Zion was in labor, she gave birth to her children.
- Isaiah 66:7-8 (NKJV)

The Third Temple Prophecy

The Bible tells us the Antichrist will confirm a covenant with Israel to set off the seven-year Tribulation. After three and one-half years, he will cause the Jewish sacrifices to cease. (Daniel 9:27; 11:31, 12:11). Christ said the abomination of desolation will be seen standing in the holy place (Matthew 24:15), and Paul wrote that the Antichrist would proclaim himself to be God in the Temple (2 Thessalonians 2:3-4). **Since this event must happen in the Jewish Temple in Jerusalem, we know there has to be a third Temple built.**

The world has only known two Jewish Temples in Jerusalem. The first was built by King Solomon. It stood for almost four hundred years until it was destroyed by the Babylonians in 586 B.C. The second Temple was built on the same site after the Babylonian Captivity. It stood for 586 years until the Romans destroyed it, in 70 A.D. Since the second Temple was destroyed and the Jews scattered to all corners of the earth, there has never been another Jewish Temple in Jerusalem.

According to Scripture, the scattered Jews would return to their land in the End Times and would become a nation again. This took place in 1948. These passages indicate that there will be another Temple built, sacrifices will be resumed, and the Antichrist will ultimately desecrate it. The Jewish people who follow the Jewish Scriptures take the promise of a third Temple very seriously. Their progress in preparing for its construction warrants consideration of how close we are to the End Times.

When ye therefore shall see the abomination of desolation, spoken of by Daniel the prophet, stand in the holy place, (whoso readeth, let him understand:) then let them which be in Judaea flee into the mountains. - Matthew 24:15-16

The Eastern Gate Prophecy

In Ezekiel 44:1-3 we are given an interesting prophecy about the Eastern Gate in Jerusalem. Many theologians believe this passage is telling us that Christ would be the first one to enter it (as Messiah) when He returns at His Second Coming.

When the remnant returned from the seventy-year Babylonian Captivity to rebuild Jerusalem, the wall, and the Temple, they built a gate on the east side of the west bank of the Brook Kidron, opposite the Garden of Gethsemane. Six hundred years later, Jesus fulfilled part of the prophecy when He entered this gate for the last time at His triumphal entry into Jerusalem, just days before His crucifixion.

The Temple was then torn down in 70 A.D. – just as Jesus had predicted (Matthew 24:2). The Romans destroyed Jerusalem, the wall and the Eastern Gate. During the next fifteen hundred years, efforts were made to rebuild the wall, but invaders repeatedly tore it down. Finally, in 1542, Suleiman the Magnificent rebuilt the wall, but for some reason he had the gate sealed off with stones.
A Muslim cemetery was put in front of the Eastern Gate, and after five hundred years, this gate remains the only one of all the old city gates that is sealed off to this day.

**Then he brought me back the way of the gate of
the outward sanctuary which looketh toward the east;
and it was shut. Then the LORD said unto me;
This gate shall be shut, it shall not be opened,
and no man shall enter in by it; because the LORD, the
God of Israel hath entered in by it, therefore it shall be shut.
- Ezekiel 44:1-2**

Christ's Prophecy on the Days of Noah

A study of the "time of Noah" is *vital* for understanding the similarities between the people of Noah's day and ours (Genesis 5:29-7:24, 2 Peter 2:5, and Jude 6). This study reveals why God had to step in and judge the entire world. The history of Noah's Flood, just like all of Scripture, was written for our instruction. In Matthew 24:37-39, Christ said that the conditions at the time of His Second Coming would be like it was during Noah's day, when God saw the wickedness was great upon the earth and acted to stop its spread.

Then the LORD saw that the wickedness of man was great in the earth, and that every intent of the thoughts of his heart was only evil continually. - Genesis 6:5 (NKJV)

God granted the people an additional 120 years (Genesis 6:3) to change their ways, but they kept right on "eating, drinking, and marrying" (i.e. going about life as normal and ignoring God's righteousness) until the day Noah entered the Ark. Just like in Noah's day, sin keeps us ignorant. Without Christ's direction, we, too, will be caught unaware and will face destruction.

"But as the days of Noah were, so also will the coming of the Son of Man be. For as in the days before the flood, they were eating and drinking, marrying and giving in marriage, until the day that Noah entered the ark, and did not know until the flood came and took them all away, so also will the coming of the Son of Man be." - Matthew 24:37-39 (NKJV)

Prophecy from Zephaniah (Part 1)

The entire book of Zephaniah has only fifty-three verses – most are prophetic. Zephaniah, the prophet and author of the book, lived at the same time as Habakkuk and Jeremiah. Zephaniah 1:1 dates his ministry to the reign of King Josiah (640-609 B.C.).

Zephaniah was commissioned by God to proclaim the great wickedness of Judah and announce the coming destruction. Zephaniah spelled out Judah's sins of rebellion, violence, and deception, as well as her disobedience and the rejection of God's correction. The country was also filled with corrupt priests, judges, leaders, and prophets. All of this resulted in God's judgment falling upon the nation. Zephaniah was told to stir the people toward repentance. **Although Zephaniah spoke about the immediate situation in Judah, he also focused on the future "day of the LORD" or End Times.** He explained how Judah's enemies would be destroyed and offered words of comfort to the faithful with God's promises of future blessings.

What Judah was about to experience would happen again in the End Times, only much worse. The prophecies relating to Jerusalem's and Judah's troubles and destruction by Babylon came to pass in 586 B.C. Zephaniah's prophecies about the "day of the LORD" have yet to be fulfilled.

The great day of the LORD is near; it is near and hastens quickly. The noise of the day of the LORD is bitter; there the mighty men shall cry out. The day is a day of wrath... trouble... distress... devastation... desolation... darkness...gloominess...
- Zephaniah 1:14-15 (NKJV)

Prophecy from Zephaniah (Part 2)

Many prophecies in Zephaniah had both a near and distant fulfillment. Some were specifically meant for the future "day of the LORD." For example, Zephaniah 1:2-3 declares a global judgment that will take place during the Tribulation period (Revelation 6-18). In Zephaniah 1:14-18, many of the same terms are used to describe this seven-year Tribulation. It is interesting that even gold and silver will be of no use to people (1:18). Zephaniah forecasts divine judgment on all the earth (3:8).

Zephaniah was also instructed to record a prophecy of great encouragement to the faithful. The Lord promised that a remnant (or small group of His people) would be protected in the "day of the LORD" (Zephaniah 2:3, 7-9; 3:13). The book closes with hope for Israel in the Millennial Kingdom (3:9-13) and Israel's comfort, healing, and glorious return to her land with Christ reigning in her midst (3:14-20).

Romans 15:4 states that prophecy was *"written for our learning."* **By studying Zephaniah, we can see what causes a nation's downfall.** God's judgment is certain, but with humble repentance and personally seeking the Lord in obedience to His Word, we also become that "remnant" God promises to protect.

The LORD thy God in the midst of thee is mighty;
he will save, he will rejoice over thee with joy;
he will rest in his love, he will joy over thee with singing.
- Zephaniah 3:17

The "Scoffer" Prophecy (Part 1)

A prophecy in 2 Peter 3:2-6, declares that "scoffers" (defined as those who mock, delude, or deceive) *will come* in the last days. We can expect this. The passage tells us these people *will walk or act according to their own desires or cravings.* "Lust" actually means a longing for what is forbidden. We are also told that they *will specifically deny that God will come back to Earth* and base this belief on the mistaken assumption that nothing has happened or changed thus far; i.e. things are the way they have always been. Verses 5 and 6 of this same passage, however, tells us the mockers *willingly ignore the biblical account of both Creation and the Worldwide Flood* when God judged sin in a catastrophic way. God left us overwhelming evidence of this Flood in the nature of the rock layers and the fossils they contain.

2 Peter 3:6-9 tells us God judged the world's sin in Noah's day and is certain to do so again. We must understand God's timing is different than ours. It is based on His patience and longing to give us time to ask Him for forgiveness and turn back to Him before it is too late.

That you be mindful of the words which were spoken before by the holy prophets, and of the commandment of us the apostles of the Lord and Saviour: knowing this first, that there shall come in the last days scoffers, walking after their own lusts, and saying, Where is the promise of his coming? For since the fathers fell asleep, all things continue as they were from the beginning of creation.
- 2 Peter 3:2-4

The "Scoffer" Prophecy (Part 2)

For over four thousand years, almost every culture in the world acknowledged that there has been a Worldwide Flood upon Earth. This is because all people descended from Noah and took the knowledge of this Flood with them across the globe. **It is only in the last few hundred years that people have started to deny this Flood.** They have become "willingly ignorant."

"Willingly ignorant" of the Worldwide Flood of Noah's day means people in the Last Days will *purposely choose* to forget or ignore the evidence of the pre-flood world. If the Bible says the evidence is going to be ignored, then this evidence must exist. Below is a partial list of the *worldwide* evidences God provided for *us* to discover. Whether we choose to ignore or acknowledge it, is irrelevant; the evidence exists.

- Polystrata fossils (fossilized plants and animals protruding through multiple strata layers)

- Complex and simple life forms found in the same strata

- Dinosaur fossils found with undecayed tissue and intact DNA fragments

- Marine fossils found on the mountain tops

- Massive fossilized graveyards

- Saltwater lakes found at high elevations

- Knowledge and drawings of dinosaurs (called "dragons") found in many post-flood cultures

- Worldwide flood accounts recorded by cultures all over the world

For this they willingly are ignorant of, that by the word of God...whereby the world that then was, being overflowed with water, perished. - 2 Peter 3:5-6a

The "Imminent" Prophecy (Part 1)

Christ's return for His Church (called the Rapture) is *imminent*. Imminent does not mean soon; it means *something can take place at any time*. **Christ taught that His followers were to be in a constant state of readiness for this event.** The apostles Paul, Peter, Christ's own brother James, and the apostle John taught this as well. A careful study of Paul's writing indicates that he and the early Christians believed it could happen in *their* lifetime (1 Thessalonians 4:13-18; 5:8-10).

The early Christians' use of the word "Maranatha" also points to the imminency of Christ's return to meet His Church in the air. The word was used among the early believers when they got together or parted company. The Christians did not use the words hello or goodbye, but used the Aramic expression "Maranatha" which is translated "Our Lord, come" and is even used by many believers to this day. It conveys the idea that **the Lord could come for His Church at any moment.** Christ Himself warned of the horrific signs that would *precede* His *return to Earth* (Matthew 24; Mark 13; Luke 21). He also stated that this time period, known as "the Tribulation", would be the *worst time in the history of the world*. The early believers were taught they would not have to go through this. This is why they could say "Our Lord, come." They were looking for the "blessed hope and glorious appearing" of the Lord God and Savior (Titus 2:13), who would rescue them from His wrath to come (1 Thessalonians 1:9-10; 5:8-10).

The purpose of Christ's teaching that His return for the Church is imminent is to produce a sense of *urgency* and *zeal* in His followers to live a life pleasing to the Lord, share Christ with others while there is still time, and be ready to be taken by Christ to the dwelling place He is preparing for us in heaven (John 14:1-3).

Behold, I am coming quickly *[by surprise, suddenly]*
-Revelation 3:11a (NKJV)

The "Imminent" Prophecy (Part 2)

Some key verses that stress the importance of our readiness for Christ's imminent return are listed below:

For our citizenship is in heaven, from which we also eagerly wait for the Savior, the Lord Jesus Christ.
- Phil. 3:20 (NKJV)

And to wait for His Son from heaven, whom He raised from the dead, even Jesus who delivers us from the wrath to come.
- 1 Thess. 1:10 (NKJV)

Therefore let us not sleep, as others do, but let us watch and be sober.
- 1 Thess. 5:6 (NKJV)

Looking for the blessed hope and glorious appearing of our great God and Savior Jesus Christ.
- Titus 2:13 (NKJV)

You also be patient. Establish your hearts, for the coming of the Lord is at hand.
- James 5:8 (NKJV)

But the end of all things is at hand; therefore be serious and watchful in your prayers.
- 1 Peter 4:7 (NKJV)

"Remember therefore how you have received and heard; hold fast and repent. Therefore if you will not watch, I will come upon you as a thief, and you will not know what hour I will come upon you."
- Revelation 3:3 (NKJV)

Is Petra in Prophecy?

Esau, Jacob's brother, traded his birthright of the land of Israel to his brother Jacob and established his own kingdom in Edom (southern one-third of Jordan today). In Edom there is a rugged area of caves and landlocked canyons, accessible only through a narrow gorge twenty to fifty feet wide. Walls on both sides of the gorge are five to seven hundred feet high. This was the capital of Esau's kingdom and was later called *Petra* (rock) by the Greeks.

The feud between the ancestors of Esau and Jacob has continued throughout biblical history. Under the Babylonian Empire, some Israelites were moved to Babylon, and the Edomites were moved into Israel. Racial mixing was one of the ways the conquerors weakened occupied territories. The Nabateans, descendants of Ishmael, moved into Petra and from 500 B.C. to 500 A.D. enlarged their territory. The Edomite stronghold of Petra declined after the Roman Empire broke up in 500 A.D. From about 600 A.D. to 1800 A.D. the world doubted this rock city ever existed until a Swiss explorer visited it in 1812 and reported on its beauty and ancient culture. Interestingly enough, Petra's roads and hotels are being restored today.

During the second half of the Tribulation Period, Scripture records a prophecy about the Antichrist setting himself up as "God" in the Jewish Temple. Immediately on seeing this, the Jews are told to flee to the mountains (Matthew 24:15-22). Additional passages support that this mountainous area is in Petra.

O God, thou hast cast us off, thou hast scattered us, thou hast been displeased; O turn thyself to us again…. Who will bring me into the strong city? Who will lead me into Edom? - Psalm 60:1,9

Prophecy from Haggai

Israel was allowed to return to her homeland from the Babylonian Captivity due to a decree of Cyrus, the Persian ruler (Ezra 1:1-4). A remnant of about fifty thousand Jews returned under the leadership of Zerubbabel and the guidance of Joshua the High Priest. The remnant had begun to rebuild the Temple Nebuchadnezzar had destroyed, but the opposition they encountered and their own indifference halted the project. Sixteen years later, God called Haggai and Zechariah to encourage the people to turn from their selfishness, obey God, and put Him first in their lives. The people listened, restored their priorities, and finished the Temple. Some older returnees, however, were disheartened that the Temple was not nearly as beautiful as the one that had been destroyed.

God gave Haggai prophetic messages to encourage the Jews. The people were told to be strong and courageous. Just as God had brought them out of Egypt, God promised He would come one day to shake up all the nations and fill a future Temple with a far greater glory and peace (Haggai 2:2-9). God also promised to destroy the wicked kingdoms forever.

Haggai closed his book with a special prophecy for the godly royal governor, Zerubbabel (Haggai 2:21-23). Even though Zerubbabel had been cursed by the wickedness of Judah's last kings, he was chosen by God to serve as the "signet ring" (a ring with an emblem unique to the king, used as a royal seal). Zerubbabel became the royal seal to God's promise of the future and final King—the Lord Jesus Christ. Zerubbabel was in the Davidic line leading to the promised future and final king – Jesus.

> **"In that day...I will take you, Zerubbabel...**
> **and will make you like a signet ring;**
> **for I have chosen you," says the LORD of hosts.**
> **- Haggai 2:23 (NKJV)**

The Rapture Prophecies (Part 1)

"The Rapture" is the event when the Lord Jesus Christ will suddenly snatch away all His true followers (called the Church) from the earth and take them to heaven. The word "rapture," which comes from the Latin word *raptura,* is a translation of the Greek New Testament word *harpazo.* **The basic meaning of every one of the fourteen times harpazo is used in the New Testament is to "suddenly remove, snatch or catch away, seize or carry off by force."** Jesus referred to it in John 14:1-3, but the Apostle Paul was the first to explain this event in 1 Thessalonians 4:13-18, 2 Thessalonians 2:1-2 and 1 Corinthians 15:51-52.

The Rapture is the first phase of the promised Second Coming of Christ. The Bible clearly describes the Rapture as the time the entire Church will be snatched off the earth and taken to heaven. Christ's return with His Church at the Mount of Olives (for the purpose of judging the world for their sins) is the final phase of the Second Coming. The Rapture is an imminent event—meaning it could happen at any time after Christ's death. Paul and the early believers thought it would happen in their lifetime.

Regarding the final phase of His Second Coming, God gave us a specific number of days until Christ would return to judge the earth. We are told this would happen seven years after a specific leader, called the Antichrist, confirms (strengthens, makes effective) a covenant with Israel (Daniel 9:27).

Then we which are alive and remain shall be caught up (harpazo) together with them in the clouds, to meet the Lord in the air: and so shall we ever be with the Lord.
– 1 Thessalonians 4:17

The Rapture Prophecies (Part 2)

In 1 Thessalonians 4:13-18, Paul was speaking to the Thessalonian Christians who were worried about their fellow believers who had died. Paul reassured the living that though Christ still hadn't come back, those in the grave would not miss the Rapture, but would actually be snatched away to meet the Lord in the air *an instant before* those still alive would (v. 13-15).

Paul then explained exactly what Jesus would do (v. 16-17) when He comes to take His followers to the place He was preparing for them (John 14:1-3).

What a marvelous prophetic promise! No wonder Paul said they should *"comfort* one another with these words."

13But I do not want you to be ignorant, brethren, concerning those who have fallen asleep, lest you sorrow as others who have no hope. 14For if we believe that Jesus died and rose again, even so God will bring with Him those who sleep in Jesus. 15For this we say to you by the word of the Lord, that we who are alive and remain until the coming of the Lord will by no means precede those who are asleep. 16For the Lord Himself will descend from heaven with a shout, with the voice of an archangel, and with the trumpet of God. And the dead in Christ will rise first. 17Then we who are alive and remain shall be caught up together with them in the clouds to meet the Lord in the air. And thus we shall always be with the Lord. 18Therefore comfort one another with these words.

- 1 Thessalonians 4:13-18 (NKJV)

The Rapture Prophecies (Part 3)

Second Thessalonians 2:1-6 gives us a prophecy as to when the Rapture will occur in relation to the Tribulation. One reason Paul wrote this second letter to the same group of Thessalonian believers was because they were undergoing persecution. In looking at the original Greek text, we get the impression that they were panicked. According to Paul, the Thessalonian believers had received word that they missed the Rapture and were in the Tribulation (2 Thess. 2:1-2). Paul reassured the Christians this information did not come from him. He told them they were being deceived and they were *not* in the Tribulation period because certain events had to happen first.

Paul prophesied there would be the "apostesia" (2 Thess. 2:3). *Apostesia* is the Greek word for "falling away" but it is also translated as "departure." The word "departure" was used in the *first seven translations* of the English Bible until the King James Bible changed it to "falling away." Later translations began using the word "rebellion."

Paul is reassuring the Thessalonians that "the departure," the revealing of the Antichrist (verses 3-4), and the removal of the one who restrains lawlessness (verses 6-7) would all have to happen before that "terrible day of the Lord." Thus, the persecution which the Thessalonians were enduring could not be the Tribulation. Paul concluded chapter 2 by telling the believers to let the Lord Jesus Christ Himself comfort them (2 Thessalonians 2:16-17).

Let no one deceive you by any means: for that day shall not come, except there come a falling away first, and that man of sin be revealed, the son of perdition.
- 2 Thessalonians 2:3

The Rapture Prophecies (Part 4)

A careful study of the Bible will reveal the sequence of events in the Rapture or catching up of "the Church" (true followers of Christ). **This is the "blessed hope" we are to be looking forward to and urgently encouraging others to do, as well.**

1. The Lord will come from God the Father's house, where He is preparing dwelling places for us. - *John 14:1-3*

2. Jesus Himself will come to receive us. - *John 14:1-3*

3. Jesus will summon us with a shout, the voice of an archangel and a trumpet call. - *1 Thess. 4:16*

4. The dead will rise to get new bodies a moment before those who are still living. - *1 Thess. 4:14-16* All of this takes place in the twinkling of an eye. - *1 Cor. 15:51-52*

5. The living believers will be snatched up together to meet the Lord in the air. - *1 Thess. 4:17*

6. Jesus will take us to our dwelling place in the Father's House. - *John 14:2-3*

7. We will be with Christ forever from here on. - *1 Thess. 4:17*

8. Believers will all go before the "judgment seat of Christ" to have everything ever done for Christ evaluated as to our true motives. Things done for Christ will be rewarded, the rest discarded. - *Rom. 14:10; 1 Cor. 3:11-15; 2 Cor. 5:10*

**Looking for that blessed hope,
and the glorious appearing of the
great God and our Saviour Jesus Christ. - Titus 2:13**

Israel's Rebirth, a Most Powerful Sign

There is a prophecy in Jeremiah which promises that the Jews will return to Israel from lands in the north and from countries all over the world. This process will *not be completed* until the regathering of all the Jewish people – *after* the Tribulation. From 1948 onward, this prophecy *began to be fulfilled*. Around 2000 B.C. God called Abraham to father the nation of Israel. In 70 A.D. and again in 135 A.D., the Jewish people were scattered over the earth. **The land of Israel laid desolate for almost two thousand years.** In 1948, this distinctly Jewish nation was reborn. Through multiple wars over the ensuing decades, overcoming impossible odds, Israel won remarkable victories in battle after battle to remain a nation – starting with the attack by five Arab nations the day after becoming a nation. In 1967, Israel achieved an amazing victory and gained control over Jerusalem – in spite of being far outnumbered and out-weaponed.

In the last seventy years, we have seen many prophecies concerning Israel's prosperity – economically, militarily, technologically, and agriculturally – come to pass. This can only be called miraculous, especially in light of the hatred and trouble Israel experiences from all sides. As this passage tells us, Israel would be regathered, and what is yet to come for her would be the incredible event that everyone will talk about over and above the miracles of the Jewish Exodus from Egypt. What a blessed people we are to *see* this being fulfilled *in our lifetime*.

**Therefore, behold, the days come, saith the LORD,
that it shall no more be said, The LORD liveth, that brought
up the children of Israel out of the land of Egypt; but,
The LORD liveth, that brought up the children of Israel
from the land of the north, and from all the lands
whither he had driven them: and I will bring them
again into their land that I gave unto their fathers.
- Jeremiah 16:14-15**

God Is in Control

In Genesis chapter 6, God had Moses include this statement about the days of Noah just before the great Flood:

The earth also was corrupt before God, and the earth was filled with violence. – Genesis 6:11

In Matthew 24:3-39, when Jesus' disciples asked Him what it would be like just before His Second Coming, Jesus answered them with the following statement:

But as the days of Noah were, so shall the coming of the Son of man be. – Matthew 24:37

As we observe the political, economic, societal, and spiritual chaos increasing all around us, God comforts us throughout His Word. We can put our total trust in Him:

- He is in control. *1 Chronicles 29:11-12*

- He is not a God of confusion. *1 Corinthians 14:33*

- He will never leave or forsake us. *Hebrews 13:5-6*

- He did not give us a spirit of fear. *2 Timothy 1:7*

- He will strengthen, help, and uphold us. *Isaiah 41:10*

By *reading* God's Word, we can *learn* who He is and *trust* His *promise* to be our refuge.

God is our refuge (shelter, hope, trust) and strength (security, majesty, praise, power), a very present help in trouble. Therefore, we will not fear, even though the earth be removed, and though the mountains be carried into the midst of the sea. – Psalm 46:1-2 (NKJV)

The Ezekiel 38 Prophecy (Part 1)

Ezekiel 38 is a key prophecy that has not happened yet. It tells us there will be a *massive invasion of Israel* in the "latter years" by a great confederation of nations. Nine specific geographical locations are given. ("Gog" is not a place, but a title, like Pharaoh. Gog is called a prince and is identified as the leader in this invasion.) The following chart lists, with their geographical locations, the nations of Ezekiel 38:1-6 that will come against Israel. These are the nations that will align themselves against Israel in the future. We should watch these nations closely.

Ancient Name	Modern Nation
Rosh	Russia
Magog	Central Asia (Islamic southern republics of former Soviet Union – could include modern Afghanistan)
Meshech	Turkey (also southern Russia and Iran)
Tubal	Turkey (also southern Russia and Iran)
Persia	Iran
Ethiopia (ancient Cush, south of Egypt)	Sudan
Libya (ancient Put, west of Egypt)	Libya
Gomer	Turkey
Beth-togarmah	Turkey

...Thus says the Lord GOD: "Behold, I am against you, O Gog, the prince of Rosh, Meshech, and Tubal....Persia, Ethiopia, and Libya are with them, all of them with shield and helmet; Gomer and all its troops; the house of Togarmah from the far north and all its troops – many people are with you.
- Ezekiel 38:3,5,6 (NKJV)

The Ezekiel 38 Prophecy (Part 2)

Ezekiel chapter 38 gives us a number of *specific details* about the end-time invasion of Israel.

- Russia, Turkey, Iran, Libya, Sudan, and the nations of Central Asia will come together against Israel (v. 1-6).

- The invasion will happen in the "latter years" (v. 8,16).

- This invasion is still in the future because nothing like this war has ever happened in the past.

- Israel had to be back in her land for these nations to come against her, which only took place in 1948.

- Israel has to be living safely at the time of the invasion. This is mentioned three times in Ezekiel 38 (v. 8,11,14).

- Russia and her allies will invade Israel for wealth (v. 11-12).

- God will miraculously intervene and punish all those who come against Israel (v. 18-22).

- Russia and her allies will be utterly destroyed with an earthquake (v. 19-20), infighting (v. 21), disease, bloodshed, flooding rains, great hailstones, fire and brimstone (v. 22).

God's purpose is to show the world He is God. He mercifully warns and gives us time to acknowledge Him, but He is also a just God and fulfills every word He has spoken.

**"...And I will be known in the eyes of many nations.
Then they shall know that I am the LORD."
- Ezekiel 38:23 (NKJV)**

The God of Prophecy

God not only gave us prophecy in the Bible to authenticate Himself but He also revealed His character to enable us to fully trust Him. The following verses are important for us to hide in our *hearts* (which in Hebrew means both our *mind* and *emotions*). Since He created us, God knows we need a firm foundation upon which to build our trust in Him. Therefore, He left us these key promises about Himself.

God is in total control.
The LORD of hosts has sworn, saying, "Surely, as I have thought, so it shall come to pass, and as I have purposed, so it shall stand:" - Isaiah 14:24 (NKJV)

God does not change.
For I am the LORD, I do not change… - Malachi 3:6a
Jesus Christ is the same, yesterday, today, and forever. - Hebrews 13:8 (NKJV)

God cannot lie.
In hope of eternal life which God, who cannot lie, promised before time began. - Titus 1:2 (NKJV)
…it is impossible for God to lie… - Hebrews 6:18 (NKJV)

Belief in Jesus is the only way to the Father in heaven.
I am the way, the truth, and the life. No one comes to the Father except through Me. - John 14:6 (NKJV)

God has a special plan for each of us.
For I know the thoughts that I think toward you, says the LORD, thoughts of peace and not of evil, to give you a future and a hope. - Jeremiah 29:11 (NKJV)

God's Seven Feasts for the Jewish People

Leviticus 23 is a chapter where God outlines the "seven feasts" that He sets forth for all the Israelites (Jewish people) to follow. **God clearly details "His" seven feasts, which seem to be a prophetic picture of the future.** An in-depth study of each feast points out an interesting pattern.

	Feasts	Event
1.	Passover	Crucifixion of Jesus
2.	Unleavened Bread	Burial of Jesus
3.	First Fruits	Resurrection of Jesus
4.	Pentecost	Establishment of the Church
5.	Trumpets	
6.	Day of Atonement	
7.	Tabernacles	

The *first four feasts* happened on the exact day of each event. The first three pointed to Christ's First Coming. The *last four feasts* seem to point to Christ's Second Coming. We have yet to see if they occur on a corresponding festival day.

For more information, read all of **Leviticus 23.**

**Speak to the children of Israel, and say unto them, Concerning the <u>feasts of the LORD</u>, which ye shall proclaim to be holy convocations, even these are <u>my</u> feasts.
- Leviticus 23:2**

Israel's Military Prophecy

Israel has been a country for only about seventy years. When we consider she is approximately the size of New Jersey and has a population of less than ten million, what we see in her military development is nothing short of astounding. Israel has an extremely powerful fighting force. She is ranked as one of the most technologically advanced armies in the world, making them "exceedingly great" just as Ezekiel predicted about 2,500 years ago.

<u>Consider some of Israel's military achievements:</u>

- This nation is a high-tech superpower and one of the world's top weapons exporters (about $6.5 billion in sales).
- Israel is one of only a handful of nations with a nuclear arsenal. They have both long-range and medium-range ballistic missiles, as well as the combat-proven "Iron Dome" defense system.
- Since 1985, Israel has been the world's largest exporter of drones (about sixty percent of the global market) and was the first to use drones in combat.
- Advanced robot technologies have supplemented soldiers in guarding the sea and borders, as well as mapping out underground enemy passageways.
- Israel was the first country with an operational system to shoot down incoming enemy missiles and to have used this defense system multiple times.
- Israel is a satellite superpower operating at least eight different spy satellites in space. These "mini satellites" weigh only about 300 kg (661 pounds), but safeguard their nation.

**So, I prophesied as He commanded me, and breath came into them, and they lived, and stood upon their feet, an exceedingly great army.
- Ezekiel 37:10 (NKJV)**

Prophecy of the Seven Churches (Part 1)

Christ addressed *seven churches* in the first three chapters of Revelation. They were all located in western Asia Minor or what is now Turkey. The apostle Paul and his fellow workers founded these churches. These churches were all located in cities that were wealthy, influential, and had large populations.

Although there were other churches in Asia Minor, **the seven churches seem to be representative of all the kinds of churches throughout the "church age"** from the time of Christ to the present. Some scholars note that **the seven churches also seem to represent seven periods throughout church history.** God's Word contains many places where passages have relevance to the people to whom it was written, but also prove to be a "prophetic type" of future events. Consider the following approximate dates:

1. Ephesus – **Apostate church**   30 – 100 A.D.
2. Smyrna – **Persecuted church**   100 – 313 A.D.
3. Pergamos – **State church**   313 – 590 A.D.
4. Thyatira – **Papal Church**   590 – 1517 A.D.
5. Sardis – **Reformed church**   1517 – 1790 A.D.
6. Philadelphia – **Missionary church**   1790 – 1900 A.D.
7. Laodicea – **Apostate church**   1900 A.D. – present

He that hath an ear, let him hear what the Spirit saith unto the churches; to him that overcometh will I give to eat of the tree of life, which is in the midst of the paradise of God.
- Revelation 2:7

Prophecy of the Seven Churches (Part 2)

The seven churches of Revelation 2-3 had weaknesses and strengths. A letter written to each church included something specific for them, but also implied something applicable to all churches as well as individual believers since then. **If we look at the churches through a prophetic lens, we can see how Satan attacks churches even today.** By paying attention to past mistakes, we can avoid them and enter into the kingdom which Christ promised to all believers who have withstood Satan's deception.

1. From the letter to *Ephesus,* we are warned not to mechanically follow religious rules, but to remember that loving the Lord with all of our heart, mind, soul, and strength is the essence of true Christianity.

2. From *Smyrna's* letter, we are warned that persecution will come and we should stay strong and faithful to the Lord. Christ promises a Crown of Life to all who trust Him to the end.

3. From the letter to *Pergamos,* we are warned of the infiltration of worldliness and false doctrine that slowly creeps into the church. Overcomers of evil are included in the Book of Life.

4. From *Thyatira's* letter, we are warned not to tolerate false teachers, and even though good is done out of love, patience, faith, and service in the church, we can never compromise truth and ignore sin. God promises a share in the rule of His kingdom to those who are faithful.

**He that hath an ear, let him hear what the Spirit saith unto the churches.
– Revelation 2:29**

Prophecy of the Seven Churches (Part 3)

5. From the letter to *Sardis* we are warned that we cannot live on the past accomplishments of the church. We can't allow the lack of interest and enthusiasm for God's Word and His command to share the gospel with others to die. We are warned to be alert and watchful for Christ's return and prove worthy as we walk with and represent the Lord.

6. *Philadelphia's* letter encourages us to cling to God's Word, persevere, and share the gospel message. This church received a most unusual prophetic promise for their steadfastness:

"Because you have kept My command to persevere, I also will keep you from the hour of trial which shall come upon the whole world, to test those who dwell on the earth."
- Revelation 3:10 (NKJV)

If we love and obey God's Word, persevere and share Christ with others, we too can have this same hope today.

7. From the letter to the last church in *Laodicea,* God gives us perhaps the most serious warning of all. The church was wealthy, arrogant and self-sufficient. They stood for nothing and received a horrible rebuke from the Lord:

"So then, because you are lukewarm, and neither cold nor hot, I will vomit you out of My mouth."
- Revelation 3:16 (NKJV)

The same kind of churches can be found throughout the world today. **As followers of Christ, we are to "hear what the Spirit says to the churches,"** a phrase God had the apostle John write seven times, once to each church *(Revelation 2:7,11,17; 2:29; 3:6,13,22).*

I Will Praise The Lord

Psalm 16: 7-9

Arlene Faith Kortright

I will praise the Lord who coun - sels me; E - ven at night my heart in - structs me I have set the Lord al - ways be - fore me; be - cause He is at my right hand I will not be sha - ken There - fore my heart is glad and my tongue re - joi - ces, My bo - dy will al - so rest se - cure, I will praise the Lord Psalm six - teen sev - en through nine

Simeon's Prophecies (Part 1)

In Luke 2:25-32, there are interesting prophecies given by Simeon, a godly man who lived in Jerusalem. Simeon was a righteous and devout Jew who was knowledgeable in Scripture. He believed God's Word and was looking for the Messiah. The Holy Spirit revealed to Simeon that he would not die before he saw the promised Christ Child.

God's providence not only led Simeon to the Jerusalem Temple on the *exact day and hour* Mary and Joseph brought Jesus to the Temple to be dedicated, but also directed Simeon *right to this couple* to make some astounding proclamations. Simeon announced that God's **promise would be accomplished through the Christ Child and that the "good news" of salvation was for all people, Jews as well as the Gentiles.** He also proclaimed that this Child was the glory of Israel. The nations of the world would indeed be blessed through Abraham just as Paul affirms in Galatians 3:8.

For my eyes have seen Your salvation which You have prepared before the face of all peoples, a light to bring revelation to the Gentiles, and the glory of Your people Israel.
- Luke 2:30-32 (NKJV)

Simeon's Prophecies (Part 2)

In the midst of Simeon's "good news," he also directed a very unusual prophecy to Mary. Simeon prophesied to Mary that her Son would cause division. Some would not believe her Son was the Messiah and fall into judgment, while others would believe He was the promised Messiah, rose from the dead, and would bring eternal life. Belief or disbelief in Christ determines one's destiny. Simeon said the Christ Child would be "a sign which will be spoken against." In Greek, this means Jesus would be rejected and denied. And indeed, Simeon's prophecy proved true. The divinity of Jesus Christ is denied by all other religions, causing division worldwide.

Christ Himself tells us in John 14:6, "I am the way, the truth, and the life: no man cometh unto the Father but by me." It is only through Christ that we can have eternal life. Simeon also told Mary that the Christ Child would cause her own soul to be pierced. A little over thirty years later, Mary fully understood Simeon's prophecy when she saw her Son and Savior falsely accused, beaten, rejected, and crucified.

Then Simeon blessed them, and said to Mary His mother, "Behold, this Child is destined for the fall and rising of many in Israel, and for a sign which will be spoken against (yes, a sword will pierce through your own soul also), that the thoughts of many hearts may be revealed."
- Luke 2:34-35 (NKJV)

The Sacrifice of the Red Heifer (Part 1)

The sacrifice of the red heifer described in Numbers 19 has a very significant spiritual purpose. **It symbolically points to the ultimate sacrifice of Jesus Christ on the cross.** Christ is our *only hope* of ever being cleansed from our sins. About 1,500 years before Christ was born, God instituted this special sacrifice, and it was to be a permanent statute for Israel (Numbers 19:10). The red heifer sacrifice pointed to Jesus Christ and His sacrifice in the following ways:

- Jesus was **perfectly sinless** as was represented by the unblemished red heifer (Numbers 19:2).

- Unlike all the other sacrifices offered in the Tabernacle and Temple, the red heifer was sacrificed as a sin offering **outside the camp.** Likewise, Jesus was crucified outside the city of Jerusalem.

- The Israelites used the ashes of the red heifer for both **spiritual and physical cleansing** (Numbers 19:9). Christ is the means by which we are cleansed from our sins and made right before our God.

- The tabernacle was symbolically **purified** with the sprinkling of the red heifer's blood (Numbers 19:4). As the temple of the Holy Spirit, we too must be cleansed through Christ's blood (1 Corinthians 3:16). The priests and all who burned or handled the ashes of the red heifer were required to be clean (Numbers 19:7-10). As followers and representatives of Christ, we should handle Scripture with a pure heart.

This is the ordinance of the law which the LORD hath commanded, saying, Speak unto the children of Israel, that they bring thee a red heifer without spot, wherein is no blemish, and upon which never came a yoke.
- Numbers 19:2

The Sacrifice of the Red Heifer (Part 2)

If a person was not purified with the water of purification made from the ashes of the red heifer, that person was "cut off" from Israel (Numbers 19:13). Likewise, God tells us that trusting Christ for the forgiveness of our sins is the *only way* to heaven. There is no other way (John 3:16-18; 14:6). Without Christ, we are "cut off" from eternal life with Him.

The sacrifice of the red heifer has not been observed since the Temple in Jerusalem was destroyed in 70 A.D. Scripture tells us that the Antichrist will stand in the Jewish Temple at the middle of the seven-year Tribulation, and he will defile it (Daniel 9:27). This means the Jewish Temple *will have to exist* in order for this to take place. We know the Antichrist will make an agreement with Israel and allow sacrifices to be resumed because Daniel 9:27 states that at the Tribulation midpoint, *"He shall bring an end to sacrifice and offering."* **The Jewish priests must have a red heifer without blemish in order for Israel to worship in a properly dedicated temple.**

Israel has been actively engaged in gathering and training the specifically identified Temple priests. It also has the priestly clothing, furniture, vessels and musical instruments ready and in waiting for their Temple. Finding the perfect red heifer is also in progress so that when the Temple is rebuilt, everything will be ready!

And he shall confirm the covenant with many for one week: and in the midst of the week he shall cause the sacrifice and the oblation to cease, and for the overspreading of abominations he shall make it desolate, even until the consummation, and that determined shall be poured upon the desolate.
- Daniel 9:27

Prophecy in Songs: Exodus 15 and Revelation 15

Of the more than 180 songs in the Bible, the first and the last ones were songs of Moses. In the *first song*, found in Exodus 15, Moses and the children of Israel sang praises to the LORD. Moses gave a detailed account of the awesome victory the Israelites experienced when God miraculously defeated the Egyptian army in the Red Sea. Moses praised God for His holiness, wonders, mercy, and strength. He spoke of how the nations would tremble at God's great power. Moses clearly understood God would plant the Israelites in the land He promised to Abraham. He prophesied not only the defeat of the inhabitants of Canaan, but also that the Lord would reign forever.

The apostle John recorded Moses' *last song* in Revelation. **This song, like the first, prophesied God's ultimate victory, and praised His holiness, justice, and ultimate power over all.** What marvelous songs we can sing, knowing God's words will come to pass.

They sing the song of Moses, the servant of God, and the song of the Lamb, saying: "Great and marvelous are Your works, Lord God Almighty! Just and true are Your ways, O King of the saints! Who shall not fear You, O Lord, and glorify Your name? For You alone are holy. For all nations shall come and worship before You, for Your judgments have been manifested."
- Revelation 15:3-4 (NKJV)

The Worthy Shepherd Prophecy (Part 1)

Zechariah was commissioned by God to play the role of a "worthy shepherd." **He was to point Israel to her true Shepherd, the coming Messiah.** The parallels between Zechariah's time (Zechariah 11) and the time of the Messiah are striking:

- Israel's wicked leaders had no compassion for the people. They used their position for financial gain and felt no guilt for their actions, even believing their gain was a blessing from God. *Likewise, King Herod of Judea in Christ's day was callous, brutal to the people, and subservient to Rome. The high priestly family also exploited the people for their own gain and felt their wealth was a gift from God.*

- Zechariah fed the nation, particularly the oppressed, with God's Word. *This was symbolic of what the Messiah, the Living Word, would do at His First Coming. Just like in Zechariah's time, it was the poor who responded to Christ's message, not Israel's wise, mighty, and noble (Matthew 11:5; 1 Corinthians 1:26-29).*

- Zechariah carried staffs like the shepherds of his time. One staff was a club to ward off wild animals; the other was used to retrieve sheep from difficult or dangerous places and keep the flock together. *The first staff represented God's grace or favor for the poor and downcast of Israel. The second represented God's provision of unity (Zechariah 11:7-14). God would keep Israel distinct and intact until Christ's return.*

So I pastured the flock marked for slaughter, particularly the oppressed of the flock. Then I took two staffs and called one Favor and the other Union, and I pastured the flock.
- Zechariah 11:7 (NIV)

The Worthy Shepherd Prophecy (Part 2)

- Zechariah loathed shepherds who abused the people and rejected his message. *This pictured God's anger with the unrepentant shepherds (leaders) who mistreated the prophets and would ultimately reject the Messiah Himself.*

- Zechariah abandoned his sheep, which was totally uncharacteristic for a shepherd. He turned them over to their own destruction (Zechariah 11:9). *In like manner, God turned Israel over to her judgment.*

- Zechariah broke the first staff, which represented God's favor. He symbolized God breaking His conditional Mosaic covenant with Israel. *When Christ died, He removed His protective grace from the nation of Israel, opening the way to destruction by her enemies.*

- Zechariah asked Israel to pay him for his service. The people offered only thirty pieces of silver, which God told Zechariah to throw to a potter, one of the lowest classes of workers in the Temple (v. 13). *The fulfillment of this prophecy was when Judas Iscariot betrayed Jesus for the exact same amount of money and then threw the blood money down in the Temple. The chief priest couldn't accept blood money for Temple use, so they purchased a potter's field outside Jerusalem for a cemetery.*

- Zechariah cut the second staff in half, symbolizing the break between Judah and Israel. *This act symbolized how the Messiah broke the unity of the Jewish people (v. 14), which was a significant factor in Israel's devastating defeat by Rome in 70 A.D.*

**And the LORD said unto me, Cast it unto the potter:
a goodly price that I was prised at of them.
And I took the thirty pieces of silver, and cast them
to the potter in the house of the LORD.
- Zechariah 11:13**

Return of the Animals

The Bible mentions lions, leopards, wild goats and oxen, camels, wolves, deer, bears, and many other animals living in Israel. After Jerusalem was destroyed and the Jewish people scattered in the Diaspora, the land was left desolate. For many centuries, there were few birds, and wild animal life was almost nonexistent. Once the Jews returned to Israel, the fauna of the land began to return, as well.

The Bible predicts a future invasion of Israel from the north and God intervening to protect His people (Ezekiel 38). The armies of the north will be destroyed and the bloodshed tremendous. This battle is predicted to occur in the "latter years." It has to take place when animals are back in Israel because Scripture tells us that animals will scavenge the blood and dead bodies (Ezekiel 39:17). **The return of animals to the land of Israel is happening in our lifetime!**

In the last two chapters of Isaiah, the prophet looks forward to the final restoration of Israel. The Lord will come in fiery judgment on the wicked. A small remnant of Jews will recognize Jesus as their Messiah and finally accept Him. This will introduce the Millennial Kingdom where Christ will reign as King. We will have peace on Earth as God originally intended, which will include the animals just as it is prophesied (Isaiah 11:6-9; 65:25).

And I will rejoice in Jerusalem, and joy in my people: and the voice of weeping shall be no more heard in her, nor the voice of crying... The wolf and lamb shall feed together, and the lion shall eat straw like the bullock...
- Isaiah 65: 19, 25

Prophecy of the Birds

Israel had been desolate for centuries. The destruction of her forests began in 70 A.D. with Titus, Emperor of Rome, and continued by the hand of the Muslims, Crusaders, and Turks. When the Jews began returning in the late 1800s, there were no trees left except for a few in some cities. Just as God had predicted through Moses in Deuteronomy 29:23-27, the land of Israel became desolate because they forsook God's covenant with His people. **Since the forests were gone and there was little grass or foliage, there were no animals and few birds of any kind in Israel.**

This, however, was predicted to change in the End Times. God said He would never totally forsake Israel. He had a purpose, and His prophet Isaiah was told to predict that God would bring the forests (Isaiah 41:19-20) and vegetation back (Amos 9:13-15). This, in turn, would bring the birds.

The Bible records there will be a battle at the end of the Tribulation. Nations will rise up in defiance against God and His people. Scripture clearly tells us God will defeat the ungodly nations, and birds will feed on the dead (Ezekiel 39:17-18; Revelation 19:17-21). Since Israel has returned to her land and its forests and vegetation are flourishing, *the birds have returned.* During spring and fall migration, over five hundred million birds fly over Israel. This migration over Israel has been called, "the eighth wonder of the world." Isn't it interesting that the birds are now in the exact location of the predicted battle of Armageddon?

And I saw an angel standing in the sun; and he cried with a loud voice, saying to all the fowls that fly in the midst of heaven, Come and gather yourselves together unto the supper of the great God; that ye may eat the flesh...
- Revelation 19:17-18

Prophetic Warning to the Nations

In Judges 2, we get a prophetic picture of what causes a nation to fall. When Israel followed God under the leadership of Joshua they were supremely blessed, as is any nation who follows God (we even see this with the early years of the United States). However, when each generation failed to pass on the knowledge of God and remember with thankfulness all that He did, the succeeding generations did not know God or the blessings He had once bestowed on them.

In Joshua's farewell address to his people, he listed what God did for Israel and warned the people not to turn from Him. Israel refused to listen to Joshua and by 70 A.D. was no longer recognized as a nation. God sent many judges and prophets to repeat the warnings, but to no avail. **Parents did not pass on the knowledge of God, and as Judges 2:11 states, the children did evil!** We can expect the same if we do not follow this prophetic warning.

We have removed the acknowledgement of God from our government, courts, town halls, and schools. We even see truth compromised in many churches. Why are we surprised that the next generation does evil in the sight of the Lord?

**And the people served the LORD all the days of Joshua, and all the days of the elders that outlived Joshua, who had seen all the great works of the LORD, that he did for Israel…. And also all that generation were gathered unto their fathers: and there arose another generation after them, which knew not the LORD, nor yet the works which he had done for Israel. And the children of Israel did evil in the sight of the LORD, and served Baalim.
- Judges 2:7, 10-11**

Health Prophecy (Part 1)

The Egyptians were the most advanced culture in the days of Moses. The great temples at Karnak and pyramids at Giza validated the Egyptians' innovative astronomical and engineering knowledge. Their level of *medical knowledge*, however, was primitive and dangerous. The Egyptians' medical practices were recorded in various manuscripts we still have today (i.e. Papyrus Ebers written during Moses' time). Many of the cures described in the ancient Egyptian documents included dung from either animals or humans.

Moses was adopted by Pharaoh's daughter. According to Acts 7:22, Moses was "learned in all the wisdom of the Egyptians and was mighty in words and deeds." Yet Moses did not include a single reference to the deadly medical practices of the pagan Egyptian society in which he was raised. Instead, **Moses recorded cutting-edge instructions on sanitation and medical knowledge in the Bible – which would not be confirmed by the science of medicine until the 1900s.**

With His scientific foreknowledge, God gave the Israelites an incredible prophetic promise. If we listen to God, He protects our health. This is still true today when we think of all the diseases we could avoid if we just followed God's guidelines in controlling ourselves in eating and drinking, hygiene, mental health, and sexuality, etc.

If thou wilt diligently hearken to the voice of the LORD thy God, and wilt do that which is right in his sight, and wilt give ear to his commandments, and keep all his statutes, I will put none of these diseases upon thee, which I have brought upon the Egyptians: for I am the LORD that healeth thee.
- Exodus 15:26

Health Prophecy (Part 2)

The presence of unparalleled advanced and accurate understanding of germs, diseases, transmission of infections, human sanitation and hygiene needs and preventive medicine in the ancient Scriptures is evidence that the Bible is truly the inspired Word of God.

It is fascinating that 213 of the 613 biblical commandments God gave to Moses in the first five books of the Bible were *detailed regulations* that promoted good health if followed by the Israelites. A few of the laws containing scientific health foreknowledge are listed below:

- *Lev. 6:27-28* When bloody clothes were boiled and washed in clay post, **the pots had to be thrown out.** When cleaned in metal pots, the pots had to be scoured and rinsed.

- *Lev. 11:35* **Anything that touched a dead carcass** was unclean.

- *Lev. 7:24* No one could eat any animal that **died naturally or was killed by wild animals.**

- *Num. 19:14-17* When a dead body was touched, people had to **clean themselves with a specific cleaning agent of ashes.**

- *Lev. 13:43-44,46* Priests served as medical control officers, **identified diseases, quarantined infectious people, and reinstated them into society only after a careful medical examination.** (The Bubonic plague epidemic was actually stopped when people began to follow ancient biblical laws of sanitation and disease control.)

All the days wherein the plague shall be in him he shall be defiled; he is unclean: he shall dwell alone; without the camp shall his habitation be.
- Leviticus 13:46

Health Prophecy (Part 3)

Here are some additional biblical insights into safe health practices:

- *Lev. 14:33-57* Specific laws were given for **decontaminating houses that were exposed to disease.**
- *Lev. 11* Foods that were **health risks were identified.**
- *Ex. 19:10* Even before the Mosaic law, the Lord told Moses to have the people **wash their clothes.**
- *Ex. 29:4* Priests who handled preparing and sacrificing animals on the altar had **strict rules on washing** themselves.
- *Lev. Chapters 12, 15* There were **purification laws** for women following childbirth and instructions for personal hygiene.
- *Lev. 4:11-12* The law required a **designated place** outside the camp to burn the internal organs and waste of sacrificed animals.
- *Num. 19* God gave Moses detailed instructions on the sacrifice of the red heifer. This sacrifice not only had important religious significance, but also the resulting "water of purification" actually had the ability to kill germs (which no one understood at the time) and prevent infection. It was made of ingredients that are **effective antiseptic, antibacterial, and antifungal agents.**
- *Num. 31:23-24* Instructions for **cleaning with fire and water** were given.
- *Gen. 17:12* The Bible records that every Hebrew male was to be circumcised on the eighth day after his birth (science now confirms this is **the best day for circumcision**).
- *Deut. 23:12-13* God told the Israelites to carry a shovel to **bury their waste outside the camp.**

These are just a *few* of the laws Moses wrote over three thousand years before science understood their importance. If these biblical principles had been followed, many people could have been treated preventing millions of unnecessary deaths.

And he that is eight days old shall be circumcised among you, every man child in your generations, he that is born in the house, or bought with money of any stranger, which is not of thy seed. - Genesis 17:12

Psalm 83 (Part 1)

Psalm 83 is an interesting chapter written about 3,000 years ago by Asaph. Second Chronicles 29:30 recognized Asaph as a "seer," which in Hebrew means prophet. In Psalm 83, Asaph identified an inner circle of Arab states which today share the common borders of modern-day Israel. At the time this was written, this "circle of Arab nations" surrounding Israel did not exist. But it does today! The nations mentioned in Psalm 83:6-8 are as follows:

- **Tents of Edom** - *Palestinians & South Jordanians*

- **Ishmaelites** - *Saudis (Ishmael is the father of the Arabs)*

- **Moab** - *Palestinians & Central Jordanians*

- **Hagarites** - *Egyptians (Hagar was Ishmael's mother, Egypt's Matriarch)*

- **Gebal** - *Hezbollah & Northern Lebanese*

- **Ammon** - *Palestinians & Northern Jordanians*

- **Amalek** - *Arabs of the Sinai Area*

- **Philistia** - *Hamaz of Gaza Strip*

- **Tyre** - *Hezbollah & Southern Lebanese*

- **Assyria** - *Syrians & Northern Iraqis*

For they have consulted together with one consent; they form a confederacy against You: the tents of Edom and the Ishmaelites; Moab and the Hagrites; Gebal, Ammon, and Amalek; Philistia with the inhabitants of Tyre; Assyria also has joined with them; they have helped the children of Lot.
- Psalm 83:5-8 (NKJV)

Psalm 83 (Part 2)

Psalm 83 presents a group of nations that formed a confederacy (Hebrew word means a treaty, alliance, or league). **The passage states these nations consulted (resolved or determined) to go against one particular group of people, the Israelites.** The author of the psalm clearly identifies these people as God's people and His sheltered ones (Psalm 83:3).

According to this passage, the sole intent of this confederacy was to not only *completely destroy Israel*, but to see that Israel would *cease to be remembered*. Has this ever happened in history or is this a prophecy yet in the future? It is debated as to whether or not the conflict of Psalm 83 happened in 1948, when Israel was attacked by five nations within twenty-four hours of her statehood because some of the confederacy members are believed to be missing. The same argument can be made for the 1967 Arab-Israel War. We know it was not possible to have happened between 135 A.D. and 1948 because the Jews were scattered worldwide and there was no Israel. There is no biblical or historical record of such a confederacy coming against Israel from Israel's birth till it ceased to exist in 135 A.D. Is it *possible* that Psalm 83 describes a war yet in the future? Today we see this confederacy aligning itself and also see their leaders *actually uttering* the words of Psalm 83 on today's news programs.

They have said, Come, and let us <u>cut them off</u> from being a nation; that the name of Israel may be <u>no more in remembrance</u>.
- Psalm 83:4

Christ's Prophecy About the Stones (Part 1)

As Jesus rode into Jerusalem on Palm Sunday, the disciples rejoiced and praised God for all the mighty works they had seen (Luke 19:36-37). However, some of the religious leaders from the crowd told Jesus to rebuke or *forbid His disciples to speak*. Jesus responded with a very interesting statement about the stones, which turns out to be quite prophetic.

Christ told the religious leaders that even if His followers did not declare Him as the King "that cometh in the name of the Lord", *the stones* would declare it. This prophecy was proven true in the last two hundred years by geology and archaeology. Both *geology* (the scientific study of the history of the earth, especially as recorded in the rocks) and *archaeology* (the scientific study of material objects of past human life) attest to the fulfillment of Christ's words.

For example, the Bible indicates the earth is **about six thousand years old**, not the millions stated in secular media. The discovery of **soft dinosaur tissue** in fossils, **widespread fossil graveyards**, **extensive sedimentary rock layers** (covering thousands of square miles and extending across entire continents), **helium from radioactive decay still remaining trapped in granite layers** when it should be long gone (if the layers were millions of years old), and **carbon 14 remaining in coal and diamonds** (when there should not be a single molecule left) are all examples of the "stones" proving the truth of Jesus and the Scriptures.

And he answered and said unto them, I tell you that, if these should hold their peace, the stones would immediately cry out.
- Luke 19:40

Christ's Prophecy About the Stones (Part 2)

Scripture tells us there was a *worldwide flood* around 4,000 B.C. The *rocks* point this out with *worldwide evidence* such as **fossilized sea creatures on mountain tops** and **fossilized trees protruding through several rock layers** (supposedly dated millions of years old). It is the *rocks* that reveal **mass burials of millions of creatures spread across hundreds of square miles.** Known as the "miniature Grand Canyon," **the stratified rock layers of Mt. St. Helens formed in hours/days** in 1980. All these rocks provide further evidence for a young earth, as God's Word records.

The Bible also tells us God made *man in His image* (Genesis1:26). Every year, discoveries in archeology cry out that ancient man was more brilliant than brute. **Tools, metal cubes, jewelry,** and **other artifacts** are found **encased in rock.** Discoveries of **ancient cities, temples, coins, tablets, pottery,** and **scrolls** all verify both the accuracy and authenticity of many places, dates and events in God's Word. Just as Christ declared almost two thousand years ago, the stones truly "are crying out" that He is Lord and His Word is true.

And God said, Let us make man in our image, after our likeness: and let them have dominion over the fish of the sea, and over the fowl of the air, and over the cattle, and over all the earth, and over every creeping thing that creepeth upon the earth.
- Genesis 1:26

Prophecy to the Day (Part 1)

Fulfilled biblical prophecy is overwhelming proof that God is in control of human history. The world is full of religious texts written by many writers, **but an in-depth study of the literature shows that not one text contains detailed prophecies that have happened.** These texts give vague generalities which can be used only in hindsight to claim accuracy. Only God knows and predicts the *future* accurately.

The Bible has around 2,000 individual predictions on a multitude of topics. Over the last two thousand years, scholars closely examined these prophecies and found historical evidence that proves which ones have already been fulfilled. No other text comes close to the reliability, accuracy and verifiability of the Bible. This alone warrants the necessity to read it.

Each of Israel's three exiles was precisely predicted, including the final return of Israel to her promised land on May 15, 1948. These extraordinarily detailed prophecies point to an all-knowing Lord God!

Remember the former things of old: for I am God, and there is none else; I am God, and there is none like me, declaring the end from the beginning, and from ancient times the things that are not yet done, saying, My counsel shall stand, and I will do all My pleasure.
- Isaiah 46: 9-10

Prophecy to the Day (Part 2)

In order to understand the *exact timing* of Israel's returns from exile, **we have to use the 360 day Jewish calendar which was consistently used to date biblical events.** In the book of Revelation, John most clearly describes the 360-day calendar when he refers to the time the Antichrist will set himself up as God during the second half of the Tribulation. John refers to a three-and-one-half-year period as 1,260 days (Revelation 12:6) or forty-two months (Revelation 13:5) to make certain the time involved is clearly understood.

The first exile to Egypt lasted 430 years. God fulfilled His promise on the Passover – which happened on the exact day that the 430 years ended. He brought Israel out from slavery to become a mighty nation. In Galatians 3:17, Paul confirmed that God fulfilled His covenant to Abraham precisely as promised.

Jeremiah predicted the exact length of the Jews' second exile, the Babylonian exile, to be 70 years.

Israel was conquered by the Babylonians in the spring of 606 B.C., which has been verified by both secular and biblical scholars. As stated in 2 Chronicles 36:22-23, God stirred the heart of the Persian King Cyrus to free the Jewish people and let them return to their homeland. The Jews' captivity ended in the Jewish month of Nisan in 536 B.C. after precisely 70 years – to the day.

And this whole land shall be a desolation, and an astonishment; and these nations shall serve the king of Babylon seventy years.
- Jeremiah 25:11

Prophecy to the Day (Part 3)

Jeremiah, Ezekiel, and Daniel all lived during the Babylonian captivity. Jeremiah prophesied it would take place and lived to see it happen. Daniel was taken to Babylon as a youth around 606 B.C., and Ezekiel followed about eight years later. Both Ezekiel and Daniel knew that according to Jeremiah's prophecy the Jews would return in 536 B.C. God gave both men unique and specific prophecies for the far future. Daniel predicted the succession of world empires, and **Ezekiel predicted how long it would be until the Jewish people would re-establish their nation in the last days.**

In Ezekiel 4:3-6 we read the full prediction. Ezekiel is told to lie on his right side for <u>390 days</u> to bear the sins of Israel and <u>40 days</u> for the sins of Judah. God said, "*I have laid on you a day for each year.*" If we add 390 plus 40, our sum is 430 years (because one day equals one year). If we then subtract the <u>70 years</u> of captivity the people served in Babylon, our result is 360 years. **In Leviticus 26:18, 21, 24, 28, we read that God would increase Israel's punishment seven times if they refused to obey Him.** If we multiply 360 years by 7, we have 2,520 biblical years. If we multiply 2,520 years by 360 days, we get 907,200 days. Converting this to our 365.25-day calendar, we end up with 2483.8 years after the 536 B.C. Babylonian captivity. Add the one year between A.D. and B.C. and we end up on May 15, 1948 – the exact day Israel again became a nation. This cannot possibly be a coincidence!

....**This will be a sign to the house of Israel. "Lie also on your left side, and lay the iniquity of the house of Israel upon it. According to the number of the days that you lie on it, you shall bear their iniquity. For I have laid on you the years of their iniquity, according to the number of the days, three hundred and ninety days; so you shall bear the iniquity of the house of Israel. And when you have completed them, lie again on your right side; then you shall bear the iniquity of the house of Judah forty days. I have laid on you a day for each year."**
- Ezekiel 4:3-6 (NKJV)

The Christmas "Seed" Prophecy

The very *first Christmas prophecy* was given in Genesis 3:15 when God spoke a curse on Satan for deceiving mankind. Adam and Eve knew their willful rebellion ruined the perfect relationship they enjoyed with their Creator. Their sin brought in a world of sin, death, and decay. **God provided this prophecy to predict His incredibly loving gift, the future Messiah.** This Messiah would redeem mankind from sin and enable people to live in fellowship once again with their Creator and Savior, the Lord Jesus Christ.

The first Christmas prophecy is tucked inside the phrase the *"Seed of the woman."* This is noteworthy because it is unique in all of the Bible. In every other biblical reference, the *"seed of man"* is used. Since we know biologically that women cannot produce seed, Genesis 3:15 can only be referring to a future descendant – one who would not have a human father. This was to be the extraordinarily special Seed, Jesus Christ. He had to be embedded miraculously in the womb of Mary so He would bypass the inherited sin nature that entered the world through Adam and spread to all mankind (Romans 5:12).

And I will put enmity between you and the woman, and between your seed and her Seed; He shall bruise your head, and you shall bruise His heel.
- Genesis 3:15 (NKJV)

Prophecy of Damascus

Isaiah 17 records a very interesting prophecy about Damascus. Damascus is the capital of Syria and claimed to be the oldest continually inhabited city in the world.

God used Tiglath-pileser III and other rulers throughout history to conquer and destroy Damascus. **In the past, however, this city has endured the ravages of war and the rule of various nations, but it has *never* ceased to exist as a city.** Since Damascus has been in continual existence throughout post-Noah's Flood history, and the passage in Isaiah 17 clearly states she will be *totally* destroyed, we can conclude this is yet in the future. It appears that Isaiah's repeated use of the phrase "in that day" found in Isaiah 17:4,7,9 points to an end-time fulfillment.

Isaiah's prophecy states that Damascus would become a ruinous heap. The Middle East is destined for an enormous upheaval in the future!

The burden against Damascus. Behold, Damascus will cease from being a city, and it will be a ruinous heap.
- Isaiah 17:1 (NKJV)

The "Ninth of Av" in Prophecy

Specific prophecies are hidden in festivals, names, and types, etc. in Scripture. **Certain dates on the Jewish calendar also seem to be prophetic, like *"Tisha B'Av"*, which means the ninth day in the Hebrew month of Av.** The day varies on our Gregorian calendar each year, but always occurs in July or August. Tisha B'Av is the day of fasting which ends the mourning period for the Jewish people as they remember the tragedies that happened on the Ninth of Av.

The following events happened on the Ninth of Av:

- **1453 B.C**. Spies returned with a negative report from the Promised Land; the 40-year wilderness wandering began.

- **587 B.C.** Solomon's Temple was burned by the Babylonians.

- **70 A.D**. Romans burned the Second Temple.

- **71 A.D.** Roman army plowed the Temple site with salt; Romans began building the pagan city of Aelia Capitolina on the site of Jerusalem.

- **132 A.D.** Bar Kokhba rebellion took place (Jews rebelled against Roman rule); hundreds of thousands died.

- **1095 A.D.** Pope Urban II declared the First Crusade. Entire Jewish communities in Rhineland and France were obliterated.

- **1290 A.D.** All Jews were expelled from England.

- **1492 A.D.** All Jews were expelled from Spain.

- **1914 A.D.** World War I was declared. Russia began persecution of Jews in Eastern Russia.

- **1942 A.D.** Germans began deporting Jews of the Warsaw Ghetto to the extermination camps.

Christmas Prophecies

Over one-fourth of the Bible tells us what is going to happen in the future. These predictions were given in a matter of hours, days, months, hundreds, and even thousands of years *before* they were fulfilled. Both biblical and secular history testify to this. Many of these recorded and fulfilled prophecies pertain to the birth of Jesus Christ. For over 2,000 years, Christians around the world have celebrated this event as Christmas. Here are a few of these fulfilled prophecies:

1. Jesus would be born miraculously <u>by the power of the Holy Spirit</u>. He would be called the Son of God. - *Luke 1:35*
2. The mother of Jesus would be a <u>virgin</u>. - *Isaiah 7:13-14*
3. Mary became <u>pregnant during</u> her betrothal to Joseph, but <u>before</u> she had a sexual relationship with him. - *Matt. 1:20, 24-25; Luke 1:34*
4. Jesus would be a <u>sanctified firstborn son</u>. - Num. 3:13; 8:17; *Matt.1:20-21; Luke 1:31*
5. Jesus would be <u>called "Immanuel"</u> (God with us). - I*s. 7:14; Matt. 1:23*
6. John the Baptist would be Jesus' <u>forerunner</u>. - *Luke 1:17, 76-77*
7. Jesus would come from the <u>tribe of Judah</u>. - *Gen. 49:8-10; Micah 5:2*
8. Jesus would be born in <u>Bethlehem</u>. There was more than one Bethlehem. The Bethlehem where Jesus would be born would be in <u>Ephratah</u>, the specific town south of Jerusalem. - *Micah 5:2*
9. Jesus would be born in the lineage of: <u>Abraham</u> - *Gen. 26:2-4;* <u>Isaac</u> - *Gen.26:2-4;* <u>Jesse</u> - *Is. 11:1-2;* <u>King David</u> - *Is. 9:7*
10. The birth of Jesus brought a <u>massacre of children</u>. *Jer. 31:15* predicts the historic event from *Matt. 2:16-18* which says: All children age two and under were killed because Herod heard that a new King of the Jews would be born in Bethlehem.
11. The kings of Tarshish, Sheba, and Seba "shall <u>offer gifts</u>...shall fall down before him..." - *Psalm 72:10-11*

All of these predictions are designed to give us an assurance that Jesus is indeed the long awaited Messiah of all mankind. For all of them to be fulfilled in any one person is *beyond* any possibility of coincidence.

And when they were come into the house, they saw the young child with Mary his mother, and fell down, and worshipped him...they presented unto him gifts...
- Matthew 2:11

The Christmas Promise

When the angel appeared to the shepherds on that first Christmas day, he made a statement of prophecy. The shepherds were told, *"Born this day in the city of David [is] a Savior [to all people]."* The angel also said, *"And this shall be a sign unto you; Ye shall find the babe wrapped in swaddling clothes, lying in a manger" (Luke 2:10-12).* A manger was a feeding trough for animals—quite an unusual bed for a newborn baby. This strange statement was a prediction assuring the shepherds they would indeed both *find* and *recognize* the promised Messiah.

Imagine the shepherds as they rushed into Bethlehem (the city of David) looking for this special Newborn. Scripture does not tell us *how* they went about finding Him. However, we *are* told when they came upon the scene of a baby *wrapped tightly* in *strips of cloth*, not in Mary or Joseph's arms but *lying in a manger,* exactly as the angel predicted, the shepherds instantly *knew* they had found the Christ Child.

The timing of the shepherds' arrival at the exact place, time and scene had to be perfect or they would have no confidence that the angel's message to them was true and from God. **For a prophecy to be a "sign," it must be fulfilled in every detail.** Because this unlikely prophecy was accurate to the last little detail, the shepherds had confidence to share what they heard, and all the people who listened to their story were amazed. Prophecy was fulfilled before their eyes.

We can also be assured that Jesus, who was found at exactly the predicted moment, in exactly the predicted position and place, *was* and *still is* the Savior *"to all people"* who accept His sacrifice for their sins and make Him LORD of their lives!

And when they had seen it [the babe wrapped in swaddling clothes, lying in a manger], they made known abroad the saying which was told them concerning this child, and all they that heard it wondered at those things which were told to them by the shepherds.
– Luke 2:17-18

The Psalm 34 Prophecy

The "angel of the LORD" is used over fifty times in Scripture. It is a title, not a name. In context it can be used as a title for Christ and can also refer to God's angelic messenger. The word "angel of the LORD" was used in the Old Testament when Christ Himself came to speak to people. For example, Christ came as the angel of the LORD to comfort Hagar when Sarah sent her away (Genesis 16:7-13). He also kept Abraham from killing Isaac (Genesis 22:11), spoke to Jacob in a dream (Genesis 31:11), and went before the Israelites in the wilderness (Exodus 23:20-23). The angel of the LORD spoke to Balaam (Numbers 22:35), Gideon (Judges 6), Samson's mother and father (Judges 13) and others.

In the book of Psalms, there is a most comforting prophecy concerning the "angel of the LORD" that gives us peace. This verse gives us two wonderful prophetic promises. First, we are told that the angel of the LORD "encamps," which in Hebrew means *to pitch a tent all around or on every side* of those who fear (reverence) God. Second, we are promised that all who fear the Lord will be delivered. The Hebrew word for "delivered" literally means *to be equipped, fought for, strengthened, and prepared*. What awesome promises we have in this verse – a verse well worth memorizing and rejoicing over!

The angel of the LORD encampeth round about them that fear him, and delivereth them.
- Psalm 34:7

God's Prophetic "I will" Promises (Part 1)

In Psalm 91:14-16, God includes eight specific "I will" prophetic promises to encourage His children.

The passage begins by telling us if we *set our love on Him* (which means we cling to, join, and delight ourselves in the Lord), **He will deliver us** (or carry us away) into security with Him.

Next, if we *know or recognize God's name* (which means His character, authority and position), **He will set us on high**. By setting us on high, God makes us inaccessible to others. No one can tear us down and discourage us because we are safe and strong in Him. God promises us His strength. (2 Cor. 12:9-10)

Finally, God tells us **He will answer** (or respond to our prayers and speak to us through His Word) when we call on Him – if we set our love on Him and recognize the Lord is our only hope and Savior.

"Because he has set his love upon Me, therefore I will deliver him, I will set him on high, because he has known My name. He shall call on Me, and I will answer him."
- Psalm 91: 14-15 (NKJV)

God's Prophetic "I will" Promises (Part 2)

The Lord God's remaining five "I will" prophetic promises are in Psalm 91:15-16. God rewards those who love and call on Him.

God states **He will be with us in our trouble**. Trouble in Hebrew means any tight spot. It includes our adversaries, adversities, sorrows, afflictions (whether they be mental, physical, or emotional), and our distresses. God promises to be with us in each and every trouble.

The passage tells us the **Lord will deliver us**. A different Hebrew word is used for deliver in verse 15. It is the word "halas" which means to pull off, to equip, to strengthen, to prepare, or to rescue. In other words, God promises to do whatever He has to do to protect us.

Not only does the Lord God prepare and equip us for what we go through, but **He will also honor us** through it, He will enrich us with Himself.

Psalm 91:16 closes with God's most wonderful promises. **He will satisfy us with long (eternal) life** and **He will show us His salvation.** We are assured from God, who cannot lie (Titus1:2), that we will see Christ's saving victory and our deliverance from eternity in hell.

"...I will be with him in trouble; I will deliver and honor him. With long life I will satisfy him; and I will show him My salvation."
- Psalms 91:15-16 (NKJV)

Christ's Name In Prophecy

The entire Bible speaks of Christ. **The inspired writers prophesied about Him throughout the Old Testament and He revealed Himself in person in the New Testament.** Many of Christ's names were given hundreds and even thousands of years *before* His birth. Each name revealed more and more about His character, position and authority which is what the word "name" means in Hebrew. Below is a *partial list* of who Christ is and where He can be found throughout the Old Testament:

- Seed of a woman - *Gen. 3:15*
- Angel of the LORD - *Gen.16:7-13*
- The God who sees - *Gen. 16:13*
- El Shaddai (Almighty God) - *Gen. 17:1*
- Shiloh - *Gen. 49:10*   • I AM who I AM - *Exo. 3:14*
- The LORD (YHWH) - *Exo. 13:21*
- Star and a Scepter - *Num. 24:17-18*
- Commander of the Army of the LORD - *Josh. 5:14*
- Peace - *Jud. 6:24*   • Anointed - *Ps. 2:2*
- Son of God - *Ps. 2:7,12*   • King over all the earth - *Ps. 6-8*
- Shepherd - *Ps. 23*   • Cornerstone - *Ps. 118-22*
- Immanuel (God with us) - *Is. 7:14*
- Wonderful, Counselor, Mighty God, Everlasting Father, Prince of Peace - *Is. 9:6*   • Rod from the Stem of Jesse - *Is. 11:1*
- Root of Jesse, Banner to the people - *Is. 11:10*
- The First and the Last *I- s. 48:12-16*
- Redeemer, Teacher, Guide - *Is. 48:17*
- Servant of the LORD - *Is. 52:13*   • Man of Sorrows - *Is. 53:3*
- Holy One of Israel, God of the whole earth - *Is. 54:5*
- Witness to people, Leader, Commander - *Is. 55:4*
- Savior - *Is. 63:8*   • LORD our Righteousness - *Jer. 23:6*
- One like the Son of Man - *Dan. 7:13*   • Branch - *Zech. 6:12*
- Messenger of the Covenant - *Mal. 3:1*

We can be assured Christ is exactly who He says He is. He is the only one who can and will ultimately prove every part of His Word true.

Christ's Return, A Sure Prophecy

Many deny that Jesus will return a second time. Their opinion is most often based on their distrust of or disbelief in the Bible. Since the Bible bases its validity on one hundred percent fulfilled prophecy, which includes well over fifteen hundred predictions, why base your belief on a personal opinion when there is a *verifiable* source, the Bible?

- **<u>Christ promised</u> to return for those who eagerly await Him.** (Heb. 9:28). He made this promise to prevent us from getting discouraged, or worse, missing this event. Throughout Scripture, we are promised Christ will come again to rule and reign:

- **Christ had the <u>Old Testament prophets</u> talk about it.** David (Ps. 2:6; 22:27-31), Sons of Korah (Ps. 47), Ethan (Ps. 89:19-29), Isaiah (2:1-4; 9:6-7; 11:1-9; 24:21-23), Jeremiah (Jer. 23:5; 33:6-18), Ezekiel (20:33-44; 37:24-28), Daniel (7:13-14,18,27), Hosea (3:4-5), Joel (3:14-21), Micah (4:1-7), Zephaniah (3:14-20), Haggai (2:20-23), Zechariah (6:12-13; 8:2-3;14:1-9)

- **Christ had <u>New Testament prophets</u> teach about His return.** Peter (Acts 3:20-21), Paul (2 Thess. 1:7-10; 2 Tim. 2:12), John (Rev. 20:1-6)

- **Christ had His <u>heavenly host</u> tell us He would rule.** Gabriel (Luke 1:30-33), four Living Creatures and the twenty-four Elders (Rev. 5:9-10), Angels of God (Rev. 11:15)

- **<u>Christ Himself</u> told us He would return and reign on Earth.** (Matt. 19:28; 25:31-34; Acts 1:3-7; Rev. 2:26-27; 3:21)

What a blessing to know that this *will* happen!

The Greatest Prophecy

All Scripture points to this prophecy that John gave us in John 3:16. Our eternal destiny rests on the full understanding and acceptance of what this verse says:

For God so loved the world that He gave His only begotten Son, that whoever believes in Him should not perish but have everlasting life. - John 3:16 (NKJV)

This verse describes the depth of God's love for humanity. God gave the world His "only begotten" (unique, one of a kind) Son. Christ humbled Himself and came to Earth as a human being. He lived a perfect and sinless life, which enabled Him to sacrifice Himself on the cross, taking the punishment for mankind's sin. He died and rose again conquering death. **Christ's prophetic promise is that every person on Earth can have eternal life with Him and avoid everlasting judgment if we believe in Him.**

The condition is that we believe in Christ. *The word "believe" means we put our trust in Christ and what He did for us. This is evidenced by our repentance and obedience.* When we recognize our sinfulness and accept His gift to be our Savior from eternal punishment, our deep thankfulness motivates us to want to live like He did. According to Christ's own words, *He alone* enables us to live with Him forever.

"Jesus said to him, 'I am the way, the truth, and the life. No one comes to the Father except through Me.'" - John 14:6 (NKJV)

How to Tackle Prophecy and Share it with Others

Though the topic of prophecy may seem to be confusing, God said He is not the author of *confusion* (1 Corinthians 14:33). God wants us to understand it since *He inspired* its writing (2 Timothy 3:16-17). Christ said He is the very S*pirit* or Breath of prophecy (Revelation19:10b).

We know that God wants His Word to give us comfort and hope (Romans 15:4; Psalm 119:49-50) and to inform us of His plans for the future (Amos 3:7). Almost every book of the Bible contains prophecy and many books have been written on this topic, so where does one begin? Our purpose and hope are that this book will be of help in your own *personal understanding* of prophecy and that you will be *spurred on* to read the Bible and be *better prepared* to share the truth of God's Word (I Peter 3:15).

The Bible tells us that God desires all of those who *want to know Him* to understand Him. He doesn't leave us with multiple contradictory meanings. If we cannot come to a common understanding, it is not because of God but because of our own lack of continued study in His Word.

Critics over the centuries have *claimed* the Bible has been corrupted over time through the handing down of the text from generation to generation, constantly altering the contents and making it untrustworthy. This *misconception*, however, was exposed in 1948 at the discovery of the Dead Sea Scrolls. Every portion of the Bible found in the Qumran caves showed that the text was unaltered. **If God inspired the Scriptures, it only makes sense that He would preserve its integrity, and that is exactly what we find. Anyone can test this out.**

Before one begins the study of biblical prophecy, one has to know for *sure* the Bible is *true*. **IF** God *inspired the writing* of the Bible, (2 Timothy 3:16), and it *is true* (Psalm 119:160), **THEN** He would also make it *testable and provable* (Psalm 18:30) -- which He did.

The Bible can be proven _true_ over and above _all other religious texts_ in the following ways:

- In the area of **GEOGRAPHY**, when examining the location of the rivers, lakes, valleys, mountains, deserts, and ancient cities mentioned in the Bible, archeology confirms them.

- The Bible's instructions, ordained by God Himself, provides a moral **ORDER** in society which proves beneficial for everyone who practices them. Societies thrived wherever God's moral order was practiced in their _government, judicial matters, marriage relationships and family life, cleanliness, health codes, work ethics, foreign relations, organization of the military, and worship services._

- Every _field_ of **SCIENCE** from archaeology, astronomy, biology, and chemistry, to genetics, geology, physics, and zoology-- points to the truth of the Bible, and _every statement_ the Bible makes concerning science can be tested and proven true. The **Bible's scientific foreknowledge**, written _thousands_ of years ago, is still being uncovered. It is found to be _accurate and unmatched in its insights._ This is something _no other religious book can claim._ For example the Bible is correct in stating that life is in the blood, the earth is a sphere, stars are both innumerable and unique in their composition, the oceans contain caverns deep enough to cover the highest mountain on Earth, fish follow ocean currents, and the sun travels in an elliptical path. Who could have inspired the writers to include things that only recent technology can verify?

- When we study recorded **HISTORY**, we find the same 100% accuracy as with the sciences. _Civilizations_ appear where the Bible indicates they are, _rulers_ are in power during the time the Bible records them to be, and specific _items, structures,_ and _events_ have been confirmed through archaeological digs. Where discrepancies are found, continued research reveals the Bible is never wrong.

It is interesting to note that the Bible has had and still has more critics than any other book on Earth, yet continues to prove its inerrancy over time. **If** God authored the Scripture and is the Creator of time, knowing the beginning from the end (Isaiah 42:9; 46:9-10), **then** it only makes sense that His history is correct in every detail.

- **PROPHECY** is the strongest proof for the truth of the Bible. Scripture says that prophecy is surer than what we even see (2 Peter 1:18-21). We are told Christ *is* the *very Word of God* from the beginning (John 1:1) and the *very Spirit* of prophecy (Revelation 19:10b).

God gave us both short- and long- term prophecies. The short-term prophecies were fulfilled a *short time after they were made.* Some include the plagues of Egypt, the birth of Samson, and the destruction of Babylon. The long-term prophecies were fulfilled many years, even thousands of *years after the time they were written.* Examples include the scattering of the Jewish people all over the earth and the rebirth of Israel, the virgin birth of Christ, His crucifixion and resurrection, and hundreds more. Some long-term prophecies have not yet been fulfilled such as a one-world government, the total destruction of Damascus, the Rapture, the Tribulation, the return of Christ to Earth, the Millennial Kingdom and many more.

God uses fulfilled prophecy to *prove* He is God and thereby draw people to a belief in Him. Since God promises to bless those who read, hear, and study prophecy (Revelation 1:3) and since almost a third of the Bible are prophetic verses, it is clear that **God considers prophecy very important for us to study**.

- Every Scripture reference that touches on the areas concerning **HEALTH** can also be proven accurate. Researchers have looked into what the Bible says about general *cleanliness, quarantining the sick, personal hygiene, best day for the circumcision of male babies, handling contaminated items, diet, times of rest etc.* They found the biblical insights proved beneficial for the people, the land, and nature in general.

These health rules were given by God to His people through Moses. When carefully followed, they kept the people, and for that matter anyone who followed them, in better health. During the times of the bubonic plague, the Jewish people were blamed for the plague because they as a people were infected less often. Later it was discovered that Jewish people were less apt to get the disease due to following the biblical rules of cleanliness. When people followed the rules, the plague subsided.

- In the area of **DESIGN,** *nothing can compare* to the Bible. Consider, for instance, the beautifully designed Hebrew language with its numerical, phonetic, and visual components. Then look at how the Bible was woven together by 40 different writers of various backgrounds and socio-economic status, writers who spoke three different languages, living on three different continents over a 1,600-year time frame. Consider furthermore that all their writings harmonize together without contradictions and with one central message: *that God made the way for all people to be able to come into His holy presence through Jesus Christ.* Surely this alone is enough to prove the Bible's divine authorship. There is no other book like it! (Josh McDowell's book, *Evidence that Demands a Verdict,* is a masterful presentation detailing this.)

We hope some of the following ideas will prove helpful to organize your study of prophecy and make it easier to understand and present to others:

1. Learning the ways with which one can TEST the Bible and KNOW for sure it is true is necessary when you share Bible prophecy. **Truth** is the reason *why* a person should study the Bible and *believe* what God says about the future.

    G - **Geographic** locations are correct and archaeology confirms them.

    O - moral **Order** is found in God's Word.

    S - **Scientific** statements can be verified. Every area of science verifies the Bible.

    H - **Historical** records are confirmed by other non-religious sources and continuous archeological research.

P - **Prophetic** statements have and are being fulfilled as well as all wise advice proven true.

H - **Health** information has been found to be accurate for both mental and physical well-being.

D - **Design** in the Bible's construction is undeniable.

2. Filing all the pages under their **topics** (*at the top of each page*) and studying one topic at a time may prove helpful. You may want to *copy pages* or *cut apart two of these books* and sort all the front sides and then the back sides of the pages by their topics or use the *Topical Index*. Some of the pages overlap topics. For example, a **Prophetic Promise** may also be put under the **Israel category**. (*You will see some of the overlaps marked in the Topical Index with a * symbol.*)

3. The pages can also be separated according to *events* (i.e., Rapture, Tribulation, 144,000 witnesses, Seal, Trumpet, and Bowl Judgments, etc.) and put in *order* according to a **prophetic timeline**. It may be easier to study the events on your own and zero in on any event we didn't have the space to cover in our book.

4. Another way to use this book and show how prophecy is being fulfilled is to study the pages that discuss what is happening to **Israel**. God chose Israel to be His "witness" that He is God (Isaiah 43:10-13). There are more *specific prophecies concerning Israel* than any other country on Earth. What happens to Israel is what we are to watch. Israel is "*the sign*" that indicates where we are on the prophetic timeline and how close we are to the end. We included an **alphabetical chart** of some signs concerning Israel that can serve as a review of the many prophecies showing fulfillment of God's final plans.

May prophecy encourage and motivate you, as it does us, to share Christ with others while we have time, as well as remind us that things are *not falling apart but coming together* according to God's plan.

Evidence of **Fulfilled** Prophecy in **Israel**

A	·Agriculture ·Animals
B	·Birds ·Birth in 1948 ·Birth before the birth pangs
C	·City names and locations ·3 Cursed cities ·Center of the world
D	·Diaspora (scattering) ·Dead Sea Scrolls ·Desert restored
E	·Exact date of return from exile
F	·Flag ·Flowers ·*most* Frequent prophecy
G	·Eastern Gate
H	·Hebrew language revived ·History prophesied
I	·Israel alone (given a land deed) ·brings on a blessing or curse from God
J	·Jerusalem-God's city ·JESUS
K	·Kinds of prophecy ·Kings/geographic accuracies backed by archaeology
L	·Land Covenant given ·Land lost ·Land bought back ·Land rejuvenated
M	·Military leader
N	·News (Israel is always in it) ·1948 prophecies fulfilled
O	**·One-word Proof of God** ·Order of return
P	·Persecution drives Jews home ·Petra ·Population
Q	·Quest by Satan to destroy the Jewish people in secular & biblical history
R	·Rebirth a most powerful sign ·Red heifer
S	·Shekel restored
T	·Temple ·Trees are back
U	·Unbiblical prophecy ·United then divided
V	·Victory prophesied
W	·Witness to the World ·Worldwide blessing
X	· X marks the chosen spot on Earth--Israel
Y	**·You can't deny the truth about Israel,** you can only suppress or ignore it.
Z	**·Zealously share the gospel** before it's too late!

TOPICAL INDEX

* symbol denotes entry that fits in
this and another category

🔖 PROPHECY BASICS

DIGGING DEEPER

▓ KEY VERSES

▣ ISRAEL

🕊 PROPHECY FULFILLED

@ PROPHETIC PROMISE

🐂 PROPHETIC TYPE

⌛ PROPHETIC WARNING

⚛ SCIENTIFIC FOREKNOWLEDGE

REFERENCES

JANUARY

2   Reagan, David R. Ph.D., Personal Communication, (Jan. 17, 2017)

3   Morris, Henry M. Ph.D., L.L.D., Litt.D., The Henry Morris Study Bible, pp. 833,841,2086,2087, (2012)

5   LaHaye, Tim D. Min. Litt.D., Tim LaHaye Prophecy Study Bible, pp. in each book's introduction, (2001)

6   Reagan, David R. Ph.D., Personal Communication, (Jan. 17, 2017)

7   Reagan, David R. Ph.D., Personal Communication, (Jan. 17, 2017)

8   Reagan, David R.. Ph.D., Israel in Bible Prophecy:Past, Present & Future, pp. 143-159, (2017)

9   Jeremiah, David R. Ph.D., The Prophecy Answer Book, pp. 5-6, (2010)

10   Reagan, David R. Ph.D., Christ in Prophecy Study Guide, p. 10, pp. 10, 26-33 (2006)
Johnson, Ken Th.D., Ancient Prophecies Revealed, pp. 60-67, (2008)

11   Reagan, David R. Ph.D., Christ in Prophecy Study Guide p. 7, (2006)

13   Reagan, David R. Ph.D., The Jewish People: Rejected or Beloved?, p. 21, (2014)

14   Reagan, David R. Ph.D., The Jewish People: Rejected or Beloved?, p. 22, (2014)

15   Morris, Henry M. Ph.D., L.L.D., Litt.D., The Genesis Record, p. 39, (1976)

16   Vallowe, Ed F.- Biblical Mathematics: Keys to Scripture Numerics pp. 80-84, (1998)

23   LaHaye, Tim D.Min. Litt.D.- & Hindson, Ed, The Popular Encyclopedia of Bible Prophecy, pp. 392-395, (2004)

24   Morris, Henry M. Ph.D., L.L.D., Litt.D., The Henry Morris Study Bible, pp. 2086-2087, (2012)
Morris, Henry M. Ph.D., L.L.D., Litt.D., Treasures in the Psalms, pp. 13,14,26,48, (2000)
MacArthur, John Jr.,Ph.D., The MacArthur Study Bible, pp. 729-730, (2006)

25   Strong, James, The New Strong's Exhaustive Concordance of the Bible, (1990)

30   Reagan, David R. Ph.D., Personal Communication, (Jan. 17, 2017)

31   Reagan, David R. Ph.D., Personal Communication, (Jan. 17, 2017)

FEBRUARY

1   Jeremiah, David R. Ph.D., The Prophecy Answer Book, pp. 186-189, (2010)

4   Hutchings, Noah W., 40 Irrefutable Signs of the Last Generation, pp. 134-140, (2010)
Lamb & Lion Ministries.www.lamblion.us/2013/09/the-reclamation-of-land-of-israel-bounty.html

5   Duck, Daymond, God has Spoken (And We Know It), pp. 22-24, (2013)

6   Duck, Daymond, God has Spoken (And We Know It), pp. 25-31, (2013)

9   Reagan, David R. Ph.D., Christ in Prophecy Study Guide, p. 8, (2006)

10   Reagan, David R. Ph.D., Personal Communication, (Jan. 17, 2017)

11   Morris, Henry M. Ph.D., L.L.D., Litt.D., The Genesis Record, pp. 119-120, (1976)

12   Jeremiah, David R. Ph.D., The Prophecy Answer Book, p. 181, (2010)

14   Reagan, David R. Ph.D., Israel in Bible Prophecy: Past, Present & Future, p. 139, (2017)
Eisen, Sara, Business is Blooming for Israel's Flowers, www.israel21c.org, (July 19, 2018)

15   Hitchcock, Mark Th.M. Ph.D., 101 Answers to Questions about Revelation, pp. 25-32, (2012)

16   Kilbourn, Mandy, Creation Illustrated- Physics and the Bible, Creation Close Up, (Fall 2016)

17   Johnson, Ken Th.D., Ancient Prophecies Revealed, pp. 4-8, (2010)

18   Johnson, Ken Th.D., Ancient Prophecies Revealed, pp. 4-8, (2010)

21   Malone, Bruce, Personal Communication, (2018)

22   Reagan, David R. Ph.D., Israel in Bible Prophecy: Past, Present & Future, pp. 133-141, (2017)

23   Reagan, David R. Ph.D., Israel in Bible Prophecy: Past, Present & Future, pp. 133-141, (2017)

25   MacArthur, John Jr. Ph.D., The MacArthur Commentary I Peter, pp. 29-48, (2004)

26   Reagan, David R. Ph.D., Personal Communication, (Jan. 17, 2017)

27   LaHaye, Tim D.Min. Litt.D., Tim LaHaye Prophecy Study Bible, pp. 1-2, 17, (2001)

28   Reagan, David R. Ph.D., Christ in Prophecy Study Guide, p. 45, (2006)

29   Kennedy, D. James Ph.D., The Real Meaning of the Zodiac, (1993)

MARCH

1   Reagan, David R. Ph.D., Christ in Prophecy Study Guide, p. 9, (2006)

2   Nobel Media AB 2014 Retrieved Aug.19, 2016 http//www.nobelprize.org/nobel-prizes/facts

4   Gallups, Carl, The Rabbi, The Secret Message, and the Identity of Messiah, pp.303-320 (2018)

5   Duck, Daymond, God has Spoken (And We Know It), pp. 33-34, (2013)

6   Reagan, David R. Ph.D., Israel in Bible Prophecy: Past, Present & Future, pp. 31-37, (2017)

7   Hutchings, Noah W., 40 Irrefutable Signs of the Last Generation, pp. 7-8, (2010)

8   Hutchings, Noah W., 40 Irrefutable Signs of the Last Generation, p. 8, (2010)

11   Thompson, Bert Ph.D., A Study Course in Christian Evidences, pp. 127-128, (1992)

12   Hitchcock, Mark Th.M. Ph.D., 101 Answers to Questions about Revelation, p. 17, (2012)

13   Ice, Thomas Ph.D., "Running To and Fro" The Prophecy Watchers, pp. 22-26, (Oct.2016)
MacArthur, John Jr. Ph.D., The MacArthur Study Bible, p. 1223, (2006)

14	Jeremiah, David R. Ph.D., The Jeremiah Study Bible, p. 1819, (2013)
15	Strong, James, The New Strong's Exhaustive Concordance of the Bible, (1990)
16	Johnson, Ken Th.D., Ancient Prophecies Revealed, p. 15, (2010)
18	Kilbourn, Mandy., Creation Illustrated, Physics and the Bible, Creation Close Up, (2016) Morris, Henry M., Ph.D., L.L.D., Litt.D.,The Henry Morris Study Bible, pp. 1831-1832, (2012)
19	Morris, Henry M., Ph.D., L.L.D., Litt.D.,The Henry Morris Study Bible, pp. 1831-1832, (2012)
21	MacArthur, John Jr. Ph.D.,The MacArthur New Test. Commentary I and 2 Thess., pp. 72-73, (2002)Strong, James., The New Strong's Exhaustive Concordance, (1990).
22	Hutchings, Noah W., 40 Irrefutable Signs of the Last Generation, pp. 134-140, (2010)
23	Hutchings, Noah W., 40 Irrefutable Signs of the Last Generation, pp. 134-140, (2010)
24	Moore, Beth, Entrusted: A Study of 2 Timothy, pp. 119-124, (2016)
25	Moore, Beth, Entrusted: A Study of 2 Timothy, pp. 119-124, (2016)
26	Strong, James., The New Strong's Exhaustive Concordance of the Bible, (1990)
29	Reagan, David R. Ph.D., The Basics of Bible Prophecy, pp. 11-13, (2018)
30	Reagan, David R. Ph.D., The Basics of Bible Prophecy, pp. 11-13, (2018)
31	Konig, George & Konig, Ray, 100 Prophecies, pp. 5-6, (1984)

APRIL

1	Morris, Henry M. Ph.D., L.L.D., Litt.D, Treasures in the Psalms, pp. 42-43, (2000)
2	Hutchings, Noah W., 40 Irrefutable Signs of the Last Generation, pp. 132-133, (2010)
3	MacArthur, John Jr. Ph.D., The MacArthur New Test. Commentary Rev. 1-11, pp. 14-22, (1999)
4	Reagan, David R. Ph.D., Christ in Prophecy Study Guide, p. 43, (2006)
7	Kilbourn, Mandy., Creation Illustrated, Physics and the Bible, Creation Up Close 23.3, (2016)
10	Fruchtenbaum, Arnold G. Th.M., Ph.D., The Footsteps of the Messiah, pp. 569-575, (2004)
11	Fruchtenbaum, Arnold G. Th.M., Ph.D., The Footsteps of the Messiah, pp. 575-581, (2004)
12	Fruchtenbaum, Arnold G. Th.M., Ph.D., The Footsteps of the Messiah, pp. 581-585, (2004)
15	Reagan, David R. Ph.D., Christ in Prophecy Study Guide, pp. 26-32, (2006)
16	Reagan, David R. Ph.D., Christ in Prophecy Study Guide, pp. 26-32, (2006)
17	Jeremiah, David R. Ph.D., The Prophecy Answer Book, pp. 3-4, (2010)
18	Morris, Henry M. Ph.D., L.L.D., Litt.D.,The Henry Morris Study Bible, pp. 843-844, (2012)
19	Hutchings, Noah W., 40 Irrefutable Signs of the Last Generation, pp. 39-40, (2010)
22	James, Terry, Deceivers, Exposing evil Seducers & Their Last Days Deception, pp.231-253, (2018).
23	James, Terry, Deceivers, Exposing evil Seducers & Their Last Days Deception, pp.231-253, (2018).
25	Jeremiah, David R. Ph.D.,The Prophecy Answer Book, p. 179, (2010)
26	Reagan, David R. Ph.D., Personal Communication, (Jan. 17, 2017)
27	Motyer, Alec, Isaiah by the Day, pp. 52-55, (2017)
28	McDowell, Josh, The New Evidence that Demands a Verdict, pp. 3-116, (1999) Morris, Henry M. Ph.D., L.L.D., Litt.D, Many Infallible Proofs, pp. 14-15, (1974)
29	McDowell, Josh, The New Evidence that Demands a Verdict, pp. 3-116, (1999) Morris, Henry M. Ph.D., L.L.D., Litt.D, Many Infallible Proofs, pp. 14-15, (1974)
30	Hutchings, Noah W., 40 Irrefutable Signs of the Last Generation, pp. 125-127, (2010)

MAY

2	MacArthur, John Jr.,Ph.D., The MacArthur Study Bible, pp. 1953-1957, (2006)
4	Hile, Michael, The Mysteries Prophecy of the Trees, Lamplighter No. 4 Vol. 38, pp. 9-11, (Jul/Aug 2017)
5	Hile, Michael, The Mysteries Prophecy of the Trees, Lamplighter No. 4 Vol. 38, pp. 9-11, (Jul/Aug 2017)
6	Reagan, David R. Ph.D., Christ in Prophecy Study Guide, pp. 59-60, (2006)
9	LaHaye, Tim D.Min. Litt.D. & Hindson, Ed Ph.D., The Encyclopedia of Bible Prophecy, pp. 309-316, (2004)
10	LaHaye, Tim D.Min. Litt.D. & Hindson, Ed Ph.D., The Encyclopedia of Bible Prophecy, pp. 309-316, (2004)
11	Mc Gee, J Vernon, Thru the Bible with J Vernon McGee Vol. 3, pp. 726-736, (1982)
12	Jones, Nathan & Howell, Steve, 12 Faith Journeys of the Minor Prophets, pp. 101-114, (2016)
14	Mc Gee, J Vernon, Thru the Bible with J Vernon McGee Vol. 3, pp. 726-736, (1982)
16	Crone, Billy Ph.D., The Rapture Don't Be Deceived, pp. 17-19, (2016)
20	Thompson, Bert Ph.D., & Jackson, Wayne, A Study Course in Christian Evidences, pp. 128-129, (1992)

21   Grady, Lee, Science and the Bible, pp. 118-119
        Kleiss, Richard &Tina, A Closer Look at the Evidence, p. Jan. 3, (2018)
27   Missler, Chuck Ph.D., Hidden Treasures in the Biblical Text, p. 17, (2000)
        Kleiss, Richard &Tina, A Closer Look at the Evidence, p. Dec. 22, (2018)
28   Johnson, Ken Th.D., Ancient Prophecies Revealed, p. 95, (2010)

JUNE
4   Reagan, David R. Ph.D., Personal Communication, (Jan. 17, 2017)
5   Reagan, David R. Ph.D., Personal Communication, (Jan. 17, 2017)
7   Thompson, Bert Ph.D. & Jackson, Wayne, A Study Course in Christian Evidences, p. 132, (1992)
        Watson, David C.C., Myths and Miracles; A New Approach to Genesis 1-11, p. 26, (1988)
9   McCoy, Shirley, Personal Communication, (Oct. 18,2017)
15   Reagan, David R. Ph.D., Personal Communication, (Jan. 17, 2017)
19   Rogers, Adrian (Adrian www.one-place.com), Israel and Bible Prophecy: What Does the Future Hold Pt.1, retrieved 7/26/18
20   Rogers, Adrian (Adrian www.one-place.com), Israel and Bible Prophecy: What Does the Future Hold Pt.1, retrieved 7/26/18
21   MacArthur, John Jr. Ph.D., The MacArthur New Test. Commentary Rev. 1-11, pp. 1-3,11, (1999)
22   Reagan, David R. Ph.D., Personal Communication, (Jan. 17,2017)
23   Hutchings, Noah W., 40 Irrefutable Signs of the Last Generation, pp. 130-132, (2010)
24   Woods, Andy, The Promise of the Eternal State - David Reagan Lamb & Lion Conference, (July 2017)
25   Woods, Andy, The Promise of the Eternal State - David Reagan Lamb & Lion Conference, (July 2017)
26   Thompson, Bert Ph.D., & Jackson, Wayne, A Study Course in Christian Evidences, p. 132, (1992)
28   Duck, Daymond, God Has Spoken (And We Know It), pp. 63-64, (2013)
29   Duck, Daymond, God Has Spoken (And We Know It), pp. 63-64, (2013)
30   Jones, Nathan, Should Christians Support Israel? Prophecy NewsWatch, Retrieved 10/5/17
        http//christinprophecy.org//sermons/in-the-box 15/should Christians really support Israel

JULY
1   Morris, Henry M. Ph.D., L.L.D., Litt.D, Sampling the Psalms, (throughout book), (1978)
2   Carson, D.A, From the Resurrection to His Return: Living Faithfully in the Last Days, p. 11, (2010)
3   Reagan, David R. Ph.D. Personal Communication, (Jan. 17, 2017)
8   LaHaye, Tim D.Min. Litt.D., Tim LaHaye Prophecy Study Bible, p. 864, (2001)
        Faculty of Moody Bible Institute, The Moody Bible Commentary, pp. 1139-1140, (2014)
9   LaHaye, Tim D.Min. Litt.D., Tim LaHaye Prophecy Study Bible, p. 758, (2001)
        Faculty of Moody Bible Institute, The Moody Bible Commentary, pp. 1139-1140, (2014)
10   Motyer, Alec, Isaiah by the Day, p. 37, (2017)
11   LaHaye, Tim D.Min. Litt.D., Tim LaHaye Prophecy Study Bible, p. 1490, (2001)
12   LaHaye, Tim D.Min. Litt.D., Tim LaHaye Prophecy Study Bible, p. 1490, (2001)
13   LaHaye, Tim D.Min. Litt.D., Tim LaHaye Prophecy Study Bible, pp. 1055-1056, (2001)
14   Motyer, Alec, Isaiah by the Day, pp. 69-71, (2017)
15   LaHaye, Tim D.Min. Litt.D., Tim LaHaye, Prophecy Study Bible, pp. 912-915, (2001)
16   Thompson, Bert Ph.D. & Jackson, Wayne, A Study Course in Christian Evidences, p. 130, (1992) Thompson, Bert Ph.D., Reason and Revelation, p. 55, (1993)
20   Johnson, Ken Th.D., Ancient Prophecies Revealed, p. 52, (2010)
21   DeYoung, Donald, Astronomy and the Bible: Questions and Answers, pp. 56-57, (1991)
22   Kennedy, D. James Ph.D., Why I Believe, pp. 4-7, (1999)
23   Kennedy, D. James Ph.D., Why I Believe, pp. 4-7, (1999)
24   Jeffrey, Grant R. Ph.D., The Signature of God, pp. 156-159, (1996)
28   Crone, Billy Ph.D., The Rapture Don't Be Deceived, pp. 41-49, (2016)
29   Crone, Billy Ph.D., The Rapture Don't Be Deceived, pp. 41-49, (2016)
30   Crone, Billy Ph.D., The Rapture Don't Be Deceived, pp. 41-49, (2016)
31   Crone, Billy Ph.D., The Rapture Don't Be Deceived, pp. 41-49, (2016)

AUGUST
3   Reagan, David R. Ph.D., Personal Communication, (Jan. 17, 2017)
8   Greenwold Doug, Greenwold on Lazarus-Barabbas Lambandlion.com, (April 1, 2018)
10   Reagan, David R. Ph.D., God's Prophetic Voices in America, pp. 225-242, (2017)
11   LaHaye, Tim D.Min. Litt.D., Tim LaHaye, Prophecy Study Bible, pp. 1545-1546, (2001)
12   Hutchings, Noah W., 40 Irrefutable Signs of the Last Generation, pp. 115-116, (2010)
15   Johnson, Ken Th.D., Ancient Prophecies Revealed, pp. 89-100, (2010)
16   Johnson, Ken Th.D., Ancient Prophecies Revealed, pp. 6-8, (2010)

17   Johnson, Ken Th.D., Ancient Prophecies Revealed, p. 92, (2010)
18   Nelson, Thomas, Nelson's Complete Book of Bible Maps & Charts, (throughout), (1996)
19   Levy, David M. Zechariah, Israel's Future and the Coming Apocalypse, pp. 7-22, (2013)
20   Johnson, Ken Th.D., Ancient Prophecies Revealed, pp. 35-36, (2010)
21   Johnson, Ken Th.D., Ancient Prophecies Revealed, pp. 38-39, (2010)
22   Johnson, Ken Th.D., Ancient Prophecies Revealed, p. 40, (2010)
23   Johnson, Ken Th.D., Ancient Prophecies Revealed, pp. 38-39, (2010)
27   Zondervan Publishing House, The Zondervan Pictorial Encyclopedia of the Bible Vol 1, pp. 452-454, (1976)
28   Zondervan Publishing House, The Zondervan Pictorial Encyclopedia of the Bible Vol 1, pp. 452-454, (1976)
29   MacArthur, John Jr. Ph.D., The MacArthur New Test Commentary I Peter, pp. 29-38, (2004)
30   Jeremiah, David R. Ph.D., The Jeremiah Study Bible, p. 1800, (2013)
31   Jeremiah, David R. Ph.D., The Jeremiah Study Bible, p. 1800, (2013)

SEPTEMBER
1   Goodwin, Dan, The Battle for the Planet, Prophecy in the News, pp. 16-18, (June 2018)
2   Goodwin, Dan, The Battle for the Planet, Prophecy in the News, pp. 16-18, (June 2018)
3   Levy, David M. Zechariah, Israel's Prophetic Future and the Coming Apocalypse, pp. 20-22, (2013)
4   Levy, David M. Zechariah, Israel's Prophetic Future and the Coming Apocalypse, pp. 29-32, (2013)
5   Malone, Bruce, Personal Communication, (2018)
6   Johnson, Ken Th.D., Ancient Prophecies Revealed, pp. 67-68, (2010)
7   Levy, David M,Zechariah, Israel's Prophetic Future and the Coming Apocalypse, pp. 33-34, (2013)
8   LaHaye, Tim D.Min. Litt.D., Tim LaHaye, Prophecy Study Bible, p. 1016, (2001)
        Crone, Billy, Ph.D., Hybrids, Supersoldiers, and the Coming Genetic Apocalypse, Vol 1 and 2, (2020)
9   LaHaye, Tim D.Min. Litt.D., Tim LaHaye, Prophecy Study Bible, p. 1016, (2001)
10   Levy, David M. Zechariah, Israel's Prophetic Future and the Coming Apocalypse, pp. 63-65, (2013)
11   Levy, David M. Zechariah, Israel's Prophetic Future and the Coming Apocalypse, pp. 71-72, (2013)
12   Beliefmap. org website, Does the Passover Lamb Prefigure Jesus?, retrieved 5/25/2018
13   Beliefmap. org website, Does the Passover Lamb Prefigure Jesus?, retrieved 5/25/2018
17   MacArthur, John Jr., Ph.D., The MacArthur New Testament Commentary Rev.12-22, pp. 309-311, (2000)
19   Levy, David M. Zechariah, Israel's Prophetic Future and the Coming Apocalypse, pp. 73-77, (2013)
20   Levy, David M. Zechariah, Israel's Prophetic Future and the Coming Apocalypse, pp. 73-77, (2013) LaHaye, Tim D.Min. Litt.D., Tim LaHaye, Prophecy Study Bible, pp. 1096, (2001)
22   Missler, Ph.D., Hidden Treasures in the Biblical Text, pp. 11-18, (2000)
        Kleiss, Rich & Tina, A Closer Look at the Evidence, p. Feb. 20, (2018)
23   Johnson, Ken Th.D., Ancient Prophecies Revealed, pp. 53-59, (2010)
24   LaHaye, Tim D.Min. Litt.D., Tim LaHaye Prophecy Study Bible, p. 210, (2001)
26   LaHaye, Tim D.Min. Litt.D., Tim LaHaye Prophecy Study Bible, pp. 1104-1111, (2001)
27   Johnson, Ken Th.D., Ancient Prophecies Revealed, p. 34, (2010)
28   Malone, Bruce, Personal Communication, (2018)
29   Johnson, Ken Th.D., Ancient Prophecies Revealed, pp. 34-35, (2010)
30   Levy, David M. Zechariah, Israel's Prophetic Future and the Coming Apocalypse, pp. 23-26, (2013)

OCTOBER
2   Watchman of Israel; Facts about Israel, Truths About our Future Agriculture in Israel (retrieved 7/19/2018)
3   MacArthur, John Jr.,Ph.D., The MacArthur Study Bible, pp. 1139-1140, (2006)
4   MacArthur, John Jr.,Ph.D., The MacArthur Study Bible, pp. 1139-1140, (2006)
5   Reagan, David R. Ph.D., Israel in Bible Prophecy: Past, Present & Future, pp. 135-137, (2017)
6   Konig,George & Konig, Ray, 100 Prophecies, pp. 133-134, (1984)
9   Crone, Billy Ph.D. In the Days of Noah, pp. 53-54, (2017)
12   Reagan, David R. Ph.D., Israel in Bible Prophecy: Past, Present & Future, pp. 139-140, (2017) Watchman of Israel: Facts about Israel Truths, About our Future Agriculture in Israel, (retrieved 7/19/2018)
15   Morris, Henry M. Ph.D.,L.L.D., Litt.D.,with Morris, Henry III, Treasures in the Psalms, pp. 110-112, (1999)
16   Konig, George & Konig, Ray, 100 Prophecies, pp. 23-34, (1984)
20   Morris, Henry M. Ph.D.,L.L.D., Litt.D. & Clark Martin E., The Bible Has the Answer, pp. 321-322, (2005)

22	Cahn, Jonathan, The Book of Mysteries, p. 160, (2016)
23	Hutchings, Noah W., 40 Irrefutable Signs of the Last Generation, pp. 124-125, (2010)
25	Konig, George & Konig, Ray, 100 Prophecies, pp. 13-15, (1984)
26	Morris, Henry M. Ph.D., L.L.D., Litt.D, The Genesis Record, pp. 373-384, (1976)
28	Malone, Bruce, Brilliant: Made in the Image of God, pp. 18,28,52,72,88,96,98, (2014)

NOVEMBER

2	Levy, David M,Zechariah, Israel's Prophetic Future and the Coming Apocalypse, pp. 18, (2013)
3	Levy, David M,Zechariah, Israel's Prophetic Future and the Coming Apocalypse, pp. 18, (2013)
5	www. Watchman Bible study.com
6	DeYoung, Jimmy, Preparing the Temple, https://israel myglory.org/article/preparing-for-the-third-temple/8/25/18
7	Hutchings, Noah W., 40 Irrefutable Signs of the Last Generation, pp. 179-182, (2010)
9	LaHaye, Tim D.Min. Litt.D., Tim LaHaye Prophecy Study Bible, p. 1078, (2001)
10	LaHaye, Tim D.Min. Litt.D., Tim LaHaye Prophecy Study Bible, p. 1078, (2001)
12	Malone, Bruce, personal correspondence, June 2018
15	Hutchings, Noah W., 40 Irrefutable Signs of the Last Generation, pp. 186-193, (2010)
16	LaHaye, Tim D.Min. Litt.D., Tim LaHaye Prophecy Study Bible, pp. 1085-1088, (2001)
17	Crone, Billy Ph.D., The Rapture Don't Be Deceived, pp. 17-18, (2016)
19	LaHaye, Tim D.Min. Litt.D., Tim LaHaye Prophecy Study Bible, pp. 1414-1417, (2001)
20	LaHaye, Tim D.Min. Litt.D., & Hindson, Ed, The Popular Encyclopedia of Bible Prophecy, p. 310, (2004)
23	LaHaye, Tim D.Min. Litt.D., & Hindson, Ed, The Popular Encyclopedia of Bible Prophecy, pp. 119-122, (2004)
24	LaHaye, Tim D.Min. Litt.D., & Hindson, Ed, The Popular Encyclopedia of Bible Prophecy, pp. 119-122, (2004)
26	https://prophecy update.blogspot.com/2017/08/the-jewish-feasts-and-their-prophetic.html
27	http:// ny post /2017 /1/29/why-israel-has-the-most-technological-advanced-military-on-earth
28	LaHaye, Tim D.Min. Litt.D.,& Hindson, Ed, The Encyclopedia of Bible Prophecy, pp. 352-353, (2004)
29	LaHaye, Tim D.Min. Litt.D.,& Hindson, Ed, The Encyclopedia of Bible Prophecy, pp. 354-356, (2004)
30	LaHaye, Tim D.Min. Litt.D.,& Hindson, Ed, The Encyclopedia of Bible Prophecy, pp. 354-356, (2004)

DECEMBER

3	Jeffrey, Grant R., The Signature of God, pp. 152-154, (2002)
4	LaHaye, Tim D.Min. Litt.D., Tim LaHaye, Prophecy Study Bible, p. 181, (2001)
5	Kranz,Jeff,overview-bible.com, bible — songs by Jeff Kranz, July 2, 2014
6	Levy, David M, Zechariah, Israel's Future and the Coming Apocalypse, pp. 97-101, (2013)
7	Levy, David M, Zechariah, Israel's Future and the Coming Apocalypse, pp. 97-101, (2013)
8	Hutchings, Noah W. with Treibich, Gilla, 25 Messianic Signs in Israel Today, pp. 101-106, (2007)
9	Hutchings, Noah W. with Treibich, Gilla, 25 Messianic Signs in Israel Today, pp. 87-100, (2007)
11	Jeffrey, Grant R., The Signature of God, pp. 137-161, (2002)
12	Jeffrey, Grant R., The Signature of God, pp. 137-161, (2002)
13	Jeffrey, Grant R., The Signature of God, pp. 137-161, (2002)
14	Salus, Bill, Psalm 83, The Missing Prophecy Revealed, pp. 12-21, 287, (2013)
15	Salus, Bill, Psalm 83, The Missing Prophecy Revealed, pp. 319-322, (2013)
17	Morris, John, Ph.D., Austin, Steve, Ph,D., Footprints in the Ash: The Explosive Story of Mount St. Helens, pp. 38-117, (2003)
	Wilson, Clifford and Barbara, Ph.D., The Stones Still Cry Out: Sensational Highlights of the Bible and Archaeology, pp.9-159, (1999)
18	Jeffrey, Grant R., The Signature of God, pp. 163-193, (2002)
19	Jeffrey, Grant R., The Signature of God, pp. 163-193, (2002)
20	Jeffrey, Grant R., The Signature of God, pp. 163-193, (2002)
21	Acts and Facts Magazine, Institute of Creation Research, The Seed Promise
22	McGee J Vernon Ph.D., Thru the Bible with J Vernon McGee Vol 3, pp. 239-240, (1982)
23	Johnson, Ken ThD., Ancient Prophecy Revealed, pp. 82-83, (2010)
24	RW Research, Inc., Rose Book of Bible Charts, Maps and Timelines, p. 129, (2005)
25	Malone, Bruce, personal correspondence, (December 2018)
29	Kalisher, Meno, Jesus in the Hebrew Scriptures, pp. 164-165, (2010)
30	Reagan, David R.,Ph.D., Living on Borrowed Time The Imminent Return of Jesus, pp. 15-24, (2013)

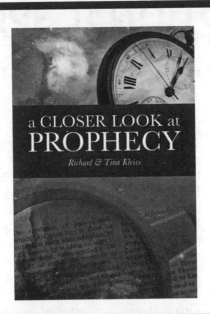

Share God's Prophetic Word with family and friends!

A CLOSER LOOK AT PROPHECY

This devotional examines prophecies from throughout the Bible - both already fulfilled and yet to be fulfilled. Prophecy is an integral part of the Bible. By revealing the future in advance, God makes the true authorship of the Bible indisputable. Prophecy is meant to instruct, encourage, warn, equip, and prepare us. This book draws from 50 expert sources to provide a sampling of the great number of prophecies contained within God's Word in an enjoyable daily devotional format.

1 book = $12
10 books = $60
Case of 24 books = $120

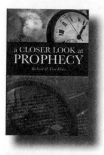

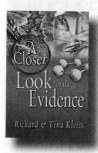

OTHER CREATION BOOKS
by Search for the Truth Ministries

Brilliant

An exquisitely illustrated, full-color hardcover book containing history from all over the world that points to and supports a biblical timeline.

(8 x11, 128 pages)

Censored Science

A stunning, full-color hardcover book containing fifty of the best evidences for biblical creation. Examine the information all too often censored, suppressed, or ignored in our schools. Every page is a visual masterpiece. Perfect for students.
(8 x11, 112 pages)

Search for the Truth

This book is the result of a 15-year effort to bring the scientific evidence for creation into public view. Search for the Truth is a compilation of 100 individual articles originally published as newspaper columns, summarizing every aspect of the creation model for our origin.
(8 x 11, 144 pages)

See all of our resources at
www.searchforthetruth.net

CREATION CURRICULUM:

Volume I **Volume II** **Volume III**

The Rocks Cry Out Curriculum

Bring the most visual, interactive, and relevant series on the evidence to creation to your church, fellowship, or youth group! Filmed at locations across America with video illustrations and animations, these lessons are not a boring technical lecture.

These 45 minute classes enable the non-scientist to bring the evidence for biblical creation to their home or church. This curriculum uses short, personal narrative-style teachings to connect God's Word with science and history, i.e "the real world". Leaders guide included with each set.

Perfect for small group, home school, or Sunday school groups of all ages, *The Rocks Cry Out* show how EVERY area of science confirms Biblical Truth in a visual masterpiece that rivals a National Geographic special. Volume I contains lessons 1-6, Volume II contains lessons 7-12, Volume 3 contains lessons 13-18

See all of our resources at
www.searchforthetruth.net

MAIL-IN ORDER FORM

See more at www.searchforthetruth.net

Call us, or send this completed order form
(other side of page) with check or money order to:

Search for the Truth Ministries
3275 Monroe Rd.
Midland, M I 48642
989.837.5546 or truth@searchforthetruth.net

PRICES

	ITEM PRICE	2-9 COPIES	10 COPIES	CASE PRICE
DEVOTIONAL SPECIAL (4 BOOKS)	$30	-	Mix or Match	-
A Closer Look At Prophecy (Softcover)	$12	$9/ea.	$6/ea.	call
Have You Considered (Full color, hardback)	$14	$10/ea.	$7/ea.	call
Inspired Evidence (Softcover)	$12	$9/ea.	$6/ea.	call
A Closer Look at the Evidence (full color, hardback)	$14	$10/ea.	$7/ea.	call
Censored Science (full color, hardback)	$17	$12/ea.	$7/ea.	call
Brilliant (full color, hardback)	$17	$12/ea.	$7/ea.	call
Search for the Truth (softcover)	$12	$9/ea.	$6/ea.	call
6 DVD Creation Curriculum (Specify Vol.) with Leader Guide	$25	-	$20/ea.	call

MAIL-IN ORDER FORM

Resource	Quantity	Cost each	Total
DEVOTIONAL SPECIAL (4 books)			
A Closer Look At Prophecy (Softcover)			
Inspired Evidence (Softcover)			
A Closer Look at the Evidence(Hardback)			
Have You Considered (Hardback)			
Censored Science (Hardback)			
Brilliant (Hardback)			
Search for the Truth (Softcover)			
The RocksCry Out 6 DVD Set (Specify Vol)			
Tax deductible Donation to ministry			

SUBTOTAL	
M I RESIDENTS ADD 6% SALES TAX	
SHIPPING ADD 15% OF SUBTOTAL	
TOTAL ENCLOSED	

NORMAL DELIVERY TIME IS 1-2 WEEKS

FOR EXPRESS DELIVERY

INCREASE SHIPPING TO 20%

SHIP TO:

Name: _____

Address: _____

City: _____

State: _____ Zip: _____

Phone: _____

E-mail: _____